Chadwick Public Library
825-684-5215

	DATE DUE		
MAR 04			

WINNING THE RACE:

THE GREG MOSER STORY

WINNING THE RACE:

THE GREG MOSER STORY

AUTHORED BY:
GREG MOSER
WITH
JOHN B. KNIGHT, Ed. D., CFBE

C. BURNS D.D.S. PUBLISHING
102 PERFORMANCE DRIVE
PORTLAND, INDIANA 47371

Copyright © 1998 by Greg Moser

All rights reserved under International and Pan-American copyright
conditions. Published in the United States by
C. Burns D.D.S. Publishing, 102 Performance Drive
Portland, Indiana 47371

ISBN D-9663857-0-5

Library of Congress Catalog Number 98-071867

Manufactured in the United States of America

WINNING THE RACE:

THE GREG MOSER STORY

This book is dedicated to all of my friends and loved ones whom I've lost along our journey including Buzz Detman, Jeff Hunter, Loran Zedyke, Virgil Dangler, Jeff Mymby, my father Paul Moser, brother-in-law Dr. Tim Burns, and my beautiful, kind, and loving sister Dr. Connie Burns Webb.

Greg Moser
March, 1998

Dear Reader

Please note:
A. "Jeff Mymby" should be "Jeff Mumby" in the above dedication;
B. Computer error has replaced the pronoun "I" with "It" on pages 55-61;
C. Human error in the photographic section reversed the captions of Bob Quadrozzi and Jeff Bickel and the caption "This is a typical "Altered" Drag Race Car" should read "This is a typical "Pro-stock" Drag Race Car."

The editors apologize for these errors.

Acknowledgments

For their dedication to professionalism in all that they do, I wish to thank first my daughter, Jackie, who spent long hours transcribing recorded tapes for this book, and second my son, Brad, who spent considerable time reading the book for corrections to be made. Of course, my wife, Whitney, and my other son, David, also contributed significantly to accomplishing the task at hand and I thank both of them.

For his hard work in making sure that my computer worked, I thank Ken Jordan who is always there to support me. I also wish to thank my secretary, Louise Pruse, at Indiana University and Purdue University Fort Wayne who continually assists me in all of my endeavors.

Of course, for their belief in me, their employees, and God, I thank Greg and Marianne Moser who have both inspired me with their love for mankind and this world. They are unique individuals who have left everything they touch better than they found it!

John B. Knight
January, 1998

I wish to thank all of my friends, teachers, and business acquaintances who helped mold who I am.

I wish to thank my parents and grandparents who taught me right from wrong and how to work to get what you want.

I wish to thank Jeff Bickel, Rosie Clamme, Donna Haggenjos, Barry Hudson, Dean Jetter, Ron Miller, Cindy Moser, Rob Moser, Bob Quadrozzi, Bob Read, Vicki Tague, and John G. Young for their contributions to this book.

Special thanks go to Marianne. What can I say? What a team, Marianne and Greg. Together, we can do anything!

Lastly, I wish to thank John Knight. Without John this would be no book. I would not have written this book without him. At the last minute when trying to talk me into it, John hit upon the magic words which were, "Some high school student might read this and be helped to chart a course for life. You could donate the profits from this book to charity." So with John's help, here's the book. Thanks, John!

Greg Moser
March, 1998

TABLE OF CONTENTS

Chapter One - Need for Speed Page 1

    Lessons Learned Early
    Hard Work Pays Off
    Revving My Engines
    Having a Great Time
    More Lessons Learned
    Lower Pay for New Opportunities
    Don't Believe "Opposites Attract"
    How Not to Operate a Plant

Chapter Two - Qualifying to Race Page 24

    Learning How to Do It Right
    Winning Time Trials Leads to My Own Business
    You Can Qualify, too!

Chapter Three - Engine Improvements Page 32

    Accomplishing Much
    Changing Your Attitude
    Fine Tuning to Make Every Second Count
    Knowledge is Power as Is Working Smart
    Tips for Engineers
    Marrying for Success

Chapter Four - Page 49
Learning from the Competition and Others

    Keeping All under Control
    Successful Techniques Used
    Moving Goals Forward to Maintain that Competitive Edge
    The Race is Wide Open so Go For It

Chapter Five - Entering the Race   Page 62

    Being Competitive is Important
    Reacting Fast is a Must
    Running the Race to Win is Never Easy
    Drag Racing is My Sport

Chapter Six - Taking the Lead   Page 71

    Racing in the Right Class Comes First
    Considering the Long Haul is Important
    Keeping an Eye on the Competition is a Must
    Approaching the Line Correctly Can Make All the Difference
    Even Reaching Top Speed Does not Satisfy
    With No Finish Line Your Goals are Always in Front of You

Chapter Seven -   Page 87
Handling Crashes and Other Mishaps

    Turning the Negative into Positive
    Moving on to Positive Learning Experiences
    Using Ethics and Integrity as Preventive Medicine

Chapter Eight - Running the Race to Win   Page 100

    Being Competitive is the Start of the Game
    Everyone Must Want to Win
    Expectations Play an Important Role
    Speed Bumps Always Slow You Down

Chapter Nine - Accelerating Beyond Top Speed   Page 114

    Helping Others is the Best Way to Accelerate
    In the Fast Lane Every Second Counts
    At These Speeds Anything Can Happen
    Other Speeding Stories

Chapter Ten - Winning is in Sight   Page 126

    Service Helps, Strikes Don't
    Clear Vision Must Continue No Matter What
    Doing the Right Thing Pays Off
    Take Risks to Give the Masses What They Need
    Quality Customer Service Says It All

Chapter Eleven - Being Recognized as the Leader   Page 140

    Communicate Clearly
    Set the Example
    Trust Others to do Their Job
    Recognize the Leader and Win
    Entertain Fresh and New Ideas
    Realize Knowledge is Power
    Practice What You Preach
    Be Mentally and Physically Fit

Chapter Twelve - Winner's Circle   Page 156

    Building our Home
    Enjoying our Home
    Making the World a Better Place
    Volunteering to Help Others

Chapter Thirteen - Sharing the Wealth   Page 167

    The Library Fund-raiser
    The Arts Council Project
    The Arts Council Speech
    Philanthropy

Chapter Fourteen -   Page 196
More Accolades from Colleagues

    Financing Our Library by Ms. Rosalie Clamme

The Optimist by Ms. Donna Haggenjos
Going to the Races by Mr. Barry Hudson
On Leadership by Dean Jetter
Greg and Marianne Moser by Bob Quadrozzi
Greg Moser by Vicki Tague

Chapter Fifteen - Life and Times with Greg Moser   **Page 209**

"Brace for Impact!" by Mr. Jeff Bickel
Racing with Greg by Ron Miller
My Years with Dad by Cindy Moser
A Glimpse by Cindy Moser

Chapter Sixteen - Working with Greg Moser   **Page 230**
by Robert Read, Ph.D.

Chapter Seventeen - Reflections   **Page 244**

Always Innovate
Curtail Inflation
Learn to Challenge Tradition
Let's All Win
Recognize Family and Friends
When All is Said and Done
Final Thoughts
Psalm 23

Glossary   **Page 262**

Time Line   **Page 266**

Winner's...   **Page 267**

Preface

Throughout his life, Greg Moser has been many things to many people. Through his business dealings, work in community organizations, and various other things in which he has been involved, many people have been influenced by him in some way. Perhaps more than anyone though, I think he has influenced me the most and I have known him in more ways than any other. He is my dad. As his son, I know or have known almost everything in this book. He has taught me basically everything he knows and shared with me everything he has.

When I was a child, we spent countless hours together in our garage working on everything from race cars to his newest machine. First, he would just let me get tools for him, but eventually he let me get my hands on just about everything I showed an interest in working on. Our time together in the garage was always about learning. Learning how to work hard, how to think, and especially how to combine the two to solve problems.

When I got older and progressed from a child to a teenager and a young man, he taught me mostly about life in general. He taught me, through both his actions and his words, that life is mainly about family and finding happiness. One's family is always the main focus. No decisions can be made about anything without first considering the effects that they may have on other family members and their lives. In short, family always comes first. I also learned that success is most often a by-product of happiness and rarely vice-versa. Only when someone is happy in what they do will they truly consider themselves successful. Without the feeling of happiness inside you, true success can never be achieved.

As I graduated from high school and went off to college, his lessons just kept on coming even though I was over 2,000 miles away. Just the fact that he and my mom let me go to college so far away from home was a lesson in itself and one I think of often now that I have children of my own. I am sure it wasn't easy for them to let their son go, but they later told me that they knew that if they had done their jobs raising me, the decisions I made would be good ones and they had nothing to worry about.

A couple of years later, I decided I didn't want to follow in my dad's footsteps and be an engineer. I remember being more nervous than ever before when I called with the news that I was changing my major from engineering to business. Much to my surprise, when I told him, he said that was fine with him and he didn't really care what my major was as long as I was prepared to give it everything I had. He had never expected me to follow in his footsteps. My happiness was what really mattered and if business was what I wanted to study, then that's what I should do.

When he and my mom came to my graduation ceremonies a few years later, they already knew I had decided to come home and work in our family business. I know that made him happy, but I think more than that, I remember him being proud that day. He was, of course, proud of me, but he was also proud of himself and my mother, too. After all, parenthood is the greatest test of all and they had passed. They had given me the freedom to go off and be myself, to make my own choices, make my own mistakes, and everything had turned out just as they had hoped. He had been successful for years in business so he knew his methods in that area were good ones. Now he knew that his beliefs and methods of parenting were also good ones.

Now that we work together on a daily basis in our family business, I think I learn something new from him every day about business, people, and even more about life. His business principles are rather simple but amazingly effective. Give people something that they need, when they need it, and at a price that is fair. Like I said, it is amazingly simple, but how many more success stories could be written if more entrepreneurs would practice these same methods?

The things that he taught me about people are some of the most difficult, yet, most valuable of all. He has shown me that life itself is almost exclusively about people and how you see them, how they see you, what makes them happy, how to motivate them, what people want, what they need, and what you can do to help them. What people want most is to be happy and to feel comfortable with themselves and what they do. No two people are the same and what makes one happy doesn't always work on another. As an employer, he taught me that one must evaluate what makes each employee happy. Whether it is money, responsibility, or something else, an employee must feel valuable to be happy. The job of the employer then is to take the needs and desires of these people and mold them into one happy and productive unit. His methods and ideas must work because in over ten years of doing business, we have never lost an employee. Our business has zero employee turnover.

Now that the success of our business has assured stability for our family, he has also taught me that there are others in our communities that also have needs. If we are able, we must also do what we can to help them and make them happy. He doesn't believe in just giving things to people because they will not appreciate what they have received. But when he finds a cause that is doing things the way he believes is right, he will do whatever he can to help. Whether it be with time, money, or some other form of aid, he has shown many times that he will put everything he can into helping an organization or a cause in which he believes.

Obviously, in addition to being father and son, much of my life with Greg Moser has been spent in the roles of student and teacher. From the time I was a child just happy to be able to spend time with him working in the garage, to the present, when we work together every day in our family business, I have spent my life watching and learning from him. As I said before, my dad has shared virtually everything he has and knows with me and I hope that through this book, a few others may be able to learn a few of the lessons I have found so valuable.

Rob Moser
February 1998

Foreword

The story that you are about to read is true. Greg Moser is winning the race and the recommendations he makes can change your life forever. Sincerely implement what he says and notice the radical change in your day to day behavior.

An example of how this book has changed my life occurred just the other day. Greg had dictated more ideas to me on an audio tape as a last statement for this book. He encouraged all individuals to "GO, GO, GO!" As I listened further, I realized that Greg is an "eternal optimist" as indicated by what he said next.

> "Just driving down the road I know who the pessimists are and who the optimists are . When you're approaching a green light, the pessimist will begin to slow down hundreds of feet before the green light in anticipation of it turning yellow. By the time this person reaches the light, it does, in fact, turn yellow and the brakes are applied suddenly to bring the car to a complete stop. The optimist, on the other hand, sees the green light, and, being continually aware of the opportunities in his or her life, this individual maintains an appropriate speed to make it through the green light. This does not mean that the optimist's car is going to make every green light, but it does mean that the little extra effort it takes to make it through the light will change the way you drive forever. Time is wasted sitting at red lights, especially when no cars are coming in the opposite direction. Beware of your surroundings and believe that all the lights in your life will be green. The result will make you an eternal optimist!"

The point of relating this to you in the foreword is that you are about to embark on an incredible story of true principles that can be applied everyday to your life. You can either use these principles to improve your life or you can remain in your present habits, stubborn in your heart, and not be willing to change. As Greg states,

> "Know what you want, know how to get it, know when you got it, and know how to keep it."

At age 45, Greg says that he has not worked in over 30 years because he loves what he is doing so much that he would not call it work. His mission is to leave everything that comes into his life better than when he found it. He sums this up by saying,

> "Do what you want to do. Enjoy what you are doing.
> Make enough to buy what you want to buy. Make enough
> to give away to make someone else's life better."

Greg Moser's motivation is to keep his business growing to help others make money, buy new cars, homes, pay for their children's education, etc. In the end he wants his employees to lead a good life. It is good to want to make money because then you can give it away. Why hoard money? You can leave some to your children but you do not wish to wreck their lives by giving so much money to them that they do not have to work. Why make money then? Greg reveals the answer in the following pages as he not only tells you how to make money but how to use it wisely as well.

Winning every time is not always easy, but Greg Moser knows how to do it and you will, too, as you read, "**WINNING THE RACE, The Greg Moser Story.**"

John Knight
February 1998

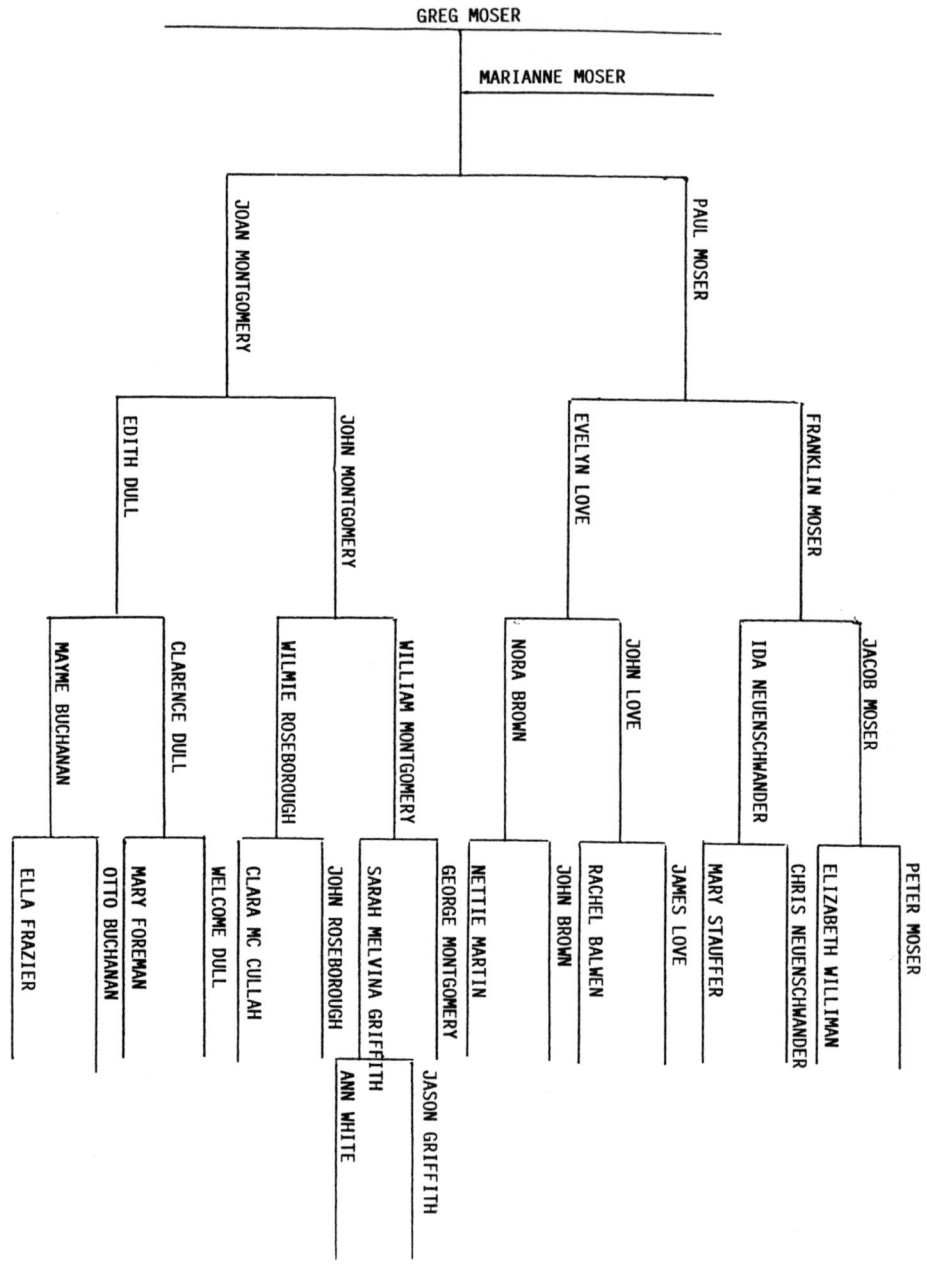

Chapter One

NEED FOR SPEED

Lessons Learned Early
Hard Work Pays Off
Revving My Engines
Having a Great Time
More Lessons Learned
Lower Pay for New Opportunities
Don't Believe "Opposites Attract"
How Not to Operate a Plant
Greg's Ancestry by John G. Young

A couple of blocks from the addition in which we lived were some people who didn't like to see us youth have any fun. I was not even 10 years old and they would turn you in and call the cops on you every chance they would get. So, what I would do is go to the garage door, open it, and hop on my go-cart, scream up and down the block, make two laps to make a sport out of it, and then come screaming back to the garage slamming the garage door behind me. Within a couple minutes, the police would show up. They would knock on the door and ask my mom, "Was your son out on the go-cart?" She would say, "Well, I don't think he was, I don't even know if he's home." She would always get me out of trouble. She always would! Then I would wait a day or two and do it again. I had the need for speed beginning at the age of nine!

Lessons Learned Early

My parents were Paul and Joan Moser, two hard workers who taught me integrity and virtue from day one. We lived in Paulding, Ohio, and my father worked for the post office sorting mail on the railroads. He worked nine days on and five days off, so I saw him every nine days for five days. Even so, I saw very little of him because he worked all the time. Actually, he would come home and paint for the local lumberyard and spray paint barns. At an early age I became indoctrinated with hard work because if you're going to spray paint barns and homes, like my father did, you must first scrape the paint off, and that was one of my jobs. I was taught the meaning of hard work by my father. In fact, my father was the epitome of a man. He could work anybody into the ground. That's where I got my ability to work.

My mother worked full-time raising us children and it was from her that I learned my values. We had a nice home, clothes, and food. I never lacked the necessities of life. If I wanted anything else, I had to work to earn spending money. It may sound strange, but **the best way in the world to raise children is by example**. Most of us don't really understand this. If we did, we would not behave the way we do. You can tell children, you can tell people in the business place, you can tell anyone anything, and they might not do as you say. But if you practice what you're teaching and lead by example, that's the greatest education you can give anyone.

WINNERS...
#1. raise their children by example

Train children in the way they should go, and when they are old they will not turn from it. (Proverbs 22:6)

As far as honesty is concerned, I can remember at four or five years old, my father had central air conditioned our home after buying a unit from Sears on credit. Believe it or not, the bill sent to the house was for only $5.60 even though the unit cost $560.00. My parents worked several years to pay that bill, when they could have just as easily paid the lesser billed amount and forgot about being honest. **They kept writing Sears, calling, and insisting that the bill was wrong. In this day and age, it would be hard to find anyone that would do that, but my parents did because they were honest.**

Children learn from example. My parents went to church every Sunday. My perfect attendance pins for ten years were a result of their example. My parents never cheated on their income tax, nor did they joke about it. Kids learn from this. My parents would never call in sick and then be found on the golf course. My father never missed a day of work and he had years of sick days available for use. Since I started working at jobs that kept track of my hours, I have not missed but three half-days in the last 30 years! It was because of my father's work ethic and my mother's support of him.

WINNERS...

#2. lead their employees, not by what they say, but by what they do

**In the same way, let your light shine before everyone that they may see your good deeds and praise your Father in Heaven.
(Matthew 5:16)**

Hard Work Pays Off

As the years progressed, I discovered that if I wanted something I had to buy it myself, so I started running paper routes. If I wanted money to buy things quicker, I needed more routes. **The truth is, the more I wanted, the harder I worked.** I literally ended up with three paper routes delivering the *Fort Wayne Journal Gazette* on two routes in the morning and the *Defiance Crecent-News* on one route in the afternoon at five.

**WINNERS...
#3. work hard because they know what they want
The plans of the diligent lead to profit, as surely as haste leads to poverty.
(Proverbs 21:5)**

The way I operated was that I woke up when the papers arrived from Ft. Wayne at 3:00 AM in the morning. I would deliver them to where my customers wanted them by 5:00 AM. Then I would go back to bed and would never really know that I had been up working. It's hard work, but if you want something, you work for it. I turned over a 10,000 mile speedometer three times on an old Schwinn bicycle delivering all those newspapers. I rode the wheels off that bike. I did this for over seven years from the time I was nine years old until I was 16.

In fact, I highly recommend working from 3:00 to 5:00 AM and then going back to bed. It should be tried by anyone too tired to work late at night or unmotivated (unable) to rise early in the morning to accomplish necessary tasks. For example, a young person who has the desire to get really good grades could do homework in those two early morning hours that would take double the time late at night because one's mind would wander or be distracted over the day's events. The same time could be used by a business person to accomplish tremendous amounts of work. When you awake at 3:00 AM, you are refreshed, undistracted, and able to concentrate unusually well. Even if you are able to return to sleep only for an hour or so, the benefit of then climbing out of bed at 6:00 or 7:00 AM is that your body believes it has had a full night's rest when, in fact, you have added two productive hours to a busy schedule and lifestyle. This may not be for everyone, but it is recommended as something to be tried if you know what you want, but just do not have the time to accomplish it!

Early on, my talent was really in organizing people. I guess that I've always been able to organize people. When I ran all those paper routes, a lot of my friends had paper routes, too. It would take them forever to collect their route. **At an early age I learned that if you provide a better service than anybody else, then you can demand something a little different from the customer you are serving. In other words, I provided excellent service and the customer would give back to me.** What I basically told my customers was, "You get your paper when you want it and where you want it. I would like to have my payment in the mailbox on Saturday morning." I literally trained all these paper route customers. The rest of my friends would spend a week collecting their routes. I would collect all these routes in a few hours going mailbox to mailbox on Saturday morning. So I guess I learned at an early age how to organize people to my benefit. It involved a lot of hard work.

WINNERS...

#4. identify and meet others' needs and in return demand more from them

Whatever your hand finds to do, verily, do it with all your might...
(Ecclesiastes 9:10)

WINNERS...

#5. train and motivate others to accomplish their goals

And the things you have heard me say in the presence of many witnesses entrust to
reliable men who will also be qualified to teach others.
(2 Timothy 2:2)

WINNERS...

#6. know where they are going so others can help them get there

Be wise in the way you act toward others; make

**the most of every opportunity.
(Colossians 4:5)**

Believe it or not, at the same time, I had my own lawn mowing service. I bought my own equipment and I mowed over 20 lawns a week. During the winter time, I shoveled, by hand, the snow on the driveways and sidewalks of these customers. It was a lot of work, but I had big goals. I had things I wanted to do and things I wanted to buy. To me, a bank account was the most important thing in the world. You have to have money in the bank, especially when you are 15 and want to buy a motorcycle and a car.

About the same time, during the summer before I was 15, I got a job at Stokley Van Camp as a human fork truck. Stokley used to take pallets loaded with cardboard cases of bottled tomato ketchup and set it in the middle of a box car and we carried each case, one at a time, to each end of the box car and packed it tight. It had to be that way so the cases wouldn't move and break during shipping. I think I worked one summer at that and that's when I decided that this wasn't for the kid. This manual labor was for somebody else and not for me. I think this was the last time in my life that I "worked" for a living.

My love from day one was always fixing and making things, and going fast. Building things at an early age was what I enjoyed doing. I can't remember, but I was probably five, six, or seven years old when I got my first erector set. Literally, I never followed instructions. I just took the stuff and built away. I didn't even look at the pictures. It was just, "Well, I am going to build this or build that." I used to build the most elaborate cranes and bridges and trusses and motorized robotic type structures. It was just build and build and build. I know I had several erector sets and I would combine them all together and make anything and everything that I could possibly imagine. What I find really interesting is that my youngest daughter is 14 and is as mechanically inclined as I was at that age. I love it because she has several advanced erector sets and she builds the most elaborate contraptions, too. She can sit down and build them and they all work just like mine used to. **I find it a blessing that I have a daughter who has this ability, and I encourage her as often as I can.**

WINNERS...

#7. build others by recognizing admirable traits and commenting on them

> **Be devoted to one another in brotherly love; give preference
> to one another in honor...
> (Romans 12:10)**
>
> **Therefore encourage one another, and build up one another...
> (1 Thessalonians 5:11)**

There wasn't a scrap of wood left around the home that I didn't have my hands on and make something out of. Whether it was a birdhouse or whatever, I used up every nail and every screw my dad had. I have to say I had a really happy childhood because I was allowed to do all of these things. I was allowed to make things and also allowed to use up all the scrap lumber around the house. We had recently moved into our house in Paulding, Ohio, and there was a lot of scrap lumber there. If any boards or any nails or screws were left over, they were gone by the time my dad got back from the railroad because I had made something out of them. I just loved to make things.

As far as my mechanical ability is concerned, I do not know where or how I got it. I do know that my father did not really have much mechanical ability, but he was a good woodworker. I would say that when I was eight or nine years old, we were already constructing go-carts out of wood. They would not hold up, but I remember picking up a Steens catalog specializing in go-carts, mini bikes, and supplies. I would take one look at it and say, "I can build that." So I went down to the local hardware store, bought some black iron pipe, hack sawed it up in lengths, and fish mouthed it so it would fit together. All that was the easy part. The hard part was finding someone who would take a nine year old serious enough to weld it together and follow my instructions as to how I wanted it welded together. Well, I found someone, and he was Virgil Dangler.

Revving My Engines

Virgil was a local guy. He ran a speed shop, 'Dragway Automotive,' with some of his friends. These guys were always up to something. They were always out drag racing or **street racing** and our paths would cross for years to come. They were people like Jeff Hunter, Rex Dangler, and Loran Zedyke. They were all six to ten years older than I was, but I was in the process of building and selling mini bikes, go-carts, and having the time of my life. But, not to get ahead of myself, I want to tell you about how I became so interested in engines.

Much of my time was spent with my grandparents, John and Edith

Montgomery, who were my mother's parents.

As farmers, they lived on the outskirts of Portland, Indiana, actually closer to Bryant. My father's parents were also farmers. They lived in the Geneva area, not far from us, and their names were Frank and Eva Moser.

My father had two younger brothers and my mother was an only child. Frank Moser was mechanically inclined, as most farmers are, and he was always fixing and repairing things. For whatever reason, we spent more time with my mother's parents on John Montgomery's farm. It was a lot of fun as a child growing up visiting them every other week or weekend. They would take me and my sister, Connie, who was two years older on special outings, too. So we always had a good time.

In fact, Grandfather and I were always playing, tinkering, and messing with things. I think that at sometime, I was probably seven or eight years old, my grandfather had a lawn mower that wouldn't run and I fixed it for him. I think the points were gone so I replaced them, set the gap, added a new spark plug, and got the thing running. This really tickled my grandfather. He thought it was great that this kid was fixing the motor on his lawn mower. Soon after that I got interested in mini bikes and things like that, including go-carts. The first few we made were actually made out of wood and he would bring these old worn out 4-cycle motors to me. I don't know where farmers find old motors but he had a few and would allow me to tinker with them.

A lawn mower motor is what you would call a vertical shaft motor because of the blade on the bottom of the mower where the shaft runs up and down. You need a horizontal shaft motor for operating a go-cart, mini bike, or something similar, so I had to make a plate to mount the thing horizontally. I know that with the first one that I overhauled, the rod bearing and piston seized up on it. "Wow," I said, "What's wrong here?" So I got a horizontal motor and tore it apart, took the lawn mower motor and tore it apart, and lay everything out to compare the two. I discovered that the horizontal motor had a little finger or an arm that bolted to a cap on the rod, the big end of the cap of the rod. What it did was to actually dip into the oil and sling it on the cylinder wall as the thing was running. The only difference between a vertical and a horizontal motor was this oil slinger that went on the rod cap. After that, I took all the vertical motors and made them into horizontal motors and went to the local small engine shop and bought the little slinger that went on the rod and that took care of that problem.

You know how grandfathers are. They'll let you do anything. I used to spend a lot of time with him. He was always there when my father was away. I used to spend a week or more with him in the summer. It was truly an enjoyable experience because he really didn't care what I destroyed. He had me farming when I was a young kid. I think all farmers do that. I got to operate all of the equipment. He let me drive his truck, too. We would drive it into Bryant where there was a little elevator. We would drive into town in the afternoon and get a nickel coke or rootbeer and I always got to drive back. I remember thinking how special it was because there was never any need for a person who lived in town to drive a car before the age of sixteen. But, as all farmers know, young people who can help with chores are taught to drive equipment almost as soon as they can walk. The opportunity was unique to me and I loved it.

The other thing that we did was to fix a lot of stuff together. He had a lot of old equipment and a lot of small equipment. I think he had 300 acres that he farmed and he had to keep everything running. We were always fixing things and that was probably the start of my love for mechanics. My love for making things, for trying to figure out how things worked, and for making them work even better, all started about this time. So I would probably have to say that my early years were nurtured by my grandfather and my father, who played an important role, too.

All my free time was spent building, making, and fixing things. I remember talking my dad into letting me change the points and spark plugs in the family car. He wouldn't even attempt it. I did things like that at an early age. I remember working hard. It was because of my father. He could work anyone into the ground and that's where I operated. I would do whatever it took to get the job done. When I yelled charge, I'd never retreat. **I would keep at it until I accomplished what I wanted to accomplish.** That's how I operated, even at a young age. I would tear engines apart, go down to the local small engine shop, order pistons and rods, and slap in the valves. Now you have to remember that I'm about nine or ten years old at this time. I look at my children at nine and ten years old and I can't believe it. I think that's impossible, but it's a fact! I was doing these things when I was that young.

Somehow through all this I developed the need for speed. Speed for me related to everything, including how fast you could fix a lawn mower motor, how fast you could deliver newspapers, and how fast you could get your mini bike or go-cart to go. Everything was based on speed! I have carried that on throughout my entire life. You brake down everything into seconds and try to knock seconds off everything that you do. **I really don't know where I got this, but I always had the need to do things as fast as I could possibly do them and as best as I could possibly do them.**

WINNERS...

#8. accomplish what needs to be done doing their best at all times

**...So whatever you do, do it all to the glory of God.
(1 Corinthians 10:31)**

Later, when I was in high school, I took shop classes and I was really good at woodworking and metalworking. My only sister was perceived as having all the brains, since I just had the mechanical knowledge. That was kind of a detriment to me. I never really tried in school because **I was never expected to do as well as my sister.** I found out later in life that I could have done as well as or even better than my sister did, but it was not expected of me at that time. I was stumbling around and could care less about grades.

WINNERS...

#9. expect others to be winners and help them to be winners

Do nothing out of selfish ambition or vain conceit, but in humility of mind consider others better or more important than yourself. (Philippians 2:3)

When I look back on those years, I did have some moments of brilliance. I'm sure there were some teachers who probably thought, "Man, this kid could go somewhere." I had design abilities and was so good in shop that Bob Follas, the industrial arts teacher, would have me come down and show the other students how to run the lathes, mills, and shaper. So I would actually skip out of classes with the blessing of the teachers because I was assisting Mr. Follas. This was a detriment to my education, too, but I was having a wonderful time.

Mrs. Snider who taught biology was big on science fairs. So I came up with this elaborate maze that had different areas with trap doors, lights, and electronic shock mechanisms in the floor. What I was attempting to prove was that mice could see different shades of color. I did prove that and I remember when I brought in this impressive maze for our local science fair, Mrs. Snider couldn't believe it. It was one of those stereo-type things. I was an industrial arts guy with no business in the science fair. You know how you always have in your yearbook the person most likely to succeed. Well, I was probably the person most likely not to succeed, but I did have some brilliance. I ended up getting a "superior" on my science fair project. I didn't win the whole thing because I wasn't even supposed to be there. But, I won my category, and by getting superior, I went on to the district. I beat everybody at district, including the people who beat me at my local fair. I also went on to state with the project. There was some academic brilliance in my life, but nothing that anybody would really pay much attention to because I was just a gear head and I wanted to go fast. That's all I really ever wanted to do. Ending up finishing in the top third of my class was bizarre, though, because it sure wasn't for trying. I absolutely did not try. I was just having a good time running around, dating girls, racing, mowing yards, running paper routes, doing my own thing, and putting money in the bank.

Having a Great Time

In fact, I had saved so much money that when I was 15, I bought a 750 Norton motorcycle and a new car! I was the youngest in my class with an early quest and a need for speed. Before I had my driver's license, I remember telling my mother, as long as I had a learner's permit which you could always obtain first in Ohio, it was legal if I had a licensed driver on the back of my motorcycle. We used to ride this motorcycle everywhere. I used to sneak in at the drag strip and at the drag races when I was 15 by lying about my age. Piles of trophies were displayed in my room. I went for the fastest bike or the fastest qualifier. It was winning. Everything was winning. Everything was speed. Everything was how fast I could do something. That's how I conducted my life by having fun in high school, making things in shop class, and drag racing.

When I was a junior, I designed and drew up a four-valve cylinder head for my Norton motorcycle. I designed it and built it in shop class. I said, "Well, it was no big deal." But later, in an engineering course in college, I didn't even redraw the prints. I turned the prints in that I drew up as a kid and I aced a college course with something I engineered years earlier!

I not only installed speed parts, I made them, and by my senior year in high school, I had done everything I could possibly do with my Norton motorcycle. It would run high-tens in a quarter mile. That was flying in 1970!

There are faster bikes now, but 27 years ago, that was fast. It was the fastest thing in the county that I know of because I raced everybody. All we did was street race. One day, just after I had turned 16, I was out riding my motorcycle and anybody who knows anything about Norton (British) motorcycles knows that they have Lucas Electrics on them. Lucas Electrics are questionable. I think it started raining and my magneto fouled out on it, so I pulled off to the side of the road in a little town on the outskirts of Paulding, Ohio. I was wrenching on this thing, pulled the mag cover off, and took thin paper to clean the points. I put the cover back on, mounted the bike, started off, and almost ran into somebody. This guy had literally been looking over my shoulder the whole time. He said to me, "Man, you really know what you're doing!" I said something like, "Well, if you're going to ride a 'limy' bike, you have to know what you're doing! If you are going to ride with Lucas Electrics, you better know how to fix them." The guy looked at me and said, "You want a job? I need a good motorcycle mechanic." That incident started my motorcycle mechanic career.

Every night I worked fixing motorcycles. I have to honestly tell you that fixing motorcycles has become the love of my life. At that time I really became good at it. I could beat almost anything in Yamaha's flat rate charge by 50%, and on some repairs, I could completely blow them out of the water. One thing that I could really do well was that I could literally take the point cover off, set the dwell, take both spark plugs out, put a dial indicator in the spark plug hole, set the timing on the left cylinder, set the timing on the right cylinder, put new spark plugs back in, put the caps on, put the cover on, and do this in less than one minute! We sold a million of those tune-ups! Well, not a million, but hundreds of these on 350 Yamaha twins. We charged 20 bucks to do that. The dealer I was working for, Dave Ganger, gave me 65% of whatever I charged. I provided all my own tools, so I made 13 bucks in one minute. It was a lucrative job. I made money for myself, I made money for Dave, and we had a good time because motorcycle shops always attract those who like a good place to stop and bench race. That's where people pull-in and mouth-off about how fast their vehicle is.

Dave would be selling bikes and I'd be fixing bikes when some guy would come in and talk about how fast his motorcycle was. "Oh yeah?" (Heh, heh, heh!) We would put the closed sign in the window and go out and race, whether it was dirt bikes, drag race, or whatever! We'd put the sign in the window and we'd be gone. We'd be drag racing or we'd be dirt biking. Everything was performance. Everything was speed. Everything was how fast you could do something. I was fortunate to work for a guy who felt the same way I did. We both had the need for speed! We also loved motorcycles and loved to travel. We'd ride anywhere and everywhere. I've ridden bikes up north and down south and on the east coast. We would just take off and go on a bike trip. So about this time, when I turned 16, I sold my paper routes, quit mowing lawns, and I started fixing motorcycles. Larry Shaw, who owned a Sohio gas station locally in town, hired me to pump gas. I pumped gas on weekends and fixed motorcycles during the evening after school. In the summertime I pumped gas every evening, worked weekends at the station, and fixed motorcycles on the weekdays. I had a lot of motorcycles including a Harley chopper that I had built from a motorcycle that was in a fire. I also had two Nortons, a road bike, a drag bike, a 650 Yamaha, a 360 Enduro, and I had a 250 all out dirt bike. So I had eight motorcycles, plus a Z-28 that I bought new and an old beat up Ford truck. I was into vehicles and totally into speed. **I was having a great time, a really great time.**

WINNERS...

#10. enjoy what they are doing and help others to enjoy what they are doing

**Enjoy life and your work that God has given you under the sun all the days of your life.
(Ecclesiastes 9:9)**

More Lessons Learned

During all this motorcycle fixing I was not applying myself to learning anything in high school, but my sister was taking college courses and planning to go off to college. My father had gone a few semesters to Ball State in Muncie, Indiana. Somewhere along the line he said, "Maybe you should go to college. You should be an engineer because you can design and build anything." The biggest problem I had was that I had not taken any advanced courses in high school, so college would be very difficult for me. I was accepted at three colleges, including Tri-State, Purdue, and Indiana Institute of Technology, all in the state of Indiana. I chose Indiana Institute of Technology for the one reason that I could commute from home and still work. I never really took college seriously. In fact, I never really had to apply myself because, other than the mathematics, everything being taught came to me naturally . I could figure anything out and I could fix anything.

As far as the mathematics was concerned, I think I received a D in my first semester in calculus. I remember telling the professor, "I have no idea what you're even doing." He suggested that I was probably not old enough or mature enough to understand the concept of calculus. I blamed my not understanding on the fact that I had always been the youngest in my class. I did find out that we were both right because the second time around I aced it, calculus 1, calculus 2, and calculus 3. I just missed acing differential equations. That was the first time in my life, while in college, that I had the sensation that I was as smart as my sister! As I attended college, I basically worked full-time at the motorcycle shop and pumped gas on the weekends. I studied while pumping gas and I studied at the motorcycle shop. My junior year, an opportunity arose, and I took a machinist job. I dropped out of school. I don't know whether that was a good move or not, but I can't picture my life turning out any differently or any better for having graduated from college. I worked as a machinist and ran into my first wife. We dated for quite a while before eventually getting married. Unfortunately, marriage wasn't for us. I'm not sure why we married, but it wasn't for future success.

As a machinist, I was working for the Haviland Muffler Company when one day my dad came in and told me that Maremont was looking for a machinist. **Talk about being at the right place at the right time! That's what life is really all about. Too many people want everything now. They're not willing to take a different path when they can see that it may lead to a great opportunity.** So I interviewed for the machinist job. It was a little more money, but what interested me most was that evidently all the machinists who worked there were hired at about the same time, over 40 years ago. The youngest guy there was about 61 and the oldest guy was about 64. Well, it doesn't take a rocket scientist to look at this scenario and say, "I could work here for three more years and be number one in seniority." Number one in seniority is what I became, and during that time, everything came naturally for me as far as machining, tool and die making, etc. I just knew how to do it. I was the only person who ever worked there who drew group leader pay and tool and die maker pay on top of machining pay. So I basically had it made. I was number one in seniority and loved what I was doing! I had to learn new methods on how to deal with older people, not offend them and still get things accomplished. The only problem was I didn't like the way my boss ran the machine shop.

WINNERS...

#11. recognize how to be in the right place at the right time

#12. are willing to take a different path when a good opportunity arises

> **Trust in the Lord with all your heart and don't lean on your own understanding. In all your ways acknowledge Him and He will direct your paths.**
> **(Proverbs 3:5-6)**

Lower Pay for New Opportunities

One day the plant manager, Bob Treinen, walked through the plant. I stopped him and said, "Bob, this place is screwed up." I told him what was wrong with it and what I would do to make it right. He basically sloughed me off. A couple of days later he called me to his office and said, "Do you know anything about management or engineering?" We talked quite a bit and the next day he offered me a new position. Probably not many people would've ever taken this job, because **I was making around $24,000 with overtime a year as a machinist. He offered me this job at $16,000 a year with no opportunity for overtime pay. I took it! Most people would say, "You're out of your mind!"** No, I wasn't out of my mind. I saw an opportunity to get into management. So I took the maintenance superintendent's job. It wasn't about money. I was married, fixing motorcycles on the side, building a new house, drag racing, drag racing bikes, and drag racing cars. **It's about having a good time and knowing where I wanted to take my life**. My wife went along with whatever I wanted to do. So I took the job and was the maintenance superintendent, while fixing motorcycles, and having a good time.

WINNERS...

#13. will accept less pay to get the right job for the future

> **"You can have anything you want--if you want it badly enough. You can be anything you want to be, have anything you desire, accomplish anything you set out to accomplish--if you hold to that desire with singleness of purpose..."**
> **(Robert Collier)**

A couple years went by, Bob Treinen had moved on, and I received a phone call from him. He said, "Greg, I need a plant engineer." "Oh, really?" Looks like I made a pretty good choice to take the $16,000 a year job because he offered me a lot more money this time. I moved out to Troy, New York, to this old plant situated where the Wyantskill River runs into the Hudson River. It was actually a total no-brainer to improve the plant's operation. The equipment was beyond obsolete. In fact, documentation has been found indicating that it was one of the first iron-making fuller plants in North America. The fuller is the hoop that holds the barrel together. (That was how it was described.) Also, documentation was found that the Garrison Rolling mills were operated by steam power originally and they rolled the plate for the monitor during the Civil War at this facility. So it was really old and it was just a total cost reduction. Every time I turned around I saved money. I think the first year I saved $2,000,000 in cost reductions and the second year it was close to $1,000,000. Even though I had a tough time persuading my wife at the time to move out there, she finally agreed and we even had a child together. I thought everything was just great.

Don't Believe "Opposites Attract"

So I was saving this company a lot of money and one of the executives from Oakbrook, Wayne Knight, invited my wife and me to a Christmas party. We really had a good time! With all the cost reductions and improvements, this company was making money hand over fist, and throwing really elaborate parties and evenings out for employees. I remember one night when Wayne told my wife, "Boy, your husband is going to go places. We want him to be a plant manager at the Portec Memphis Railroad Products Plant." My wife responded by saying, "There's no way I'm moving to Memphis, Tennessee!"

Wayne instantly got a hold of me and said, "You have got a real problem. Your wife just told me she will not move!" My wife and I had a long talk and she was just unhappy. She didn't want to move anywhere, anywhere except back home to the Fort Wayne, Indiana, area. That was at the point in my life as a young kid when I still believed in the vows I took when I had been married. I thought I would try to save my marriage, so I gave up all and took a job with International Harvester in Fort Wayne, Indiana, where she wanted to live. I gave up being a plant manager and being a plant superintendent. I gave up running everything! I basically gave up all of that to be a spoke on a wheel in management at International Harvester.

We lived where I grew up in Paulding, Ohio. I thought she would be happy, but I was wrong! My wife said, "You're just too difficult to live with and I want to move out." That's when it dawned on me, wait a minute! I gave up a very promising career to try to make you happy, but you're not happy. What I discovered was, we were opposite people. They say,

"Opposites attract," but that's simply not true. At least, not if you're going to be successful. **You have to be on the same wavelength, have the same ideals, have the same morals, and the same basic goals. This really means that your spouse should come from the same economic background, religious orientation, etc.** We weren't happy. My whole goal in life was advancement and she had no interest in that. In the '70s, I signed my name in the front of books and drew an arrow straight up off the page. If you're going to succeed and dominate your little end of this world, you have to want to go to the top.

WINNERS...
#14. create synergistic energy by finding others of similar mind

Iron sharpens iron, so one man sharpens another.
(Proverbs 27:17)

As I have stated previously, **I believe that no matter what you do, you should do it to the best of your ability and you should do it to be the best.** If you want to be an electrician, then you should want to be the best electrician. If you want to be an engineer, you should want to be the best engineer. If you want to be a toolmaker, you should want to be the best toolmaker. One of my faults is that I expect everyone to do their best. When I run into half-baked service, my thought is, "Why are you a waitress? If you don't want to do the job right, why do you do it?." That's my philosophy of life. I've got a lot of philosophies, but one of the most important is that if you're going to do something, then you do it the best you can possibly do it.

WINNERS...

#15. are competitive and want to be the best

Do you not know that those who run in a race all run, but only one receives the prize? Run in such a way that you may win.
(1 Corinthians 9:24)

So my goal in life has always been to run the company and to go straight to the top. Whatever company employs me, I'm going to run it. I realized that was not my wife's goal and we parted ways. We divorced.

How Not to Operate a Plant

I got back into drag racing, having dropped out of it for the few years I was on the east coast. I ran into Donny Whirrett who helped me with a lot of the work in building a race car. The result was an altered which was completely home built. It was another one of those deals, just like the mini bikes and the go-carts that I had constructed, built, and sold to the neighborhood kids. I literally looked at a picture and constructed it. We went to a car show and saw an alcohol funny car chassis and duplicated it. Everything was made from scratch. The headers were even hand made, as was the body, all the bracketry, all the steering, and the front steering knuckles. Everything was hand fabricated and not purchased! It was actually fabricated at my little machine shop with an old lathe, an old mill, and many parts.

Now I had a real challenge at Harvester at this point in my career. I was a spoke on a wheel and it was 99% political. That was really tough. This was about the time management was trying to bankrupt the International Harvester Group by promoting a strike to get some concessions back from the union. I don't really want to elaborate on unions, but everybody's always pointing a finger at them saying it's their fault. Well, the whole deal is that when you sign a contract, there's a management signature on it as well as the union's signature. So I think everybody's at fault for all the giveaways and all the benefits driving prices up.

During the Harvester strike, I worked as a maintenance man on third shift, fixing everything that everybody broke trying to make production. I worked twelve hours a day and seven days a week. I made a literal fortune, so I had a lot of money to spend on race cars. Between all the partying that I was doing, I kept my home with a pool, the acreage, all my tools, and basically paid off my first wife, keeping everything else. I was really having a good time, but I think I was down to about 167 lbs. and at 6'2", I was looking pretty bad. I had a friend of the family, Sandy Bandy, who came to the house. She took one look at me and said, "Man, you look rough. You need to get yourself a wife. Get your health back." I was completely burned out. She said, "I have this friend you have to meet. She'll be good for you." "Yeah, yeah, right," I said, "That's what everybody tells me. You want to set me up?" She said, "No, no, no! This woman works just as hard as you do." I said, "Yeah, it's impossible." She said, "No, it's not impossible. Her husband left her when her kids were three and one. She waited tables and finished her college education. She has a teaching degree, teaches school, and waits tables while she's raising the two kids. She works all the time." So I called Marianne and we spent some time together!

That was when it dawned on me that an important rule in life is marrying for success. I now knew from my first marriage what didn't work. I remember one time when I was over at Marianne's apartment looking for something under the sink and I saw this plastic tray. It had wrenches, spark plug wrenches, spark plug boxes, a couple of oil filters, and five quarts of oil. I said, "What's this stuff?" She said, "That's my stuff for the car. I have to keep it serviced." I thought to myself, "This is hard to believe, a woman who changes her own oil, and spark plugs! I'm going to marry this woman." We did some drag racing together, and she liked it as much as I did. We really got into it and ended up getting married. I adopted her two children and we had one of our own. With the children from Marianne's previous marriage, we now have Rob, who's 26, Cindy, who's 24, Angie, who's from my first marriage and is 22, and Danielle, who is Marianne's and mine and is 14 as this book is being written.

After we were married, I was employed by Harvester in Fort Wayne, Indiana. The person who hired me, Mel Bye, left right after I was hired, going to the Wagner, Oklahoma, plant. It was at this time that I first experienced a taste of politics in the work place. **I believe that there is really nothing negative in this world.** No matter how bad a situation is, it can always be viewed as a positive learning experience.

WINNERS...

#16. take a potential negative and make it into a positive

"In the middle of difficulty lies opportunity."
(Albert Einstein)

So, being employed for Harvester was a good learning experience. It was where I learned how NOT to operate a plant. It was just crazy the wages they'd pay people. I remember when I was running maintenance in the A&T (axle and transmission) division. I said something about not being able to get the floor sweepers to follow instructions! One person was sweeping the floor in the brake area and I could not get him to do what I wanted him to do. They said, "Well, you should be able to. He's got a master's degree." I said, "A master's degree!?" They said, "Well, yeah! They make more money here sweeping the floor than they do teaching school." I couldn't believe it! I would tell them, "You can't operate a plant like this." They would just poo-poo me by saying, "This place has been here forever and it will be here forever." Well, it's not! They succeeded in running it into the ground and ended up laying everybody off.

Before any layoffs, I narrowed the rear end of a race car that we built. We built the whole car but I figured out a way to hard spline the axles. You see, an OEM axle shaft is 58-60 Rockwell on the surface that's hard. Everybody who was narrowing rear ends, at least the low budget method, would cut the axle in half, take a section out, and weld it back together. If you were a metallurgist, you would just cringe if I said something like that because what was created was a piece of worthless junk. What we engineered was a way to cold cut the splines in the axle shaft. The first machine I used to accomplish this took about an hour to do an axle and the job was well done. We were racing everywhere and by word of mouth, a few people asked me to narrow their axles for their race cars. We needed the money because we were spending a lot of money racing. We would race at Avilla, Indiana, on Friday night, Muncie on Saturday, and Wayne Trail on Sunday. Racing three times a week, we would win a lot. They had a quick eight at Van Wert, Ohio. We'd win that about half the time and if we didn't win it, we were usually runner-up. So I was racing cars, narrowing axles, and working for Harvester until that day came when they laid me off.

Greg's Ancestry
by John G. Young

While what follows has everything to do with the very existence of Greg Moser, it has little to do with Greg Moser's life and background since he started to work in Jay County in 1982. What follows is an amazing story about Greg's ancestors. It is important because it helps to define something of what life was like for those ancestors and of the kind of stock from which Greg comes. The input for the story is a combination of written recorded evidence and reliable word of mouth information.

The earliest relevant background information for the story dates to 1835 and to Beallsville, Washington County, Pennsylvania, where Jason Griffith and Nancy White were married. To this union were born nine children with the eldest being Isaac Allen, who was born on May 8, 1836. As the eldest son, Isaac was expected to help assure the well-being of the family. In addition to working, Isaac educated himself and received a teaching certificate and taught school in Pennsylvania. In about 1859, it was decided that a new home should be found for his parents and the entire Griffith family. At the age of 23, Isaac undertook a 350 mile trip from Pennsylvania to Indiana on foot and the trip is best described in his obituary which appeared on July 8, 1919, the day following his death.

"No network of railroads covered our

> country then by which he might be conveyed the seemingly great distance to his destination. As he walked from his home to Pittsburgh no automobile with its accompanying cloud of dust passed by him--no buggies or fancy carriages overtook him. That was in the day of ox-teams and corduroy roads--the day of blazed trails."

During his stay in Jay County, Indiana, he contracted to purchase 40 acres of land and immediately set out on foot again to carry the good news to the family in Washington County, Pennsylvania. Quoting the Isaac Griffith obituary again,

> "...within a short time the father, mother and nine children were on their way to the then 'far west.' Their destination reached, a one-room log cabin was erected and their permanent abode began."

While it is recorded in the obituary that Isaac loved to relate the story of the "memorable trips," there is no known written account of the trip. Sarah Malvena (Griffith) Montgomery was the youngest sister of Isaac and the great-great grandmother of Greg Moser. Sarah did later relate to grandson Ted Montgomery her recollections of following the covered wagon and picking flowers along the way.

It fell to Jason and Isaac, and probably any other family members who could help, to build a log cabin and start the clearing of the 40 acres. While there is again no known written record of what life was like during that first year in Jay County, there is a letter from Jay County to members of the White family back in Pennsylvania describing the difficult farming conditions at the time.

Within one year of the arrival of the Griffith family, they contracted "black diphtheria." With no known cure available at that time, the family was nearly wiped out over a period of 20 days in the fall of 1860. The tombstones which still stand in the picturesque Mt. Zion cemetery in Noble Township in Jay County, Indiana, are testimonials and grim reminders of what Nancy White Griffith went through. During the days which started on September 25, 1860, the following is recorded on those tombstones:

Jason Griffith (father)	Died--September 25, 1860	Age 58
Mary Eliza Griffith	Died--October 3, 1860	Age 13
Martha Ann Griffith	Died--October 7, 1860	Age 22
Jason Alex Griffith	Died--October 9, 1860	Age 18
Emma Viola Griffith	Died--October 11, 1860	Age 4
Benjamin White Griffith	Died--October 12, 1860	Age 15
Jacob Fisher Griffith	Died--October 13, 1860	Age 11
Esther Edith Griffith	Died--October 14, 1860	Age 9

Another son, Benjamin, had died at age 4 in 1844 before the family came to Jay County.

"Grandma" Griffith, as Nancy was known until her death, her eldest son Isaac, and youngest daughter Sarah Malvena were the only survivors of this plague. Sarah, or Aunt Sade (Sadie) as she was fondly called, married George Montgomery on August 3, 1872. The George Montgomery's lived in Bryant, Indiana, where George went into business with brother-in-law Isaac Griffith, who had established a general store in nearby Westchester near the land owned by the Montgomery family. George Montgomery felt strongly about the issues raised by the Civil War and, after mounting some obstacles, became a soldier. He was kicked out of one unit because he lied about his age and eventually became a member of the 89th Regiment Co. E. While little is known about his military career, a story survives that he accidentally shot himself in the arm while firing his rifle. George Montgomery was a respected merchant and for two years prior to his death was also President of the Farmers and Merchants Bank of Bryant.

Obituaries at that time were flowery and following are excerpts from the obituary of Sarah Griffith Montgomery, who died on July 29, 1935:

> "'The stream is calmest when it nears the tide;
> The flowers the sweetest at the even-tide.
> The birds most musical at the close of day,
> The Saints divinst when they pass away.'
>
> So it was with Sarah Montgomery, whose earthly
> life came to its close at the age of 81 years, 11 months
> and 5 days.
>
> She was the daughter of Jason and Nancy Griffith
> and was born in Beallsville, Pa, Aug. 24, 1811.

She was united in marriage to George Montgomery
Aug. 3, 1872. The two tread life's pathway lovingly
and happily together until Sept. 7, 1919
when her companion was called by death.

Mother Montgomery possessed a lovely personality,
a sweet and kindly spirit which endeared her to a host
of friends, both young and old.

She lived a model Christ-like life, was a lovely mother
and kindly neighbor.

She leaves to cherish her memory five children...,
13 grandchildren and 5 great-grandchildren and many
other relatives and friends.

'Tears of Joy today are blended.
Tears for loss and Joy for again.
Mothers stay on Earth is ended,
God has called her from her pain.

Thanks to God who gave her to us,
As we lay her neath the flowers.
Sweet memories always with us,
Of that Mother Dear of ours.'"

    To Sarah Griffith and George Montgomery were born 6 children and it was son William H. Montgomery who was to marry Wilma Rosenbloom. William and Wilma were the great grandparents of Greg Moser. William Montgomery was a farmer and owned land north of Westchester where the general store was located. One of William and Wilma's sons was John, who was to marry Edith Dull. John and Edith were the grandparents of Greg Moser. Their only daughter Joan was to marry William Moser.

    Greg Moser is the only son of William and Joan Montgomery Moser. Greg, who grew up as a city boy, has fond recollections of visiting grandparents John and Edith Montgomery on the very farm where Greg now lives. He credits grandfather John Montgomery for providing the first spark of his all-consuming interest in cars and motors, which has led to his incredible career. Grandpa John Montgomery also let "Greggy" drive the farm tractor at a very young age. Even more exciting was the approval to drive the pickup truck into Bryant, even though he could barely reach the pedals. Greg has a fond memory of the readiness with which Grandpa John Montgomery would ply him with root beer floats and sodas until he became ill. When chided by Grandma Edith, John's retort was, "But he kept asking for more."

Grandpa John continued to farm the land owned by his father, William Montgomery, and it was in the woods of this farm that Greg would play and hide when he was a boy. Greg learned to love these woods. In about 1990 Greg and Marianne Moser acquired this property and in 1995 built a lovely home there.

The generosity of Greg and his wife in sharing their lovely home with friends and associates is surpassed only by their generosity in sharing the fruits of their hard work and ingenuity with the entire Jay County community.

Could it be that the hard work and ingenuity characterized by Greg Moser can be linked to that Griffith family walk into the wilderness in 1859? Could it be that the willingness to live through adversity to reach a difficult goal can be linked to the struggle of privation and the untimely deaths of those who went before? I think that the pioneer spirit that existed in the lives of Greg's ancestors lives today in Greg as it does in the lives of so many Americans who are proud of their roots and are not ashamed of the blood, sweat and tears that are necessary to make things happen.

All who know and appreciate Greg are grateful that Sarah Malvena Griffith was one of the survivors of the "Black" death that nearly wiped out the entire Griffith family in 1860.

Chapter Two

QUALIFYING TO RACE

**Learning How to Do It Right
Winning Time Trials Leads to My Own Business
You Can Qualify, Too!**

Four days after being laid off, I received a phone call. "Hey! I want you to set up a machine shop for me at a new plant in Columbus, Ohio." I only went there because **it's a lot easier to find a job while you're employed, doing well, than it is to find a job if you're unemployed.** While I was working there I started actively looking for a job and I ended up with three offers. I took the best job offer which was a Teledyne position in Indiana at its Portland Forge.

WINNERS...

#17. find it easier to get a new job if they are doing well

"There is no future in any job. The future lies in the
man who holds the job."
(Robert Crane)

Learning How to Do It Right

They made me plant engineer which had to be the ultimate job. I talk a lot to students now in entrepreneurial classes and I do keynote speaking engagements and I basically tell them, "I haven't worked in 25 years." That's because I haven't. I don't consider what I'm doing, as an engineer, work. It's playing. **In fact, anyone who enjoys his or her job as much as I did at this time cannot help but succeed.**

WINNERS...

#18. enjoy their job so much that working seems like play

**Delight yourself in the Lord and He will give you
the desires of your heart.
(Psalm 37:4)**

At Portland Forge, it was a blast because we were always building things which made the jobs easier and made the people more productive. We wouldn't lay anybody off. We would automate, reduce manpower, and, in that sense, eliminate unnecessary labor through attrition and efficiency, saving the company money. I was given the responsibility of designing one of the most modern forge shops on the face of this earth.

Our plant had its own Citation jet, and when I was promoted to the position of vice-president of manufacturing and engineering, I started flying everywhere. I traveled all over Europe looking at equipment other plants operated. We put together a brand new state-of-the-art forge facility in Lebanon, Kentucky, which had screw presses in it and had automated steel storage racks where you could go to get the material. It had shear tables where you could bar unscramble the bar stock. It allowed you to feed stock through induction heater coils. We also had a hot shear that actually sheared the material at forging temperature. We had an adjustable stop-gage on the shear so that the operator could add or subtract gram weight as he was running, because as the die wears, you need more material to fill it. The part was placed on the die from the descaler that knocked any scale that was on the part, off the part, and it was transferred from the machine to the trim press. Trimmed, using micro-alloys, it was put on cooling tables to actually heat treat it. It was probably one of the most technically advanced forge shops ever conceived and it was fun to design.

That was one of my projects along with maintaining the Portland Forge plant and EPA (Environmental Protection Agency) standards. I went through all the material safety data sheets and the hazard communication exercises, and with engineering and production, I was busy. I must have done a good job because I was promoted the whole time. At the same time, I was building race cars and engines, and racing everywhere. I'd take my vacation one day at a time and drive all night, qualify Friday and Saturday, race Sunday, and tow all night to be back to work with no sleep on Monday morning. I'd do this all the time and still did a good enough job to be promoted. You might say at the plant that I was qualifying to race because I was meeting all of the time trials, so to speak, and experiencing success in all that I did. It was very difficult to leave that kind of a scenario. It was very difficult because I was having such fun designing and engineering things and working with and helping people.

Winning Time Trials Leads to My Own Business

We got the national event bug so all we wanted to race were national events. That takes a lot of money, so Marianne and I were trying to decide if there was enough money to be made in the business of resplining axles. We basically invented that word. **The true definition of an entrepreneur is someone who discovers a product or a service that people don't even know they need, convinces them that they have to have it, effectively dreams up a method of manufacturing it, sells it to them, then makes a buck doing it.** We basically invented the word, respline, because the stock axle has splines on it. So if you're going to cut it off, what are you going to do with it? You're going to respline it.

WINNERS...

#19. are entrepreneurs meeting needs by selling profitable products

"If there's a way to do it better...find it."
(Thomas A. Edison)

So, by simple word of mouth, we were making money--race car money--by doing one to three pairs of axles per week. We were contemplating going into business, so we sent for some media kits and they proved to us that there was no short cut or cheap way to advertise. If someone is going to sell you a sixth of a page or a twelfth of a page for 100 bucks, you're going to get a circulation to 100,000 people. If you advertise in *Hot-Rod* magazine, they want 600 bucks for a little bitty one inch ad because the circulation is 6,000,000. We had to sign up for three consecutive months minimum at $1,800, so even though we put it off and put it off, I believe it happened for a reason.

It was a week or two after we got all these media kits that I received a phone call from Pete McHenry, the vice president for Industrial Furnace Service Corporation (IFSC). He called me up and said, "I have a problem. We just bought a brand new Chevy truck with a 350 in it, and we hauled these heavy-weight furnace ladle tops to the steel industry with it. This truck only had a 456 gear in it and wouldn't pull the weight. This one plant was up on a hill and we couldn't even deliver the load even though it was a brand new truck. We need to run about a 5-something gear in it." The lowest gear Chevrolet made in the thing was a 456. So he said, "I'd like for you to put an older rear end in and put a 5-series gear in it." So I checked around and I found an old Dana '70 rear end. The local salvage yard wanted

100 bucks for it. I called up my friend Loran Zedyke and said, "Hey, do you have a set of gears to put in this truck?" "Yeah, I happen to have a 587 ratio which is what you need." "What do you want for it?" "Oh, a 100 bucks."

So my cost was 200 bucks total and I called up Pete and said, "Yeah, I'll do it for $1,000. I'll swap this rear end and set the gear up in it for you." He started laughing and said, "Man, that's way too cheap." So I asked, "Well, what were you planning on paying for it?" He said, "Well, I can't even get it done around here. You're my only hope to get it done. I'll give you $2,000 to do it." How's that for coincidence? With a couple of weekends of work, I had my $1,800, and we sent it off to *Peterson's Hot Rod* magazine, took out the ad, and the very first month, I think we made 1200 bucks over and above the $600 for the ad. My wife and I couldn't believe it. We could not believe it. Just amazing!

That's what started the business. This was in '87. My wife answered the phone, took care of tech questions, and at night I unboxed what came in, did the job, boxed it back up, and shipped it out. The two of us did it all. I did my work when I got home from Portland Forge. The pricing structure that we had was based on nothing. It was not based on what I actually had in it. We basically reasoned that the average UPS shipping was 15 bucks. So we thought, well, let's just charge $85 so that the person has 100 bucks cash on delivery due when he gets it back. That's how we came up with our pricing schedule.

We have not raised a price on any product that we have manufactured since 1987. We've lowered pricing. There are only a few items that I have someone else make for me that we've had to raise the price on because if I didn't, I'd be selling at a loss. But on what I have manufactured, we have never raised a price.

We came up with $85 to spline a pair of axles. Every year, we'd double our advertising. This will work when you're talking about a product that no one else makes or a job that no one else on the face of the earth does. The more people that know about it, the more business you have. So, we started advertising, and every fall we'd double our advertising. Sometimes we'd double the size of the ad, and sometimes we'd leave the ad size the same and go to another magazine. The need for speed, more production, greater efficiency, a supportive wife, and all that I had brought from my childhood and family resulted in success. From '87-'92, the business grew at an average of 93% a year. It basically doubled every year and all the time, I was having fun!

Nonetheless, we were having some upper management problems at Teledyne which was affecting my life at Portland Forge. Corporate people came in and had some big meetings and on a Friday they offered me the president's job. There was one stipulation. While my boss, Bob Reed, had tolerated my business, which might have been considered a minor conflict of interest, the new corporate people would not. They said I'd have to sell my company.

My wife, Marianne was saying, "I need help! You have to get over here and help me run this place," because by this time we had built a new building in the industrial park. We had moved out there from our two-car garage. When they said I would have to sell my business, it was a no-brainer. I wasn't going to sell the company. At that time, our business was making sales of $1,500,000 at 30% profit. So I was making $450,000 a year. I knew I couldn't sell this. I basically told them I had to go home and talk to my wife and I would let them know Monday morning.

What I really wanted to do was to go home and enjoy being the President of Portland Forge for two days. Then, on Monday, I said, "I'm sorry but I have to decline your offer." I gave them a couple of months notice and left. **The reason I did that was because throughout my entire career, my objective, no matter where I worked, was to end up running the place.** I had accomplished that goal. So now it was time to go accomplish my own goals. As soon as I started working my business on a full-time basis and talked to my customers on the telephone, I became more aware of the needs in the market. So we started selling more and doing more. The business doubled every year and in 1992 Marianne and I thought, "Well, if we're this efficient with a remanufactured OEM axle, why don't we make a new axle and make an instant axle?"

WINNERS...

#20. develop their leadership qualities to be the boss

...I do not regard myself as having laid hold of it yet; but one thing I do: forgetting what lies behind and reaching forward to what lies ahead, I press on ...
(Philippians 3:13-14)

People buy products for only three reasons: quality, price, and delivery. You can have one of those three things and sell your product. If you have super delivery you can have a high price and bad quality and people will buy your product. You can have a cheap price, terrible quality, terrible delivery and people are going to buy your product. Or, you can have terrible delivery, a super high price, but the quality's impeccable. It'll last forever. Guess what? People will buy your product.

WINNERS...

#21. succeed by insuring product quality, price, and delivery (service)

Finally, brethren, whatever is true, whatever is honorable, whatever is right, whatever is pure, whatever is lovely, whatever is of good repute, if there is any excellence and if anything worthy of praise, let your mind dwell on these things.
(Philippians 4:8)

You Can Qualify, Too!

In starting my business from scratch, **I decided to do right all the things I had seen industry do wrong.** If we were going to engineer a product, I wanted to make it the best and the cheapest on the market and provide two-day delivery, which is instant compared to the way my competitors were doing it. They'd take weeks to deliver a pair of axles.

WINNERS...

#22. profit from their mistakes as well as from the mistakes of others

Like a dog that returns to its vomit
Is a fool who repeats his folly.
(Proverbs 26:11)

We hired one employee when we worked in our two-car garage and spent a long time looking for that perfect person. When you have the luxury of starting a business from scratch, you want the perfect employee-- **someone who is healthy, who has never missed a day where he used to work, is intelligent, who wants to be responsible, and who wants to be given responsibility.** That is a good employee. If you start out with good employees, they will make sure all the others you hire are good employees, too, or they will run them out the door.

WINNERS...

#23. surround themselves with responsible people who in turn do the same

**He who walks with the wise grows wise,
but a companion of fools suffers harm
(Proverbs 13:20)**

So, we're plugging along here and we come out with these new axles. As we rolled out this new product, what I found ironic was that nobody in the industry really knew how good or bad their axles were! **The key in any industry is to know where your product stands against the competition.** So I built a torque testing machine that could literally test the torque of the axles, the degrees of rotation, and then the cycle fatigue life of the material. Then, I engineered a total of about 30 different types of axles. There were five different heat-treats and five different materials. That's a total of 25. I started doing testing and when I finished, I found out just how good my product was. Since I had developed the automated equipment to do this, it took an hour to do an axle when I first started, then I got it down to 20 minutes, and then down to 15 minutes. I would keep reengineering my machines building them in house. The computers are interfaced with indexing heads. I can spline an axle in two minutes now, and do it unattended. I have six of those machines. It takes that many because we are now averaging 166 pair a day. We've done as many as 272 pair in one day. In fact, every Monday in the month of March, April, and May we do 400 to 500 axles a day!

WINNERS...

#24. know and test their products and the products of their competitors

**"Hold yourself responsible for a higher standard than anybody else expects of you. Never excuse yourself."
(Henry Ward Beecher)**

We continually build equipment. I have some equipment now that I have just finished. We drill holes in an axle flange for the studs. We can drill five holes in 27 seconds, floor to floor time, and we can tap five holes in 15 seconds. This is the kind of equipment that you need if you are going to make a commitment like I have to myself and to the world, that I am not going to add to inflation. It's just total lunacy for people to raise the price of their products in order to pay for their wage increases. Because all they're doing is adding to inflation. **We, on the other hand, give our people pay raises based upon productivity increases.** We have the highest paid employees in Jay County, Indiana, period, and I have not raised a price since 1987. **In 10 years, we have not contributed to inflation.**

WINNERS...

#25. increase productivity in order to give pay raises

#26 absolutely do not contribute to inflation by raising prices

"The world is blessed most by men who do things,
and not by those who merely talk about them."
(James Oliver)

Chapter Three

ENGINE IMPROVEMENTS

**Accomplishing Much
Changing Your Attitude
Fine Tuning to Make Every Second Count
Knowledge is Power As Is Working Smart
Tips for Engineers
Marrying for Success**

Growing up with parents who hold you accountable for your actions develops integrity at an early age. In all the work I did and all the paper routes I ran, I never failed to deliver. It didn't matter what the weather was. Basically, I had the papers out anywhere between 3:00 AM and 5:00 AM in the morning. **When I told somebody that I was going to do something, I did it.** And when I told them I wasn't going to do something, they didn't expect it to be done. I think that has a lot to do with being successful in this world.

WINNERS...

#27. do what they say they are going to do or communicate otherwise

Simply let your 'Yes' be 'Yes,' and your 'No' be 'No.'
(Matthew 5:37)

Accomplishing Much

It seems like from an early age, I had the ability to plan ahead. I always thought out what I was going to do for my next move. To get a lot accomplished, you have to do that. **You cannot waste time.** I didn't waste time when I was a youngster. As I grew up and circumstances pointed my life in new directions, it became even more critical that I not waste time. I didn't even waste seconds, because I knew they all added up. **I think one of the soundest pieces of advice you can give to anyone is to just forget** the word "procrastination." While people are worrying or thinking about how to do something, they could have already had it done. Consequently, if you put something off until the next day you have just wasted that day. In fact, not only did you waste the day, but you probably are going to spend the next day doing what you should have done the day before and, thus, you're going to miss an opportunity today because you have to work on something that you could have done yesterday. Miss an opportunity today and you have missed life, because that's all life is: an opportunity! Probably one of the hardest things for people to recognize is an opportunity. But even harder than that is to take advantage of an opportunity after it has been recognized. **If you're busy catching up from the day before, you'll never be ready for and recognize an opportunity, let alone take advantage of it.**

WINNERS...

#28. plan ahead to never waste time or procrastinate

Commit your works to the Lord,
And your plans will be established.
(Proverbs 16:3)

WINNERS...

#29. not only recognize opportunities but they take advantage of them

"The people who get on in this world are the people who get up and look for the circumstances they want, and, if they can't find them, make them." (George Bernard Shaw)

My desire to work hard was ingrained in me by my father. We worked together when we could since he worked all the time. In fact, as I was growing up, I worked a lot of hours and a lot of jobs, at least two or three at a time. When I worked at Maremont, before I went into management, overtime was allocated by seniority. After a couple of years, when I had seniority over everyone, I told the maintenance superintendent at the time, "Don't bother asking me if I want to come in for overtime when I'm up on the list. Just tell me when to come in." That was my philosophy. If you want me to work, and if you're going to pay me to work, I'll be there to work!

The secret to getting a lot of work done is to do the work. Numerous situations I've had later in life indicate to me that any decision is better than no decision: right or wrong. If you're making no decision whatsoever, then all of your subordinates and the people you work with really know that you're clueless. It's hard to manage people by procrastinating and worrying about what you're going to do next, not to mention the fact that you're never going to get anything done. Just do it! Sense your gut reaction to a problem and you will probably have the correct answer. It's just like when you're taking a test. Usually your first answer, your first inclination, is right. It's usually right when you're making a management decision, too.

WINNERS...

#30. get a lot of work done by doing the work that needs to be done

"The mind is the limit. As long as the mind can envision the fact that you can do something, you can do it--as long as you really believe 100 percent."
(Arnold Schwarzenegger)

Not only did I get a lot done but I also learned from what I was doing. Over these early years, I had a quest for excellence. **If you're not going to do something right, then don't do it at all.** In fact, I try to tailor that to everything I do. For example, what if you're not a good baseball player? Then, maybe you shouldn't play baseball. Or if you're not a good football player, then maybe you shouldn't play football. If you're good at something that's probably what you should pursue. It'll give you a lot more satisfaction in life.

WINNERS...

#31. do it right or don't do it at all

"The quality of a person's life is in direct proportion to their commitment to excellence, regardless of their chosen field of endeavor."
(Vincent T. Lombardi)

Another philosophy that I developed early around 10 or 11 years old was one that I believe is a philosophy of engineers today. Something is either right or it's wrong. It's black or it's white and there is no in between. I think I developed that with my theories on making a decision. **You do not vacillate in making decisions, getting things done, or being on time.** It all comes with right or wrong, and black or white, because if you can't make up your mind, you can't make a decision, and then you can't move forward. That's how I manage to get a lot of things done. In fact, to this day, people wonder how I get all the things done that I do. Well, it's because I do not procrastinate. When someone asks me to do something, I do it. I'm meticulous about that.

WINNERS...

#32. do not vacillate in making decisions, getting things done, or being on time.

One of the teachers at the high school recently asked me to speak at the academic excellence banquet. It was a month away. As soon as I hung up the phone, I roughed out my speech so that I could work on it periodically. I basically roughed out the outline within an hour after agreeing to do it. That is how I get a lot of things done.

Changing Your Attitude

Throughout the time when I was 9 to 23 years old, I was basically working three jobs, having a good time, saving money, and enjoying life. I didn't have much to do with anybody and developed an arrogance and an intolerance for most people in general. I had a few friends but I wasn't concerned with friends. As I was going to school, I really wasn't going, at least in my mind, to learn anything. I was basically going through the motions because it was kind of understood that my sister had the brains and I had the mechanical knowledge. She could get A's and if I received C's, that was okay. So that's all they expected of me and I do realize now that if my parents had expected A's out of me, I would've gotten A's. In college, when I knew I had to do it, I did it.

Somewhere along the way I developed a quest for excellence. I can honestly attribute a change in my behavior to an individual in high school. This person was the industrial arts teacher, Bob Follas, whom I mentioned in an earlier chapter. I remember it like it was yesterday. We were in the wood shop and we were building folding lawn chairs. He had passed out some wood to me, and I don't remember what I said, but it was a smart mouth comment. Mr. Follas grabbed me by the throat, threw me up against the wall and said, "Moser, you're never going to go anywhere in the world if you don't get rid of that attitude!" Then he just walked away, and after thinking about it, I went into his office. I apologized and said, "I really wasn't being smart." I showed him the wood that he gave me and said, "This wood has a couple of knots in it. I want my lawn chair to be immaculate. I don't want knots in my lawn chair. I want it to be beautiful and I want it to last. That's why I was complaining about the knots. I really wasn't bad mouthin' you." I was a freshman in high school at the time, and we got along really well after that. It was during that time that I changed my attitude towards other people. **I realized right then the importance of getting along with others.** I attribute the lesson learned to Bob Follas on that particular day.

WINNERS...

#33. recognize the importance of being able to get along with everyone

Pursue peace with all men...
(Hebrews 12:14)

My philosophy throughout high school, then, was to do it right or don't do it at all, but that didn't mean we didn't have fun! In industrial arts class, I built all kinds of things from a solid oak gun cabinet to that four-valve cylinder head for my drag bike. We were always overhauling motors in class. We were just having a good time, dating girls and drinking beer on weekend nights. We were in Ohio so we could get 3/2 beer which was a special beer with less alcohol for those over 18 years of age. My whole life was working to do it right or not at all. That was my philosophy. And even when I reflect on my years of weekend drinking, I remember looking at an alcohol/weight chart to see how much alcohol I could drink and still be under my state's legal limit for alcohol in the blood. I stopped drinking at that point. If not, I would have someone else drive me home! I have lived by these rules for over 20 years with the most important being never to drink and then drive.

Fine Tuning to Make Every Second Count

When I was a sophomore in high school, my dad was diagnosed with cancer of his lymph glands . He was given six weeks to live and that was it. He went through chemotherapy. He not only lived that six weeks, but lived over 22 years. In fact, at the time of his death, he was the oldest living oncology patient that Parkview Hospital in Fort Wayne, Indiana, ever had. He went through three separate rounds of chemotherapy and lived to be 62. Someone claimed that each round of chemotherapy takes ten years off your life, so he should've lived to be 92. That's how strong a heart he had.

A lot of my strength in life was gained as I experienced the strength of my father during this time. The man never complained. In fact, most people never knew that he had a problem either undergoing chemotherapy or fighting cancer. The doctors would build his blood cells up and then knock them down. While they were building them up, that's when we'd take off and go fishing together. It's the one thing that my father loved to do all the time. He loved to fish.

We kept in touch even after I was married. When I started seriously running the national event circuit drag racing, my dad was always there. He was my pit-crew. He actually scheduled his treatments so that he was feeling good on the weekends when I went racing. In fact, no one racing with me ever had any idea that my father had a problem. I remember when Loran Zedyke, who passed away in 1996, was first diagnosed with cancer. I remember he was down and out and I told him, "Well, I wouldn't even be concerned about it. My dad has had cancer now for 17 or 18 years, and he's still alive." Loran said, "What? Your dad's got cancer?" I know it changed his outlook and he lived for 5 or 6 years after that before he passed away.

WINNERS...

#34. gain strength from the One who is strong

He gives strength to the weary,
And to him who lacks might He increases power...
(Isaiah 40:29)

What was ironic was that, even though my father had a profound impact on me, it didn't change my outlook on life when he died. He was supposed to have died 19 ½ years ago, but he didn't. He died when he was in his 60s. It wasn't a shock because many people die when they're 60. Sixty and 70 year olds die and it's a sad affair, but it's not something new. His death didn't really change my outlook on life. Even prior to my father's passing away, my sister's first husband, Dr. Tim Burns, who was a dentist, died from cancer and that really didn't have any profound impact on my life either. But years later, when my sister, who was also a dentist, had her second child, she was diagnosed with cancer. That really struck home. It completely changed how I felt, and how I operated. I thought, this really can't be happening because Connie is just two years older than I am. When her husband passed away, he had had problems his whole life but ignored them. When they opened him up, he was completely eaten away with cancer. They just closed him up and he died the following day. Two weeks prior to this, we were on the golf course. But there, again, it did not have any effect on my life.

Connie was a beautiful person. She was artistic and a nature lover. She was a kind and committed person, and just wonderful. In fact, after her husband passed away, she went back to college and got her dental degree because they already had the dental office and now she wanted to run the business. That is exactly what she did. When she was diagnosed with cancer, it was amazing to me that God would allow me to live, but take my sister's life. I really felt guilty about the whole thing because growing up, my sister was always presumed to be the smartest. She may have always received better grades than I did, but when she'd find a quarter on the side walk, I'd find a ten dollar bill. It was as though everything always worked out for me. I was always at the right place at the right time and she hardly ever was. Then she was at the wrong place at the wrong time with the cancer.

With the realization that her life had been cut short, that she would never see her children grown up, and that she would never see any grandchildren, I decided to live my life for both of us. I was allowed to live and she was not, so the main way I changed my outlook on life was that I decided to do the volunteer work for two people. When individuals say that is what I do, they don't know it, but they are correct. I'm doing volunteer work for my sister and for myself. I'm trying to fill the void that was left by my sister's passing away.

Looking back now, I never really realized how much alike my sister and I were until Connie had her first child. My wife, Marianne, had spent two weeks at her home in Bay Village, in the Cleveland area, to assist Connie. When Marianne came home she said, "I just can't believe it. You two act alike, your mannerisms are alike, your attitudes are alike, your outlooks are alike, and you even laugh the same way. It's just amazing because numerous times when I was talking to your sister, if I could deepen her voice, it was as if I were talking to you." This was all very interesting to me because I had never really realized it.

Another thing that changed me when my sister passed away was that I really started living every second of every day. I tried to do everything that

I could. Anything that I wanted to do, I would do. My sister passed away, and it could also happen to me, so I wanted to be sure that I had done everything with no regrets. I also wanted to help people, to do everything that I could possibly do so that, if I died in my sleep, I would know and **God would know that I had done a good job.** God indeed has a plan for each of our lives and it is His will that you find joy and happiness by following that plan!

WINNERS...

#35. recognize God and are motivated by His power

**And we know that God causes all things to work together for good to those who love God, to those who are called according to His purpose.
(Romans 8:28)**

Knowledge Is Power As Is Working Smart

From my experience, along with making each moment count in your life, you should take advantage of everything that school has to offer, because **knowledge is power**. I spent all my time thinking about working in the industrial arts department or what I was going to be doing after school. I basically ignored school. Well, I found out the hard way, but when I got into college, I knew I had made a mistake. It's been my observation that when you have the opportunity to take advanced courses, **you should take every advanced course that you can**. There are several reasons for doing this and I found them out the hard way. The first reason is that up through high school, the courses are free. You have to pay for them when you get into college. The second reason is that when you take those courses in college, and you've already had them in high school, it's like you're taking the course over again. It's easy! The third reason you want to take all the advanced courses that you can possibly take is that you can actually test out of courses. I know my oldest daughter at Jay County High School had calculus 1 and calculus 2, and she tested out of both of them at Worcester Technical Institute, Worcester, Massachusetts . That gave her more time to take electives and have fun! Remember that life is a journey, and to get the most mileage out of it, you must start with a good foundation. Everything you do from seven, eight, and even nine years of age until you die should be done with the idea that you are building a foundation and continually adding to it every second, minute, and hour of each day.

WINNERS...

#36. challenge themselves early on to make life easier for themselves later

"Better to have tried and failed than to not have tried at all."
(Unknown)

Besides taking advanced courses in school, **it's imperative that you pay attention and get good grades as well.** That is probably the only thing in my entire life that I look back on and wish I could change. I wish I would've done better in school. I'm not a person that looks back and I'm not a person that says, "Well, what if?" because I really don't have any "what ifs?" I've done everything that I can possibly think to do. Nonetheless, if I could have paid attention and received more education, I would be a more well rounded person today and my college years would have been much easier. I'm telling all the young people out there to get their education even though they can look at me and say, "Well, this guy didn't do much. He wasn't very smart and look where he ended up." Well, I attribute a lot of my success to being in the right place at the right time and by working smart.

WINNERS...

#37. pay attention in school and get the best grades possible

"Knowledge is Power!"
(Francis Bacon)

Earlier, when I talked about working at Maremont and all the people there were older than I was, it was obvious to a blind man that you only had to work there a couple of years and you'd be number one in seniority. Well, that's what I call working smart. When the opportunity came up to be a maintenance superintendent, I consider accepting that position working smart. In fact, a lot of things in life revolve around working smart and this is something I tell young students when I talk to them. I always give them this example. I say:

"Let's say you're a sales person and that you're looking for a sales person's job. Let's also say that your whole goal in life is to be the vice-president of sales for some company. So you're interviewing with a company and you're talking to a sales person who's three years older than you are and he's the vice-president of sales. You look around and all the people sitting at all the desks are basically your age. The guy offers you 50 grand to start. So now, you're interviewing with another company. You go in, sit down, and talk with the vice-president of sales who is 60 years old. You look around and all the sales people are his age or older. Looks like a bunch of fossils sitting around and the guy offers you 40 grand to start. Which job would you take?"

Now, believe it or not, every time I tell this to high school students, every time, they all take the $50,000 per year job. Then after I explain to them where I'm coming from, they all change their mind and take the $40,000 per year job, which is the correct answer. So when the fossils retire, you're trained and ready to move up and take their place. That is what I call working smart. **By working smart, you put yourself in the right place at the right time, so that when an opportunity arises, you are available to grab it.** I honestly believe that probably 70% to 80% of all promotions in this world do not go to the most qualified individual. They go to a qualified individual who happens to be available.

WINNERS...

#38. work smart to insure their success

**"Always bear in mind that your own resolution to succeed is more important than any other one thing."
(Abraham Lincoln)**

Unfortunately, I've seen some bazaar management styles. Some managers tell no one under them what they're doing. They think that if they run the whole show, it will be job security. That's the worst mistake any management person could possibly make because I have seen it backfire so many times. I've seen people totally protect their job such that nobody knows what they're doing. When a job opens up, higher on the ladder, upper-management looks at this guy and they all say, "Oh, he's perfect for the job but he has never trained anybody to do his job. Who will we get to do his job?" Well, he doesn't get the promotion for the very reason that he thought he would get the promotion. He doesn't get it because there's nobody to replace him. So what it boils down to is that not everybody can put themselves at the right place at the right time unless they work smart. I know I've been fortunate in this regard, but my advice is to get as much education as you possibly can, because knowledge is power as is working smart.

Tips for Engineers

Here's some valuable knowledge that I have gained over the years. **If you're going to be a successful engineer, you've got to keep moving.** You cannot stay at a job any longer than three years. The first year that you start working for a company, your ideas are fresh. Everything that you do is meant to be. You work to make this process better or that process better. It's a no-brainer. The second year you're on the job, the cost reductions get harder. They're harder to see because you basically picked all the good ones the first year and what you're doing now are the more difficult cost reductions. Well, by the time the third year arrives, you look at a problem or a process and your mind says, "Well, that's not running too bad." Now, you're starting to think like the plant management. You're starting to think like the workers. That is when you are no longer effective as an engineer. That is why you have to keep moving.

The other reason to keep moving is that it's a lot easier to find a job while you have a job. If you're a gainfully employed engineer and somebody's paying you big bucks when you start looking around to move, other companies will try to increase your pay and your benefits. By bouncing around every three to four years, you'll end up with an above average salary and above average benefits. Whereas, if you stay with a company too long, "they've got you" so to speak. Once they've got you, they've got you. After you've been there for so many years, they don't think you're going to leave, so raises are smaller, your benefits are smaller, and, thus, you literally have to "break away" and move around to get back on top of the world. If you don't, you're going to stagnate and never go anywhere.

WINNERS...

#39. change jobs as frequently as necessary to remain effective

> "Success...seems to be connected with action. Successful men keep moving. They make mistakes, but they don't quit."
> (Conrad Hilton)

I have received a lot of job offers and have accepted a lot of them. Many times it was a result of an excellent resume. How do you get people so interested in reading your resume that they have to talk to you? It is easy. **Research the company at which you wish to work.** So many people send a generic resume. Each month I get hundreds of resumes sent to Moser Engineering. Most of them I just look at and can't believe it. People will send me a resume in answer to our need for a clerical person or an order-entry type person. The resume will state that they are looking for a health care job and want to be a nurse. These people are clueless. They are clueless about the needs of the management and about what the company does. There is no way on earth that they are ever going to get an interview, let alone be hired. You need to be serious enough about the company that you are going after by researching that company.

To give an example, when I was working at Harvester in Columbus, Ohio, there were several companies that interested me. I researched the companies by finding out what kind of equipment the companies had. Like in the Teledyne case, I found out they had Chamberburg hammers, Erie hammers, and Ajax upsetters. They had National upsetters, National presses, an Ajax press, one induction heater, and everything else was slot fired fossil fuel furnaces. They converted all their steam hammers over to air and they ran them off compressed air instead of steam. I found all of this out before I ever wrote a resume. When I wrote the resume, I included that a **Chamberburg** hammer has less maintenance than an **Erie** hammer and that an Ajax upsetter is a better upsetter than a National upsetter. I put in information about which brand of hammer broke less rods, which brand of upsetter had a better clutch on it, and why I like National presses over Ajax presses. After I wrote my resume and submitted it, I know for a fact that the president and the vice president of Teledyne got hold of it, passed it around, and said, "We have to meet this guy. We are not even going to have to train him. We won't have to do anything. He knows all of our equipment." That is how you get your foot in the door.

WINNERS...

#40. thoroughly research a company prior to writing any resume

"Destiny is not a matter of chance; it is a matter of choice.

> It is not something to be waited for; but, rather
> something to be achieved."
> (William Jennings Bryan)

A generic resume does not put your name on the top of the list of job applicants. How bad do you want a job? **If you want it bad enough, you should totally research the company that you wish to work for and never lie on a resume. Slant everything and all your accomplishments, without lying, to show that you know what that company's operations are.** I guarantee that you will get an interview. I always said, "Once I have my foot in somebody's door, I would get a job offer." I always have. I have always received job offers once I have interviewed.

The interview is another thing which is important in getting an offer. So many times people come in to my company for me to interview them. They have long hair, one earring, and their clothes are atrocious. I think that the younger generation seems to think that, "Well, this is me and I am not going to change for anybody." They are missing the point. **If you are trying to get the job, then you should impress the person who is interviewing you.** I have had people in my office I look at and say, "This guy really wanted to impress me. I have never seen him in a suit before in his life and he comes in here in a three-piece suit. He is clean-shaven with short hair and no earring!" Well, the guy impressed me because of cleaning himself up just for me. I knew he did it just for me. After he comes to work, maybe he will grow his hair long and maybe he will put earrings in, but the fact is, he knew how to get his foot in the door and to look good. Obviously, he was doing it just for me, but it worked for him because he got the job!

WINNERS...

#41. Never lie on a resume and always dress to impress

> "Each time you are honest and conduct yourself with honesty,
> a success force will drive you toward greater success. Each
> time you lie, even with a little white lie, there are strong
> forces pushing you toward failure."
> (Joseph Sugarman)

Marrying for Success

Okay, here comes the biggie. This is what I call, "Marrying for

Success." The first time I got married, whether it was for love or for infatuation, I made a mistake. When I look back on that, I realize it was impossible for me to make a correct choice for marriage. I mean it is impossible for anyone that age. If you don't know what you are doing or what your plans are, how on earth when you are 17-23 years of age, can you choose a partner who will help or benefit you in your plans? You can't. It's impossible. Hindsight is 20/20. Even though some of you will probably not listen to your parents as far as marriage goes, believe me and listen to what I am saying, because I've learned this lesson the hard way.

To marry for success, you first have to know what your goals are and have a plan to accomplish your goals. Once you do that, then you can start looking around for a person to help you achieve those goals. I know that my first marriage, after about five or six years, was a total flop. Simply, my whole goal in business was to "run the company" and that has always been my goal. It didn't matter where I started working in a company, my goal was to run the company eventually. My goal was to be on top. My goal was to be the boss. That meant moving around, and it became painfully obvious to me that my wife at that time had no desire to move around, had no desire to get ahead, had no desire to work, and had no desire to mow the yard when I was off working. We were leading a good life and making a lot of money, but she could care less. I look back on that and think, "The worst mistake I ever made was to marry someone like that."

WINNERS...

**#42. set their goals and know where they are going
before getting married**

**In his heart a man plans his course,
but the Lord determines his steps.
(Proverbs 16:9)**

But how could I have known that? I had aspirations and I had goals back when I married her. I guess I honestly thought that by being successful in my career, she would conform to what my ideals were, just simply because we were being successful. I guess I was kind of naive in thinking that everybody wants to have a good time, have a good life, and be successful. But believe me, not everybody does. At that time of my life, I made a severe mistake. When that marriage finally ended and I was single, I literally tried to work myself to death. I normally weighed between 240 and 245 pounds. Several years after my divorce, I was down to 175 or less, and that was because I was building race cars, drag racing, chasing women, and just basically having a good time. That was the time when I was introduced to my present wife, Marianne. The main reason I was interested in meeting her was because I heard how hard she worked. After I met her, I found out that her goal in life was to be on top. Her goal was to do whatever it takes to get on top, which was my goal. She liked to drag race and she liked to ride motorcycles. They say "opposites attract," but that is simply not true. As I have said previously, **I really believe that you need to be totally in synch with each other as God intended man and wife to be, that is, one in flesh, mind, and spirit.** Marianne and I even have the same levels of tolerance. Somebody can be annoying us, like one of our children, and we will both ignore it for a little while. It's kind of ironic because when we both have had enough, and it has happened more than once, we will both get up at the same time to correct them. It is like we both have had enough at the same time. We are totally on the same wavelength!

WINNERS...

#43. are in total synch with their spouse

If I do not trust someone, I have no room in my life for them and that applies not only to my spouse, but to a relative, or anyone else as well. It is just wasting your time to even associate yourself with people you are unable to trust and respect. When you respect someone it is apparent in your communications, actions, and dealings with that person. **To be successful in this world, you have to trust and respect your spouse.** In all the years that Marianne and I have been married, we have never raised our voice at each other. There is no reason to do so. Neither one of us would ever consider doing something that would make the other one angry. Why would you do that? It doesn't make sense. If you truly have respect for your spouse, then neither one of you would do anything to offend the other one or to even remotely make them angry. **Marianne and I make each other's life easier.** If we see something that needs to be done, we do it. I don't wait for her to do it and she doesn't wait for me to do it. We both recognize that there is much to accomplish in this world and we just cannot do it alone. A little cliché is "behind every good man is a good woman" or "behind every good woman is a good man." Well, those are true. Many things in this world require help in doing and if you expect to have help from a partner, **your best partner is also your spouse.** It is very difficult to take on a business partner and get along, but if you are married to your partner, then you have a lot better chance for success.

WINNERS...
#44. trust and respect their spouse
#45. unselfishly and constantly help their spouse to make life easier
#46. have their spouse as their partner

Nevertheless let each individual among you also love his own wife even as himself; and let the wife see to it that she respect her husband.
(Ephesians 5:33)

As Marianne and I run the business together, she runs her end and I run my end. If one of us is not there, we take care of each other's responsibility. If someone has a question, whoever is passed in the hall first gives the answer. **We both have enough confidence and enough respect in each other's abilities that if one of us makes a decision, then it must have been the correct decision at that time.** A lot of people don't understand that statement, but usually when people are hindsighting or second guessing someone, they totally forget the fact that when the decision was made, it was a different time and a different day. They look at it and say, "Why on earth was this decision made?" Well, usually, the decision was right at that time. Everybody forgets about the circumstances a week later and they all look at it and say, "Boy, that was a dumb idea," or "That was a dumb decision." In reality, it wasn't. So you always have to keep in mind what the circumstances were when the decision was made. Marianne and I have enough confidence in each other that it doesn't make any difference. If that is what you said, then that is what we are going to do. That's how we operate and that is why we have a very successful marriage and a very successful business.

WINNERS...

#47 accept spouse's decisions even when hindsight may prove them wrong

Do you see a man who is hasty in his words? There is more hope for a fool than for him.
(Proverbs 29:20)

My wife is attractive, but even if she weren't, I would have still married her. Many people think the grass is always greener on the other side because the person is new and exciting and different. You should never marry someone for their beauty. You should marry them for what is in their heart and in their mind. You should be able to relate to them, respect them, and trust them because then your marriage will last forever.

WINNERS...

**#48 do not marry for outward appearances,
but for what is within a person**

**...for man looks at the outward appearance, but the Lord
looks at the heart.
(1 Samuel 16:7)**

When I was growing up in Paulding, Ohio, there was an Apostolic church there and that particular church used to have arranged marriages. We always thought that was crazy. Well, now that I'm in my 40s, and I look back and think about it, I believe that such arranged marriages are not so crazy after all. If you raise your children correctly, and you raise them by example, then your child will act like you, the parents. These Apostolic church parents used to get together with other parents and discuss which children would match each other. If the children were raised with the morals and the examples of their parents, then the outcome is that they are very compatible. Those kids will learn to love each other, but before that, their minds, their morals, and their goals will be in synch. That means that their marriage is really going to work. They are going to make an ultimate duo in business and in life, and it will be a lot easier for them to conquer the world because they are a pair. They are a partnership. Of course, I realize that the freedom of choice is lost in such arranged marriages, but my point is to bring people of like minds together.

Another consideration before you marry is whether or not you want children. Believe me, you cannot change a person. Most people will think, "Well, we'll get married and then we can decide about children later." That is not going to happen. That is why marrying for success involves knowing what your goals are before you can possibly think about choosing a spouse. Once you do know these goals, you want to find a person with the same goals, and then you will make quite a pair. You will have married for success and success will be yours.

Chapter Four

LEARNING FROM THE COMPETITION AND OTHERS

Keeping All Under Control
Successful Techniques Used
Moving Goals Forward to Maintain that Competitive Edge
The Race is Wide Open so Go For It

Most people don't think about it, but almost all businesses start in a one-car garage, a basement, or a shack behind someone's house. Almost all businesses start that way. All businesses follow a bell curve, too. In fact, both life and business follow a bell curve. Once you get to the top, there is usually no way from there but down. So the object is to keep that curve continually going up. I have worked for companies that have employed 11,000 people and I have worked for companies that have employed 300 to 400 people. While these companies have been mostly unionized, a lot of the things that I have learned throughout my life have been learned from these large companies. Unfortunately, I am sorry to say, a lot of the things that I have learned have been what *not* to do with the work force.

Keeping All Under Control

Most big companies have their job descriptions too finite. For example, at International Harvester, there were seven or eight unions in one company. Now I'm not saying there is anything wrong with unions. In fact, in Harvester's case, the union actually helped the company run the plant. I believe what can be wrong with a work force is what can be wrong with a lot of things in general. That is, if people or the union become so full of themselves, they think, "We are the company. Management can't run this place without us. When it comes time to negotiate, we will just go on strike and they will give us whatever we want." That's what usually happens when you get a work force which is really large. The sad thing is that everybody always looks at the company and says, "Oh, the company this and the company that." Well, the company is owned by people. It's owned by stockholders. It's not just one individual or two individuals. It's owned by people who want to make money from their investments. Since they have invested their money they have a right to make more. The thing that I always found wrong with Harvester, for example, was the fact that they paid way too much money and expected too little from their employees. It always amazed me that, like on the A and B line, in heavy duty truck, there were more people at the end of the line fixing the trucks than there were people assembling the trucks. Was that crazy or what? You can't operate that way. It took just as long as to assemble the thing wrong as it did to assemble the thing right.

The things that I really learned while working there were first, you can't let the company get out of your control, and second, if you are going to do something right, you do it right. If you are going to pay somebody to do it, you have that person do it right. The other thing that I really found that drove me crazy was there were so many management layers that nothing could get done. If you had a good idea, it was virtually impossible to institute the idea because of company politics and the many hurdles you had to clear to get anything done or get anything approved.

WINNERS...

#49. keep it simple by doing the job right with as few people as possible

Go to the ant, O sluggard,
Observe her ways and be wise,
Which, having no chief,
Officer or ruler,
Prepares her food in the summer,
And gathers her provision in the harvest.
(Proverbs 6:6-8)

At the plants that I set up myself, my own company as well as at Teledyne and at Portec where we employed several hundred, we had to fill out some minor paper work for cost reductions for automation projects, but mostly, these projects were a gut feeling. The way you succeed in this world is with speed. If you decide to come out with a new product, a small company can develop it and bring it to market in a month, month and a half, or two months. A big company will take years. It will take months just to get people in the meeting to decide what to do. It's crazy.

I learned something else while working at Haviland Muffler Company in Defiance, Ohio. Their overtime was 100% seniority. I could be working eight hours fixing something and come 3:00 PM, this guy with the most seniority would walk around and say, "Well, tell me what you've been doing." He would take up where I left off. You'd go home and he would stay for the overtime. It used to drive me wild.

When I started my own company, we had and still have 100% equal overtime. There are a lot of other things we do that are different from other companies, too. The way we can get away with the equal overtime is because everybody can basically do everyone else's job. The object is to get the product out the door. So everybody works to that end. They do whatever it takes to get it out the door and they work 100% equal overtime. They all work a half hour over or they all work an hour and a half over. They all get paid the same number of hours. No one has more hours than anyone else, no one has a problem worrying about someone else making more money. They have equal overtime.

Something that I discovered, and this was the case in maintenance at Harvester, Portec, and Teledyne, is that if you give people responsibility and accountability, and respect them for it, they will, in turn, give it back to you. We do not have a time clock at Moser Engineering. We never will have a time clock. The people are responsible for being there on time. If somebody's car breaks down and is a half hour late, well, with the type of work that we do, he or she works a half hour over for a total of eight hours. We work a straight eight and that is how all is kept under control.

Successful Techniques Used

First, let me describe how our business operates. We originally started out remanufacturing OEM axles, housings, and narrowed rear ends. Whatever came in, we would do the next day and ship the next day. This philosophy started with no employees except for Marianne and me doing one or two pair of axles or rear ends a day. Once we were in that mode we could build upon that.

We employ enough people so that in August, September, October, and November I can keep them gainfully employed for eight hours each day. During February, March, April, May, June, and July we work overtime to get the job done. How much overtime we work is totally at my work force's discretion. We lay out the work we have to do. It's all marked when they come in each morning. If there's a lot of work, we have them come in an hour or two early, and they work until the job is done. They all finish at the same time and they all get the same overtime. When and where I hire someone is totally up to my work force. If they do not want the overtime or if they are tired of working overtime, then they say, "Well, why don't you hire somebody?" Then and only then do I hire somebody. It is at their decision and is their choice. So the work gets done. We have never failed and we never will fail to honor our two day turn around time because that is what we have all set as our goal.

When I started my business, my competition spent six weeks delivering a pair of axles. Six weeks! They charged more money than I did, they had the same or lesser quality, and they took six weeks to deliver it. I want to tell you right now that the two day turn around that my company offers is the slowest service that we do. So my competitors charge an extra $100 to get the product out in a week. Well, we charge nothing extra because our standard service is two days. For about ten people a day, we do what we call quick ship. That is, if you order it today, we will do it tomorrow and ship it tomorrow. So we offer a one day service (there is no charge for this). That is still not our best service, believe it or not. For people that are in emergency, like they have broken down, or they have really given us a good sob story, or they are mad at one of my competitors and they want to buy our product, we honestly, if you place the order by 9:00 or 10:00 in the morning, will make it and ship it the same day. There is no extra charge for this service. So we offer no-day, one-day, and our slowest service (which is the standard for us) is two-days. If you really analyze what our company does, it's basically a no-brainer why we are successful. I am a drag racer and I know what drag racers need. They want the product now, they want it to last forever, and they don't want to pay a whole lot for it. Well, we provide that product and service and we make a buck doing it.

So, here we have a business that has no time clock and has no problem with overtime. Another problem that I ran into working for other corporations is the old first shift against second shift, second shift against first and third, and third shift doesn't like anyone syndrome. Well, since I personally build all my own computerized equipment, I basically have little investment in that equipment, compared to purchasing high dollars CNC equipment. This means that I do not have to run this equipment two or three shifts a day to get my money back. I will never run on an off shift. I don't want to have to worry about someone getting hurt. Basically, I consider my employees and their families to be a part of our larger family and I do not want to have anyone else have the responsibility with other shifts, so we run a one shift operation. That way I have no one following someone else and no one mad because someone else is not doing their job. Nobody is going to leave the lathe dirty or the floor dirty, because if they do, they just left it dirty for themselves, because I work a one shift operation. Like I said before, it's a no-brainer. People like to work day shift and do not want to work second and third, so I don't have those shifts.

The other thing that we do that I have learned over the years, based upon our business and our two day turn around, is that I honestly do not care when the work is done. I don't care. The guys set their own hours. If they want to come in at five and leave at one, that's fine. If they want to come in at 4 and leave at noon, I don't care. As long as the job gets done. It is their responsibility to get the job done and to do the job correctly. They are held accountable for that. Consequently, we pay the highest wages in Jay County, Indiana. I think that is my responsibility if I'm going to expect this much from my employees. I believe my responsibility is to pay them well. We also have a good benefits package and we also, at Christmas time, have a company meeting where we discuss what we are going to do for the next year. At these meetings, I normally give out $3,000 Christmas bonuses to each employee. I have done this every year since I've been in business. We also have these company meetings at various locations including Chicago, Las Vegas, and Paradise Island in the Bahamas. We basically have a good time. My philosophy is if you work hard, you play hard.

So now we have a business that has all homemade CNC equipment, everybody's working, everybody gets the job done, and everybody's responsible for their job. Other areas save even more money. It is just like the no-time clock. We don't have a time clock, so guess what? You don't need a time keeper! You don't need time cards, you don't need anything. My controller writes down how many hours everybody works every day. At the end of the week, if everybody worked 45 hours, then everybody gets 45 hours pay. Simple.

Something that we also started with this business is the philosophy which dates back to my paper route days. When I delivered the paper on time, I expected to be paid on time. Everybody else was messing around collecting their routes, taking all week to do it, but I could do it in a couple of hours on Saturday morning. If you are providing super-service, then you can demand different things from your customers. We don't have and we don't need open accounts. We already provide the best product, instant service, and a cheap price. We send everything out C.O.D., and thus, we have no open accounts. We don't have a bookkeeper, we don't have someone that enters the money or figures out who owes what. We don't have a billing department, we don't have a collection department, we don't need any of that. UPS collects the customer's money, UPS sends us a computer read-out every day, and our money rolls in five to seven days after we ship our product. We keep it simple. Consequently, we don't have bounced checks. It's all C.O.D. We don't have any problems. All we have is a total steady cash flow.

We give our employees substantial raises each year, too. We have never raised a price, yet we give substantial raises. As I mentioned before, we had to mark up our cast iron cases since someone else builds them for us. Thus, we've had to raise the price on one item, but we have done nothing but lower prices in the last 10 years on all products that we manufacture. You can say, "Well, that's hard to believe." Well, it may be, but it's a fact and that is my business philosophy. I am not going to add to inflation. I'm just not going to do it. What we continually do is automate our equipment. I talked about taking an hour to spline an axle when I first started out. Right now, I can spline an axle in about 90 seconds. We have just completed some automatic, computer controlled drilling machines to drill the bolt pattern and the flange of the axles. The equipment to do that would cost in excess of $100,000, but I have only $14,000 in each machine and my floor-to-floor time (that's the time it takes to pick the part off the floor, put it in the machine, punch the start button, have it do its thing, bring it out of the machine, and set the axle on the floor) is 27 seconds. That is how you save money.

On top of that, I just completed an automatic tapping machine. I can tap five, ½ x 20 holes in an axle flange in 15 seconds. Every year we just keep getting better at what we are doing. We produce more product with less man hour input. In fact, we will do $7,500,000 in sales with only 21 employees this year and we are just a machine shop. Now you might find a better sales dollar per employee in other businesses, but it's probably a warehousing business where all they are doing is filling orders. We are actually manufacturing with that kind of dollar value. That's about $357,000 of product generated per employee each year!

WINNERS...

#50. make more money by increasing the productivity of each employee

All hard work brings a profit, but mere talk leads only to poverty. (Proverbs 14:23)

The thing that I really enjoy with my business is the fact that I don't have to write up ROI's, cost reductions, or anything. When we think up a new product, we take a look at it and say, "Yep, that should work." We just do it! When I want to automate something I don't have to write any ROI's. I look at it, and my gut says, "This thing will work. This will save man power." We just do it. That is the advantage that we have over any company on the face of this earth. We can react instantly to changing problems, to changing market share, to changing product lines. We can do it almost instantly while everyone else is going to have to have a lot of meetings to do it.

Something else we have in our facility is air conditioning everywhere. Any business that It ever have is going to be air conditioned because of all those years seeing people go home early because it was too hot to work in the forge shops. It don't want to lose any productivity in the summer months whatsoever. If you create a pleasant work place with the appropriate atmosphere, then the people will want to come to work, and they will come to work, and they will work.

WINNERS...

#51. create the ideal working atmosphere for their employees

**And just as you want men to treat you,
treat them in the same way.
(Luke 6:31)**

When local presidents and CEO's of companies get together and talk about problems and successes, we discuss what each plant in Jay County is doing. These meetings are sponsored by the Chamber of Commerce. Numerous times the question will come up as to workmen's compensation and what each company is experiencing as far as the percentage of sick days. When it gets around to me, It say, "Well, It have none." "You have to have a percentage," they say. "No, It have none." We have worked years without a sick day or without someone calling in sick. It is probably a small reflection of myself and it is a total reflection of the quality and the caliber of people that It employ.

My first employee was Greg Imel and It basically hired him because he was intelligent, he was prompt, he had worked for another company for ten years, and had never had a sick day. On top of that, he was trainable. So after It hired him, It realized that It really had a winner. My next employee was Chad Franks and It basically hired him for the same reason. As It started hiring people, It tried to hire them for those same reasons and It accomplished that. Now it's to the point with the number of employees that It have that It still look for all these same qualities in an employee, but even if It don't get what It think I'm getting, the person has to conform to the rest of my employees. It's a self-fulfilling prophecy. You can take the adage that you can put one bad kid with four good kids and you are going to have five bad kids. As the sayings go: "Bad company corrupts good morals" and "One bad apple spoils the barrel." (1 Corinthians 15:33--"Do not be deceived. Bad company corrupts good morals.")

That doesn't work in my plant. You hire someone who is not holding up his end and he will be chased away or have to conform. They will conform to our business philosophy or be forced to leave. That's another reason why you can be successful if you know your work force is going to show up. It know. It worked for big companies that hired hundreds of extras for all those sick days. Teledyne hired a lot of extras just for people who were going to call in sick. If you hire extra people to take care of people who don't come to work (sick or otherwise), what kind of message are you sending to your people? "Oh, it must be okay to call in sick. They have people to replace me." Let's just turn that around. Let's say you don't hire anyone to replace sick people, like we do. If someone doesn't come in, everybody else has to take up the slack, or, if it's vacation time, It have to go out and help make the product, and It do. Then, no one calls in sick! Because they know there's no one to take their place, so they come in to work. There are two things accomplished by this. Number one, It have a successful business and all my products are sent out on time. Number two, It have a wealthy work force because they are all making good money and they are all getting paid. They don't take time off without getting paid and they come in to work and get paid.

Like It said, It think it's my responsibility to take care of my employees. In fact, It have nothing against unions and unions can be justified when a company is not taking care of its employees. If the company is taking care of its employees, there is really no need for any representation. In this day and age, **the person who takes care of his employees is the person who gets the good employees.** It know It have absolutely no problem hiring employees. They beat my door down. It have never yet advertised for any employees and It probably pick up five to six resumes a day. This is a small community. That's a lot of resumes. It have thousands of them! It's my work ethic and it's my employees' work ethic that make this business successful. **Everybody does whatever it takes to get the job done.** It guess that has been my philosophy since It was nine years old. You do whatever it takes to get the job done. Like when It was running those paper routes and It had my customers organized to pay their bills, well, It organized this business so it pays its bills so It do not have to worry about chasing my money down. Why should It? If It have the best product, the cheapest price, and the best delivery, why should It worry about getting paid for it? It shouldn't and It don't!

WINNERS...

#52. take care of their employees who in turn are diligent in their work

The generous man will be prosperous,
And he who waters will himself be watered.
(Proverbs 11:25)

Moving Goals Forward to Maintain That Competitive Edge

We went from a two car garage to one containing 3,000 square feet. It remember standing in there telling my wife at the time, "We will never fill this up." To that 3,000, we added on 6,000 square feet. This business grew out of a two car garage and there's no secret to our success. **You give people what they need, when they want it, at a competitive price, at a quality level that makes it as good as anything on the market, and you will sell your product, even beating out the competition.** In fact, what we have started doing is value adding things. We are going into the circle track market with ring and pinions, spools, and what It call "Value added to the rear end differentials." The whole philosophy is to keep moving, never hit the down side of the bell curve. Our bell curve has slowed down, but it has not flattened out. When you start out from zero market penetration, you have to have some fantastic growth years. We grew almost 100% for the first five to seven years. Now we are back down to the 15% to 20% growth years. We are starting to act like a normal business. We are at the top of the bell curve and we are just like any entrepreneurial business. The whole key is to keep the business moving forward and to get it out of the entrepreneurial stage. That's what we are working on now. We have hired a comptroller, sales people, and we actually have a management structure now. We have a plant manager, a sales manager, and an office manager.

WINNERS...

#53. give people what they need, when they want it, at the best price and quality possible

Give, and it will be given to you; good measure, pressed down, shaken together, running over, they will pour into your lap. For whatever measure you deal out to others, it will be dealt to you in return. (Luke 6:38)

What all of this means is that we are trying to structure and run our company like a real company, but unlike any other. It do not want to get into the rut in which these other companies find themselves. It want to be at a level of management so that everyone knows that they are responsible. It want to have enough people that It can get around my desk, make a quick decision to pick up something in the market place, get the job done, and get it moving.

The one thing that It dearly love to do in my business is build equipment. That is one of our keys to success. The fact that we can react and build equipment makes us more productive and efficient. It dearly love to build this equipment. It really enjoy doing it. That is one reason why we are ultra competitive with our products – we can literally build or make anything. **"Better, quicker, cheaper," is what It like to say.** Since we are into differentials and rear ends, those are the products we wish to improve. Anything that has to do with a rear end, we can build it better, quicker, cheaper. People will just beat your door down for that. My business philosophies can be adapted to anything. They can be adapted to any other business because they are sound philosophies and they work.

WINNERS...

#54. are constantly looking to do it better, quicker, cheaper

**Do not withhold good from those to whom it is due,
When it is in your power to do it.
(Proverbs 3:27)**

When It used to set goals, It would approach the goals and would always move the goals out farther. Well, obviously, the goals were too easy or It wouldn't have approached them that easily. So I'm always moving the goals forward. As It speak, my goals right now are to keep my business moving forward at an above industry growth rate. Also, It wish to continue to treat my employees right.

We take our employees racing, canoeing, and out to dinner. We have Christmas parties, and we go all over the country, even all over the world, for parties. We give them Christmas money, we have interest free loans, we provide vacations, we encourage good health and the best life possible for them. It honestly believe that a person should not make a buck off the sweat of his employees without sharing it with him. It think that a reasonably intelligent person should be able to think up an efficient enough business that, number one, makes you a buck but, number two, also allows your employees to live an above average standard of living. It know that all my employees have new homes, they all have new cars, they all have a family with kids, and it's just a win-win situation for everyone.

Something else that It require, and It developed this philosophy from the years It spent working with the Chamber of Commerce and the Jay County Development Corporation, is that all of my employees must live in Jay County. Why do It do that? Well, when It built a new plant, It am given tax abatements which do not take any money out of the county. The first year It don't pay any taxes, second year It pay 10%, and so on, up until a 100%. If It had not started the company, then there wouldn't be any tax dollars. However, It feel it's my responsibility to require my employees to live in Jay County so that they pay taxes in Jay County. It guess what goes around, comes around. It just want to make sure that It make money, the county makes money, my employees make money, and everybody's happy.

You can look at all this and you can say, "Wow, this is really something. This guy is really successful." Well, that's another mistake most people make. **As the Chairman of Southwest Airlines says, "Never think you are successful, because about the time you do, is about the time that you become complacent, and that is about the time you get run over from the rear by somebody hungrier, meaner, and more aggressive than you ever were."** It fully plan on moving this company forward forever. Maybe, just maybe, when I'm on my death bed, and It know I'm dying, then It might let up. It might even admit that It have been successful. But until then, It am not. It am going to keep running as hard as It can run. That way it's going to take one heck of a person to catch me, and It don't think it can be done.

WINNERS...

**#55. run hard to insure success but remain humble
less they become overconfident and stumble**

**Pride goes before destruction,
And a haughty spirit before stumbling.
(Proverbs 16:18)**

A lot of people ask me where It think this business is going. While It have many ideas, the one goal that I've already done some calculating on is, once the business gets to ten million in sales, It am going to purchase a Citation jet. **That's just to save me minutes.** It have stated this before, but you have to watch the minutes, and even the seconds. Seconds add up to minutes, minutes add up to hours, and hours add up to days. That is one reason why It do want a jet because It spend way too much time waiting for planes in airports which drives me crazy. It drives me absolutely wild.

WINNERS...

#56. watch the seconds to make every minute count

Therefore be careful how you walk, not as unwise men,
but as wise, making the most of your time,
because the days are evil.
(Ephesians 5:15-16)

The Race is Wide Open So Go For It

Believe me, you can either invent your own product or you can find someone else's product and make it better, quicker, and cheaper. It is easy to do. You can apply the principles that It have described and with a lot of hard work, set your company up correctly so it runs itself, and you will succeed. That is how Marianne and It did it and It would imagine that in our company, in the new after market axle business, we went from 0% to probably 60% to 70% of market share. We will sell between 40,000 and 50,000 axles this year. There are all kind of businesses out there. You can pick up any magazine, newspaper, or look at anything and see something that someone else is manufacturing at which you can make a buck doing the same thing. There are a lot of things out there that are not being manufactured that you can make a buck out of as well. **You just have to believe in yourself. You have to communicate what you want to achieve and work hard.**

WINNERS...

#57. believe in themselves, their employees, and their product

A man will be satisfied with good by the fruit of his words,
And the deeds of a man's hands will return to him.
(Proverbs 12:14)

Set your company up, select your employees wisely, and you will end up with something that will basically run itself, make you money, and make your employees money. Not only that, we actually benefit our customers. We sell them a quality product and save them money. In fact, It know that is where a lot of our sales came from, especially when we used to respline OEM axles. Our new race axles are so cheap, that people actually can afford to buy them. So they have a quality product at a cheaper price. We are helping everyone not by trickery, but through excellence. As Proverbs 13:11 says, "Wealth obtained by fraud dwindles, but the one who gathers by labor increases it." That is what your business should do. It should help everyone in an honest way with a quality product.

The best advice that It can give someone is that if he or she has a good idea, go with it as soon as possible and get the business off the ground. It have quite a few friends who had small businesses on the side. After It talked them into going full time, you can't believe how their businesses grew. As soon as they left and went into business full time, their comment was that they should have left their jobs years earlier. Between '87 and '92, Marianne basically ran the business. She answered the phone and took care of shipping and receiving. We had one or two employees who helped with the work, and then It would finish up when It got home from Teledyne. It think the only reason It stayed at Teledyne was because It had such an excellent job. It just love people, love responsibility, love making things, love engineering things, and Teledyne offered all of this to me. But when It left in '92 and went full time with my wife, It realized that It should have left years sooner. **So, if you have a good idea, go with it.** Don't do it part-time. Jump into it and make the most of it. People look at my business and say, "Boy, it's really successful." It look at it and think, "Boy, if It had left my other work two or three or four years earlier, my business would be twice as big as it is now." That's the best advice It can give you. If you have a good idea, have faith and go with it as quickly as possible.

WINNERS...

#58. get a good idea and move with it rather than sitting on it

**For just as the body without the spirit is dead,
so also faith without works is dead.
(James 2:26)**

Chapter Five

ENTERING THE RACE

**Being Competitive is Important
Reacting Fast is a Must
Running the Race to Win is Never Easy
Drag Racing is My Sport**

We are going to talk about racing and business. I've met a lot of successful individuals in my life, including presidents and CEO's of different companies. The interesting thing about all of them is that, once you have gotten to know and talk with them, at some point in their life they all raced something. Whether it was radio-controlled planes, or dirt bikes, or go-carts, they raced something. Racing something and success in business are one and the same.

Being Competitive is Important

For me, I started racing mini-bikes and go-carts when I was in my single-digits. When I reached 15 or 16 years of age, I started racing motorcycles and cars. I raced **flat track,** I raced **motor cross, hare and hound, hill climb, and** I even **ice-raced motorcycles**. I developed my love for racing at an early age, but I really think my niche in life was drag racing. Drag racing has been my love. Drag racing and business have a lot in common. Drag racing involves the skill to react quickly so that when you leave the line you can gain an advantage over your opponent. It is highly competitive. You have to build enough horsepower so that the car will qualify to race. In other words, you have to qualify just to have the chance to race. Qualifying is probably the hardest aspect of racing simply because you are dealing not in minutes, seconds, tenths, or hundredths, but you are actually dealing in thousandths of seconds. Our racing team has literally missed qualifying by two-thousandths of a second. Thus, you have to first qualify if you want to race.

Success, business, racing, and winning are one and the same. Thirty years ago, when I was 15, I was drag racing a bike and knew that I had to win. **You do basically whatever it takes to win, just like in business.** The one thing that racing will teach you, though, is the realization that you cannot win all the time. **So you have to develop the ability to be a good loser because you can't win them all.** I'm not saying that you want to be a happy loser because a happy loser is a loser. But you need to learn from your experiences so that you are better prepared the next time you race to win the race.

WINNERS...

#59. are competitive to the point that they want to win every time

**The soul of the sluggard craves and gets nothing,
But the soul of the diligent is made fat.
(Proverbs 13:4)**

WINNERS...

#60. experiencing loss are good losers learning from their mistakes

**...for though a righteous man falls seven times, he rises again.
(Proverbs 24:16)**

In drag racing, we have won a lot of races. My motorcycles have taken their class and many times top bike over all others. When we started drag racing cars we won a few times, but we were never really successful with the '70 Camaro I used to race. We just were not successful at the drag strip. On street racing we were very successful. My drag bike was only beaten once on the street and that was by Loran Zedyke in a roadrunner. The only reason I got beat was because I had never run a car with open headers on the street before and I did not have a tachometer on this drag bike. My bike was as light as it could be made. When you run somebody illegally on the street, you are on a narrow road and you are right beside the competition. I couldn't even tell if my motorcycle was running, let alone how to bring it out to the line and when to shift it. I honestly can run cars at the drag strip, but I couldn't hear a thing on that street! This was back in the late '60s. This motorcycle would run high ten second quarters and the car that beat me was an 11 second car. But that was the only vehicle that ever beat my drag bike. We used to run my modified production Camaro around and this car would run ten-60s to ten-70s, that's E.T. or elapsed time. That was a street driven car. That may not seem fast to anybody, but bear in mind, this is 1970 and that was 28 years ago, a mid ten second street car.

This car was never beaten on the street. It made a lot of money. We would usually run it for $100 a pop back then. Great fun!

Later on, after I got back from working in upstate New York, we decided to build an altered. This vehicle was completely homemade including the chassis, the suspension, the steering, and the body which was hand formed out of aluminum. The rear end we narrowed ourselves. Having always been a machinist, I always had machining equipment at home. We made everything. This particular vehicle was very successful for us. We used to run a quick eight in Van Wert, Ohio, and we won that, I'd say, 50% of the time. The times when we didn't win, we were runner up. We ran all over the area. We never really left more than a 70 to 80 mile radius, running Avilla, Indiana, on Friday night, Muncie on Saturday, and Wayne Trail, Ohio, on Sunday. We had a lot of fun.

The interesting thing with this altered that we built was that it drew a lot of attention and a lot of people asked, "Who did the rear end?" and "Whose axles are you running?" People would ask this and that. By word of mouth, that car actually started our business. We were narrowing maybe a rear end every other week and that was funding our race car habit. If you look around at national events and see all the individuals there, they almost all have a business that's funding their race car. Believe me, no one, and I repeat, no one actually makes money racing cars. They either have a major sponsor or somebody who has found a way to make a buck off advertising or business to be able to channel money into the racing. I call racing a habit. Racing is addictive. It's worse than any drug you can possibly take because the faster you go, the faster you want to go. We basically got hooked on running in the national events circuit and that takes a lot of money. That's where the altered actually started the business. We actually created a business to pay for our racing.

Reacting Fast is a Must

There are a lot of parallels between drag racing and running a business. On the drag racing side of it, you have to first decide what you want to do, what kind of vehicle you want to run and in what class you want to run it. A lot of that decision is based upon the competition that's out there and how fast they are going, just like in business. Once you decide what you want to do, it takes a lot of preparation to get the vehicle ready, just like in business to start your own company. When you get your car prepared, you must be ready for the start line and the Christmas tree.

You've got to be alert, you have to have had enough repetitions in the car to know what you are doing and how you are going to do it. **You** have to have good reaction times to catch a good light to win the race. Just like a business, you have to react to your competition and you have to react quickly. Speed is the whole key with drag racing and in business. The key is how fast your car can run down a quarter mile or how fast you can react in business.

WINNERS...

**#61. are experienced to react fast in order to
take the lead and win**

**And let endurance have its perfect result, that you may be perfect
and complete, lacking in nothing.
(James 1:4)**

If you are to win the race in a 16 car pro-stock field, you have to win 4 rounds before you are declared the champion. So you win a round only to go back to get prepared for the next round. The joy of winning a round is short lived. Basically, it is forgotten right after you have won the round because you have to be prepared to win the next round. It's a good learning experience to understand how to run a business. You never take your competition lightly, and **you are never satisfied with one victory**. As soon as you complete or win a race, it takes total preparation to try to win another one. This is basically the way you should run your business. In racing, you never really think you are successful because there is always another race. Success in racing is a very fleeting moment in time and that's the way you should treat your business.

**WINNERS...
#62. appreciate victory but are always anxious
for the next challenge**

**...not that I have already obtained it,
or have already become perfect,
but I press on...forgetting what lies behind
and reaching forward to what lies ahead.
(Philippians 3:12-13)**

Running the Race to Win is Never Easy

We ran the altered from about '80 to '89, had a lot of fun, and won some races. I believe it was 1986 when I met up with an individual named Ron Miller who was an excellent engine builder. He had been racing just as long as I had and had won a lot of national events. He was in the same dragster class that I was running at the time and was getting faster and faster so I needed a lot of horsepower to qualify against him. Finally I had Ron build me an engine. We qualified nicely with his expertise.

As previously stated, my father would race with me when he was on the upside of his chemo treatments. My son always went with me, too. At one of the races in 1988 (I believe it was the Sports Nationals at Marion, Ohio), my father wasn't able to join us. It was a time run to qualify. There was a terrible bump in the right lane. The track was not that good and I had some funny car tires on my car which was a hard tailed altered. I was in the right lane with Ron Miller racing in the left lane. I pulled the parachute at the same time I hit the bump causing what I call with an altered, basketball bounces, where the back end dances two or three feet off the ground. When it comes down the front end goes up two or three feet and you just see-saw back and forth as the car bounces down the track. The only way you can get out of it is to accelerate to take the bounce out of your tires. Well, in this particular instance, I was bouncing sideways at probably 120 mph! I have it on film bouncing sideways down the track. I actually got the car out of it by accelerating! At the instant I got it straight, I saw a parachute. I was in Ron's lane and he had slowed down to probably 50 mph when I hit him in the back doing probably 140 mph. It knocked us over the guard rail and barrel-rolled us both. I hopped out and ran down and made sure he was okay. It destroyed my car and didn't do Ron's any favors. We helped him a little bit and he took it to Spitzer's Shop where Mike Spitzer did some work on the rear end. They got it back together and he raced the next day. My altered was really destroyed so I drug it up to the trailer, took it home, and started to rebuild it. That was in '88.

It was about a month after that when my dad became worse. He was at the end of his third round of chemo and he had somehow contracted shingles, which you wouldn't wish on anyone. The doctors had to quit treating him with chemo and he passed away later in '88. I spent a lot of time with him before he died. He was my pit crew. I basically told him, about two nights before he died, that if he didn't make it I wasn't going to race anymore so that when he was in heaven he wouldn't have to worry about me getting hurt racing. I honestly believe that is why he always went along with me anyway . He just wanted to make sure I didn't get hurt.

Nobody really knows that, but that is why I quit racing in 1988. Here we had a business that we had started to fund racing operations and now I could race because the money was there. I took a different direction.

We did not do anything at the beginning of '89, but I happened to run into Ron and said, "Hey, I'd like to do some sponsoring, would you be interested?" So we started sponsoring Ron and that was in '89. In '90 we bought a car and really put some sponsorship dollars into it. Basically, we went with Ron to all the races. We were really successful with this top dragster and won a lot of races. They used to have a quick eight at the IHRA (International Hot Rod Association) national events and in 1992 we won 12 quick eights out of 14. We won one national event, too, which was unheard of back then for a six second car to actually win a bracket race because the Sunday race was a bracket race, the quick eight was heads up racing where the fastest man wins. I guess drag racing, here again, is just like business, because Ron and I both felt that while it was great to win, we both thought that there was something missing. We really needed to step up our competition. So, we decided in '93 to go pro-stock racing.

WINNERS...
#63. not only compete but actually search out better competition

**Poor is he who works with a negligent hand,
But the hand of the diligent makes rich.
(Proverbs 10:4)**

Pro-stock racing has really been a learning experience. When we started racing, we bought an old Rickie Smith car in which he had won the '89 world championship. We qualified for one race that year because we just didn't have the horsepower. This motor was built without any dyno whatsoever. So the next year we decided that if we were going to be competitive and we were going to stick with running mountain motor pro-stock we needed to have a dyno. So we put in a complete dyno facility. That really helped as we started developing horsepower. Our biggest problem the next year, though, was that we could not get the parts. We were always behind. The engine builders who were currently building motors would change the spread of the bore on their blocks. We had a block ordered for six months and by the time we got it they already had a larger bore spread on their blocks which meant they could run a larger piston with a shorter stroke. That is one reason why, and most people don't really understand it, a NHRA (National Hot Rod Association) 500 inch motor, which has a 4.650 bore, has a three something inch stroke, where a mountain motor engine has a 4.800 bore and a 5.625 stroke. Our piston speed was outrageous because any NHRA motors have gone up and down three plus inches, but we were going up and down five plus inches. That's why a NHRA motor can develop a little over two and one-half horsepower per cubic inch which is outstanding for a push-rod motor, four-cycle non turbo charged pump gas motor. While in the IHRA, we have actually gotten our motors up over two horsepower per cubic inch and our limits are 815 inches where an IHRA is 500 cubic inches.

So the next year, we had the dyno but we couldn't do anything with it because we didn't have the parts. So then, the next year, we had some parts and we did pretty well. We won a round and we qualified at a few races. Finally, in '96, we had enough parts to do some serious dyno work. Basically because as a major (I have always been a major sponsor at IHRA and NHRA national events) my company and I played politics long and hard to put a limit on the spread bore. The NHRA had one of 4.900 inches and since there were already shot gun Fords with five inch spread bore out there, I talked them into going with the five inch spread bore. Now they just can't keep coming out with a 5.100 and a 5.200. It has to stop at the five inch spread. Which means now we are done buying blocks every six months. Five inch spread bores are standardized so you only have to buy the block once. So last year we qualified for I think every race but two, winning a few rounds, and finishing eleventh or twelfth in the points.

Most people would think that was a great year. Well, it was miserable. We were not happy with it. But that's the way you should be, just like in business. **You should not be happy with mediocre performance.** We got some more parts, did a lot more head work, a lot of intake manifold testing, and right now our pro stocker is competitive with anybody. This year we should actually win a race or two, not just win rounds. We are gearing up and have some tricker parts and some tricker heads that we are working on for next year. We also have some 500 inch motors, heads, blocks, cranks, and cams that we bought from Dale Eicke when he went with Mopar . So we have a lot of parts and a few great cars. We have a '96 Jerry Haas Oldsmobile Cutlass. We have a '94 Rick Jones pro-stock Camaro. We just picked up a Jerry Haas 1998 Monte Carlo and we still have the original '89 pro stocker that we bought from Rickie Smith which my son races. He's a tough sportsman and he's won rounds with that. It won't be long until he'll win a race, and even a national event.

Drag Racing is My Sport

We are totally committed to drag racing. In '94 and '95 we

sponsored Todd Payton's Alcohol Funny Car. When we went pro-stock racing in '93, we sponsored Bruce Litton's top dragster and he won a lot of races, a lot of quick eights. In fact, he won the quick eight shoot out finals three years in a row with the top dragster that we were sponsoring. In '96 and '97, we sponsored Bruce Litton's top fueler. He has run some 480s with it which is really fast at the IHRA's tracks. So we are totally committed to drag racing. It's what we want to do. It's what we love to do. Ron works for my company now and we have several people who do nothing but work on the race cars. Ron drives the pro-stocker. My son, Rob, drives the top sportsman car. He will eventually race pro-stock and we will have a two car team. The only thing that's holding us back from having a two car team is the experience I want Rob to have in the top sportsman car. I want him to have about everything and anything that can go wrong happen to him when he is running a slow car because the car he's running runs 730s and 740s at 180-190 in the quarter. The mountain motor pro stockers that we raced run low 670s at 205 or 206 mph in a quarter mile. That's the kind of speed these vehicles obtain!

We are one of the few pro-stock teams that actually builds its own motors. There are people out there who buy trick heads from Joe Clark or whomever or Dale Eicke and then they bolt them on their motors. There are other people who buy Sonny Leonard Motors and John Kaase Motors and they all buy the same thing. They can never get ahead. It's very difficult to have your own engine program because to truly have your own engine program you need to do your own heads and your own intake manifold. It takes a long time to get ahead that way, but once you are ahead, and you do not sell your technology, it will be very difficult for anyone to catch you. So we have our own engine building program and we do the whole thing. We do our own intake ports. We do our own porting. We do our own intake. We do everything. There are hardly any teams that do that anymore and that's our plan. **We want to do it ourselves or we don't want to do it.** It's my business philosophy, too.

WINNERS...
#64. create to lead the pack rather than follow others

Give instruction to a wise man, and he will be still wiser.
Teach a righteous man, and he will increase his learning.
(Proverbs 9:9)

It's really kind of unique when you go to a national event and you look around and you see all these big rigs and all this cubic money. That's what I like to call it, cubic money, as it is invested in racing. There is a successful business behind every one of these operations because, like I said before, speed is addictive and everybody wants to go fast. The faster you go, the faster you want to go. Speed costs! How fast do you want to go?

So, in wrapping up this discussion on racing and business, a lot of businesses were started, including my own, to go racing. Now that the business is picking up we can really go racing. If you look around, a lot of successful business people race vehicles. It rubs off on their operation because they have a successful racing team.

Chapter Six

TAKING THE LEAD

**Racing in the Right Class Comes First
Considering the Long Haul is Important
Keeping and Eye on the Competition is a Must
Approaching the Line Correctly Can Make All the Difference
Even Reaching Top Speed Does Not Satisfy
With No Finish Line Your Goals Are Always in Front of You**

So many people that I've observed in life try to tackle something that they have no business tackling. It is just like a game. If you are good at a game, that's the game you should play. If you are not any good at it then you probably should consider not playing it. Take golf for example. If you are good at golf, great! If you are not, then don't play the game, unless you're just going to play for rest and relaxation. Why set yourself up for a fall? Any profession you choose to participate in or make a living from, you should enjoy. In this day and age, and in the '70s, '80s, and '90s in the United States, a person can do and be anything he or she wants to be. So you need to find something that you like to do, something at which you are competitive, something in which you would like to improve, and something at which you are good at least some of the time. If you are going to start your own business, you want to start a business that you would like to do, one that you are good at doing, and something at which you can make a decent living.

Racing in the Right Class Comes First

Whether you're racing or in business, you want to race in a class or work in a business at which you are, or can be, good. If you don't have a lot of money as far as racing, and you want to be competitive, then choose one of the dial-in classes. When you run off a dial-in, you are all equal, so it all boils down to the driver's skill. Race that type of race. That is how you get good. You become good by choosing a class in which you can excel.

When we were running top dragster we dominated the class. Well, that got old, so we decided to step up to pro-stock. That is quite a step. In fact, it is really hard to believe that we can even be competitive in it. But we are and we like what we're doing. It is so competitive in pro-stock that we are one of the last of the independents. As I have stated before, everybody else buys their horsepower from either John Kaase or Sonny Leonard. They are all buying the same horsepower. If you are going to dominate the class, how can you do that if everybody has the same horsepower that you have? You can't! The only way you can dominate the class is to develop your own horsepower which is the route I have taken with Ron Miller. As noted earlier we have constructed and built a complete dyno facility. We do the machine work in my shop and he works on the dyno night and day. We make horsepower. We are very competitive. It is actually quite an accomplishment just to qualify for a pro-stock race in this high dollar game.

Same goes with business. **You have to excel at what you are doing and enjoy it.** In other words, you have to be smart enough to pick something, either a profession or a business, at which you are good and can have fun.

WINNERS...

#65. excel at what they are doing and enjoy it

**He who tills his land will have plenty of bread,
But he who pursues vain things lacks sense.
(Proverbs 12:11)**

Considering the Long Haul is Important

If you use all the best components that money can buy because you want what you are going to build to last, you want to do it right. You don't want to take any short cuts. You want to construct your motor so that you have reliability. So many people build with huge rocker arm ratios and really thin cylinder walls. They try to make maximum horsepower for five or six runs before the motor wears out on a pro-stock car. We don't do that. We build motors to last. We don't drop valves, break rocker arms, seize top rings, etc. We prevent problems like that. In fact, we run our main bearings the entire year. Same goes with your business. You want to build your business for the long haul. You don't want to do anything crazy or stupid. You don't want to take short cuts. You want to do it right. You want to build upon a solid foundation. **You want to build a foundation under your business so that your business is there for years, so it will last just like a quality engine being built for a race car. You are looking to** build for reliability, longevity, and especially, like in our case, success so you can pass an inheritance onto your children and they can pass it onto their children. That is what you want to do.

WINNERS...

#66. build their business on a foundation to last

> I will show you what he is like who comes to me and hears my words and puts them into practice. He is like a man building a house, who dug down deep and laid the foundation on rock. When a flood came, the torrent struck that house but could not shake it, because it was well built. But the one who hears my words and does not put them into practice is like a man who built a house on the ground without a foundation. The moment the torrent struck that house, it collapsed and its destruction was complete.
> **(Luke 6:47-49)**

WINNERS...

#67. want to leave a legacy for future generations

> A good man leaves an inheritance to his children's children,
> And the wealth of the sinner is stored up for the righteous.
> **(Proverbs 13:22)**

Keeping an Eye on the Competition

The best way in the world to take the lead in business is to see just what your competitors are doing. You are checking out their business to see who is making a product like yours. In our case it was Strange Engineering and Mark Williams Enterprises. You see what they are doing, how they are doing it, and why they are doing it. It is really amazing when you check into the actual performance of your competitor's product. I know we had to build our own torque testing machine to do that. To the best of my knowledge, we are the only company that even has that capability. But we had to check out what the competition was doing. You have to see what they are doing, how they are doing it, and why they are doing it. You go from there and you engineer a better product. Then you engineer a way to make it quicker, and a way so that you can make money selling it cheaper. Basically quicker, cheaper, better, and if you can meet those criteria, you have a product that only a fool would not buy. Since we have started our business, we have completely dominated the axle after market business. The competition is not even remotely close. We sell in the neighborhood of 40-50,000 axles a year. That is a lot of race car axles. The competition is lucky to sell 15,000 and one of our competitors might not even sell 1,000 axles a year.

The same goes with racing. You have to check out the competition, see what they are doing, and you have to keep an eye on them. No matter how much market share you have, no matter how dominant you are in the market, no matter how dominant you are in your race car class, you still have to keep your eye on your competitors.

One of my favorite statements was made by Chrysler's Chairman, Lee Iacocca. In one of his advertisements, when he was stumping for Chrysler years ago, he used to say, "Lead, follow, or get out of the way." In other words, you either have to lead or get out of the way because if you don't, you are going to get run over by your competition. He is right. You need to keep an eye on your competition, keep an eye on what they are doing, how they are doing it, and why they are reacting the way they are reacting to you. If you keep your business small and keep your management core small, you can react instantly. You don't need a dozen board meetings to figure out what is happening. If you have an idea that is going to save you money, use your gut feeling, and do it. It is just good business. It is not good business to spend days, weeks, or months trying to decide what to do. I guess it boils down to making a decision. Like in the military, the worst thing you can do is to make no decision. **Whether it is the right decision or the wrong decision, make a decision.** That way, you have a direction in which to go and all of your work force can go in the same direction. This is how you get things accomplished.

WINNERS...

#68. get things accomplished by making decisions as quickly as possible

**He also who is slack in his work,
Is brother to him who destroys.
(Proverbs 18:9)**

In all of the years that I have raced personally, especially when racing top dragsters, I would check out my competitor before making a run down the drag strip. I would actually go back and look at the records to see what kind of a light this guy catches. It's all an equal playing field. You have to run fast to qualify the car, since they take only the fastest 32 qualifiers out of a field which usually numbers 50 to 70 cars. It's the top dragster in which Ron and I have run for years.

You have to run fast enough to qualify. Once you are qualified, they have a quick eight with the eight fastest qualifiers. There is no break out. On a Saturday night, the eight fastest cars race to find out who is the fastest car there. On Sunday, it's the bracket race. Let's say you run 6.5 seconds in the quarter mile and somebody else runs a 7.0. Well, you have to give the guy a half of a second head start. They use a computer and they put that in the Christmas tree, so his light comes down a half a second before yours. Now think about that. If you both catch the same light and you both run the same E.T. that you dialed-in on your car, you would have a tie. In other words, if you wrote 6.50 on the side of your car, and he wrote 7.00 on the side of his car, theoretically, when you would cross the finish line, it would be a dead tie, given that the tower and computer running the race are working correctly. Now you are dealing with thousandths of a second. That is impossible. Well, it's not impossible, but highly improbable. That may have happened once in the history of the sport. But if you leave too soon before the last green light comes on, then the red light comes on and you are automatically disqualified. The lights on a pro-tree are 4/10 lights or 0.4. On a regular tree they are 0.5 or a half of a second. A perfect light is how close you can get to 0.500 or 0.400 depending on what class you are running. Real hot dogs in the sport catch a double 0 light. They will catch a 0.406 or 0.408, which are fantastic lights. Now, think about that. Let's say you caught a 0.410 light. Let's say the guy you are running caught a 0.490 light. That's eight hundredths of a second head start. You dialed-in a 6.50 and he dialed-in a 7.00. He could run a 7.00 and you could run a 6.579. Got that! You would beat him because you beat him eight hundredths on the Christmas tree and took off eight hundredths quicker than he did. You could run 7.90 hundredths slower than your dial-in and still beat the guy. So that is why you scope out the competition. You find out just how good they are because you don't want to, as we call it, "squeeze the tree." You don't want to squeeze that last bulb unless you have to do so.

I know that in all of the years that Ron and I have run the top dragster, Ron has been so good on the tree that we have played with the delay box to actually delay his start so he wouldn't red light this on a pro tree. We'd check on the lights that someone was getting, and we would dial-in some delay on purpose just so that we wouldn't red light. I know a lot of people do that. That is what you call scoping out the competition as far as race cars go.

Approaching the Line Correctly Can Make All the Difference

In drag racing, a person needs to be so familiar with his staging routine that he could do it in his sleep. When you stage the car in a drag race, you are trying to position your front wheels in the lights. There is a Christmas tree with colored bulbs that individually transcend down. It has three yellows, a green, and a red light. If you leave too fast, the red light is tripped and you are disqualified. There are two little yellow bulbs on top of the tree. The first one is the pre-stage beam and the second one is the stage beam. When you pull your car into the lane, you edge the front wheel until it trips the first pre-stage bulb. When you trip the second bulb (stage bulb), and the other person you are racing in the other lane does the same, then the starter activates the Christmas tree. You get yellow, yellow, yellow, then green. Like I said previously, you are trying to leave as close to the green light bulb as you possibly can but not before it actually comes on since, if you do, the red light comes on and you are automatically disqualified.

People race the eighth mile, fifth mile, and quarter mile. Believe it or not, you can do what they call "deep stage." You know exactly how much roll out your car has and after you roll in and trip the pre-stage light, you roll forward and your pre-stage light goes out. Now if you roll too far and you trip the stage light and your competitor has his stage light lit, that's a red light. You are disqualified. If you accidentally lunge forward and roll past the stage beam, and your competitor does not have his stage beam lit, you can back up quickly and properly stage the car.

Believe it or not, one inch difference in where your car stages can mean a hundredth of a second in E.T., a hundredth of a second! You say, "Boy, that isn't much," but I can tell you from experience that we have failed to qualify by zero, not a hundredth, not a thousandth, not a millionth, but we have failed to qualify by zero. I will elaborate on that a little bit.

At one race we ran about a 6.864. Thousandths of a second is as far as the timers go. We were tied for 16th place. But because there is no tie, the tiebreaker is how fast of the mile an hour you went in producing that E.T. We've been bumped out of the field to first alternate by someone running just a hair faster mile an hour with the exact same E.T., down to the thousandths. So it is critical where you pre-stage and stage the car. The second thing that is critical about staging the car (and this just makes sense if you think about it), when you pull the car in you want the car to be within a quarter inch of the same place in the beams every time you stage a car. That way you have a more consistent light. You have a better chance of red lighting if you deep stage. A lot of people with a slow car, like a 14 second or 13 second car, deep stage. Because the car reacts so poorly, it reacts so slow, that you can't get a good light unless you deep stage.

So to correlate this with business, it is like being prepared when opportunity knocks. You approach the line or opportunity to win knowing that you have the skills, talents and horsepower to succeed. **In other words, you come up to the line where you know you can be successful due to positive attitude, confidence, and knowledge.** A person needs to be smart enough or have enough common sense to be in those situations, but you can literally put yourself in those situations by working hard and by working smart. You can create your own opportunities in life simply because you are ready. Most people never reach their dream because they never had a dream in the first place. It is really easy to think up an idea to make money. What's harder is to actually develop it, figure out how to market it, and present it to the public at exactly the right time when somebody needs to buy it. If you are able to do that, and you can if you have the desire, then you know how to make a buck.

WINNERS...

#69. use positive attitude, confidence, and knowledge to take the lead

**A worker's appetite works for him,
For his hunger urges him on.
(Proverbs 16:26)**

Most people procrastinate and put things off and that is why they don't get much done in this world. It is easy to get a lot done. I've been involved in many organizations. I have served on many boards. I have been asked to be the director of this and to help out on that, be the chair of this and the head of that, and I know people say, "Doesn't he sleep? How does he get this much stuff done?" Well, it is because I subscribe to the theory that if you want something, or someone asks you to do something, you do it. You don't put it off until tomorrow, because if you do, you have to do it tomorrow. If an opportunity comes up tomorrow and you are busy taking care of business that you should have done yesterday, how are you going to jump on the opportunity that comes along. I am a stickler on this. I get asked to speak to a lot of organizations and groups. The second I get a phone call and someone asks me to speak, I say "yes" because I think it is my responsibility to try to help other people. You have heard me say it before, but by helping other people you help yourself. You make the world a better place in which to live, which, in turn, makes the world a better place for you. I have had people call and ask me to give a talk and I'll say, "What do you want me to talk about?" I write it down. "What time do you want me to be there?" I write it all down. "Okay, great, I'll do it." The main reason why I say I will do it is because I want to help people and I think it is my responsibility. The second reason I talk or speak to people is because I like to and the only way to get better at being a speaker is to continue to do it.

When someone asks me to give a speech, as soon as I hang up the phone, guess what? I clear up whatever I had been doing at the moment when the phone rang and I sit down and rough out my speech. I don't put it off until the next day or the next week, even if they ask me to give this talk a month from now, I sit down and I rough out the speech's outline right then and there. That way I can be thinking about it over the month and the material will come together naturally. It will be a good talk and I will get it done. Most people don't do that and I don't know why. You just have to train yourself. **If you need something done, you do not put it off.** You can't put something off and get a lot accomplished in this world. You have to do it when the opportunity arises and when you have the time to do it. In fact, you have to make time, so that tomorrow, when an opportunity comes around, you can grab it! You have to create the opportunity by working smart and by putting yourself in a position to take advantage of the opportunity. Then you have to have the guts to grab that opportunity and see it through to the finish.

WINNERS...

#70. accomplish much by focusing on what needs to be done and doing it

**Laziness casts into a deep sleep,
And an idle man will suffer hunger.
(Proverbs 19:15)**

"Should've, could've, would've" is an old saying. Well, most people should've done it, and they could've done it, but they just wouldn't do it. I think the fear of failure is the driving force behind it all. **The fear of failure is something you just cannot have.** Unfortunately, it just gets worse the older you get. When you are young, when you don't have much responsibility, that is the time to take advantage of opportunities. They are easier and you have a lot less to lose. I like to think of it as a merry-go-round where you are reaching for the brass ring. You are on the edge of the merry-go-round, rotating in a circle, and all the opportunities are right there. All you have to do is reach out and grab one. Well, as the years go by, the opportunities are farther away from the perimeter of the merry-go-round so you are going to have to really reach out to grab an opportunity. As the years continue to pass, the opportunities keep moving farther away from you. Before long, you are going to have to jump clear off the merry-go-round to grab an opportunity and most people won't do that. The fear of failure is too great and they will not take the chance. You cannot put off until tomorrow what can be done today. If something comes along you want to be ready to pounce on it. You have to be prepared when opportunity knocks.

WINNERS...

#71. do not fear failure because they are prepared when opportunity knocks

For Thou art my rock and my fortress
For Thy name's sake Thou wilt lead me and guide me.
(Psalm 31:3)

Even Reaching Top Speed Does Not Satisfy

In drag racing, E.T. is what counts. The person who crosses the finish line first is the winner. The faster you can cross that finish line, the lower E.T., is how you set your qualifier. The only time miles per hour comes into play is if you are tied for a particular qualifying spot.

In racing we are never satisfied. We have made beautiful runs. The joy of looking at a beautiful E.T. on the scoreboard lasts for only a matter of seconds. Your brain looks at it and says, "Wow, this is great!" Then you look back at the run and your mind replays a video in your head and you think, "Well, the car went a little left," or, "The car went a little right." "It got loose out there and the driver had to drive it a little bit. There were probably two hundredths left in that run." You go back, download the computer information, stick it in the computer, look at it, and what you saw was correct. There were two hundredths left in that run. We are never satisfied. It doesn't matter how good you are, and it doesn't matter how fast of an E.T. you run. You can never be satisfied. **In business, you can never be satisfied**. You can't! The only time you can ever be satisfied in business is if you're done. If you say to yourself, "Well, I feel like I have accomplished everything I can accomplish. It is time to let someone else take over," then you can sell your business and get rid of it. But if you decide that you no longer want to be number one or you no longer want to lead the pack, there is no way from the top but down. It's a big bell curve. Clear at the top, your business is starting to mellow out and you have to keep that curve going up. It's very hard to catch a moving target. It's very hard to hit a moving target. That has always been my business philosophy. It's always been that way when I worked for other companies. You were never satisfied without something being done. You always tried to figure out a way to make it better, quicker, or cheaper! You can't look at something and say, "Well, that's okay. That works pretty good. They are getting enough production off of that." You can't do that. You can't look at something and say that's okay. There are thousands of things with which I have been involved over the years in these companies and the one thing I know that has made these companies successful is that outlook. They are never satisfied.

WINNERS...

#72. are never satisfied due to their desire to always do better

"Winning isn't everything, it's the only thing."
(Saying in 1953, often attributed to football coach Red Sanders)

It's like when I was working for Teledyne. Ever since I have been working in business, we have found better ways to do it. When I was working for Maremont we were constantly looking at new things and building new equipment. We made brake lining there and we were constantly looking for ways to cut costs to improve the product. In fact, one story about saving money at Maremont involved our clutch facings. We made heavy duty truck clutches. We molded the fiber and actually made a clutch disc. Sometimes a major cost reduction is thought up by someone who doesn't know that it can't be done. I find this really interesting because that is why I think engineers should move all of the time. **They should always try different things and try different companies. If they don't know that it can't work, then they try it and find out that it will work!**

WINNERS...
#73. don't assume that something can't work, so in trying it,
it does work

"You see things; and you say, 'Why?'
But I dream things that never were;
and I say, 'Why not?'"
(George Bernard Shaw)

What I am going to tell you saved hundreds of thousands of dollars. It is beyond belief. At one job, they used to mold clutch facings for trucks: multi-platen, hydraulic presses, steam heat, electric heat, and we had to cook them. There was a die cavity with little serrations. As I recall, they were probably 20 to 24 inches in diameter with a six inch center hole and were about 1/4 or 3/8 inches thick. An operator would load the material into a seven platen press. The operator would then stick these in and fill the next slot and then when he got them all loaded up he would hit the hydraulic pressure and would bake them. Then, from what they were molded in, he would pry them out. After these things were all done and cooled down we had multiple spindle decka drills. I am talking like 60 holes. We needed carbide tip drills and a welder to weld all the carbide tips in them. We needed a tool grinder to grind all the tips in these things, and then we needed another toolmaker to set up the depth so we had all 60 holes the same depth. These were rivet holes or counter bore rivet holes. We would rivet the facings to the steel clutch hub. It was an enormous amount of work to set this up. Then we had to take this whole set up and install it into this decka drill. The deckas had many universal joints that were constantly wearing out along with the bearings. Then somebody would ding one and we'd have to go in and, instead of pulling the whole head, we'd have the maintenance set-up man change bits scraping half a dozen facings getting the hole debt right. For some reason, I looked at this and said, "Don't these facings shrink the same amount every time with the right heat after they are molded?" "Yeah they do!" "How about if we mold the rivet holes in the facing?" "Well, we tried that years ago, and that won't work." "Oh, really?"

So I did some investigating and I went out back in the scrap pile and sure enough, there were these pins. Guess why they would not work? Somebody had thought up this idea years ago. They figured out all the shrink and everything, and they had pressed all these pins in, and on the back side countered them, drilled them, and put little Allen head flat heads to hold them in place. It was really neat! On top of this pin hole they had about a half inch tall pin with the rivet hole. On the top plate they then drilled 60 holes for the pin to go into this hole. Somebody had already thought of it but it absolutely didn't work!

There are several reasons why it didn't work. First, the presses weren't accurate enough for the pins to hit the holes in the top of the plate when they pressed them down in place. So they were constantly shearing the sides of the pins off. Second, the mixture of rubber and glue that held the friction yarn together would go up in these holes and after two or three pieces, it would clog the pins and would stick the plate down to the rivet hole.

You know how I solved the problem? This is amusing and is so simple. The clutch facings were all ground on both sides after they were cooled. All we did was make the pins with about a .010 (10 thousandths) flat top pin on top of the rivet. We didn't have it sticking up half an inch. I just had them ground down so they were actually five thousandths below the rim of the mold so that when the plate came down and hit the top side of the mold it never touched the pins. If you looked at the facing after it was molded you saw the rivet hole and you saw the head clearance in the hole. Then there was a little bitty five thousandths wafer in the bottom. If you turned it over you couldn't even tell there were holes in it. Guess what? We ground ten thousandths off the clutch disc. So when you ground it off you uncovered the hole. We saved hundreds of thousands of dollars. It was just because I was a kid, fresh out of college at 21 years old, and basically said, "Well, guys, this will work." What I then found out was that we were just getting into molding disc brake parts. Guess what? They tried it there, too. The pins were stuck in the presses so we did the same thing. You have to revolutionize the manufacturing of these parts. Unbelievable! It was something that some kid looked at and said, "Why do you do it that way? Let's just do it this way." There are so many things in this world that you can do better by never acknowledging that the way you are doing it at present is the best way. **Never reach your top speed and say, "I can't go any faster. I can't go any quicker."** Never look at a process and say, "This is just the ultimate. I am never going to do any better." Because you are doomed. You are doomed to have someone pass you by if you become complacent in your thinking.

WINNERS...
#74. are never satisfied at top speed because they know they can go faster

"What this power is I cannot say; all I know is that it exists and it becomes available only when a man is in that state of mind in which he knows exactly what he wants and is fully determined not to quit until he finds it."

(Alexander Graham Bell)

Another cost reduction idea actually won the National Conservationist of the Year Award for me from the Eutectic Castolin Corporation when I was working for Portec in 1977. This was another one of those things I did when I was probably around 24 years old. I was a kid who didn't know anything. We had a product at Portec that was called a weld strap. We rolled rail joints (railway track components). They were starting to weld rail instead of bolting it together. They couldn't trust it if the weld broke. The train would derail so they made a bar called a weld strap that took the place of the rail joint. It was a little cruder than a standard rail joint, but it was just there to hold the track together so if the weld broke, the train wouldn't derail. This particular part, we rolled it, punched four slots in it so it was adjustable to bolt to any rail, and forged an offset in the middle to clear the weld on both sides of the rail. We form forged it so that when you bolted it to the rail it would clear the weld, and since it was coming out around the track to clear the weld, it had to come down so that when the edge of the train wheel rolled across it it didn't hit the side of the rail joint. It had to have clearance down and out. We rolled it, punched it, had people line them up, and stick them in a reheat furnace. We brought them back up to forging temperature, loaded them in the press, and forged them. Somebody unloaded them out of the press, down a conveyor, and into a quench where they were heat treated. Then they were taken out of the quench, stacked on the dirt floor, and allowed to cool.

When they completely cooled they had burrs all over them from the forging operation. We had to grind all the burrs off. We ran the total production by hand grinding these things. We made about 18% profit on this product. We could not get through two hours of forging before the die burred up so badly that we had to stop production and the die maker had to hand grind and rebuff the die, or change the die, whichever was quicker, because if you kept grinding on it then you were out of tolerance and you would be grinding off your offset of the die. I looked at that and thought all we had to do was to figure out a way to put some material on the die so that it wouldn't wear out so quickly because we were using Finkle hot work die steel. This is one of those deals where I contacted the local Eutectic salesman whose name was Jerry. He was a part of a group of high-tech salesmen offering very expensive high dollar welding rod from Eutectic Castolin Corporation. I wanted coating for a die. They had just introduced this spray. You actually took a torch, which they sold, and got the metal hot. The torch had a button which dispensed this powdered metal and you sprayed it on the die and it adhered to the die. They had Diamax spray and they had Boron spray and we settled on the latter. We sprayed this die with Boron, stuck it in the press, and this stuff worked so slick that you could run a ten hour shift and never shut the machine down. Well, it was so slick, that we didn't need to reheat the part to forge it. As it came off the rolling mill, we would punch the part and transfer it to a high speed conveyor to this press. The forging press would forge the offset in the part and the operator would take the part out at the correct temperature to quench it. Once quenched it would come out and we would stack it. Guess what? There were no burrs on it. It didn't need to be ground. We eliminated nearly half of the production people on this particular job. It became the highest profit margin part in our business. Since the industry was going to more welded track, we were making a lot more of these weld bars. We ended up with over a 40% manufacturing margin on this part. It was all because somebody didn't know any different, know any better, and know that it wouldn't work. I looked at it and said, "Why don't we do it this way?"

This all took place over a period of one year. You have to bear in mind that when I started working in this particular facility they produced about $12,000,000 a year in sales. The total savings in a year on this particular part, over and above the profit margin, was in excess of a million dollars. After I showed him all the facts and figures, the Eutectic Castolin Corporation man said, "No way! This is unreal! We have to enter this in a contest! We have an annual competition for the person who saves the most money with our products." He turned it in and we won it hands down. This was a little $12,000,000 company that won this award. So the bottom line here is that you should never be satisfied with anything.

Actually, I would have to say in my life I am only satisfied with two things. I am satisfied with my children and I am satisfied with my spouse. Other than that, there is nothing in this world with which I am satisfied. I am always trying to figure out how to make things better, cheaper, quicker, and how to reach top speed and low E.T.

One major cost reduction at Teledyne had to do with natural gas and this was back when they were deregulating the pipe lines and you could buy gas at the well head. It's a good lesson in dealing with people, but you need some power to deal with people or you need an edge. We had some large propane tanks at Teledyne but nothing really efficient to actually run the gas fired forge furnaces off propane. So we put in a mixture system with which we could actually mix the propane at the exact B.T.U. burn rate of natural gas. Then we could switch back and forth from natural gas to propane (L.P.). No one could tell the difference. The heaters couldn't tell the difference and the forging operation couldn't tell the difference. Nobody could tell a thing. This is what you call dealing from a position of power. Once we had the capacity where we could say, "Hey, we're not buying natural gas from you," we had it made. We were the largest natural gas user in the area. We never received any complaints out of them whatsoever. With the ability to have back up with L.P., we could purchase natural gas at the well head, and just pay to have it transported, or put in the pipe line to use it. We could actually sign up for totally 100% interruptible gas which gives you the most ridiculous gas rates you have ever seen.

The other thing that was so amusing about all this was the fact that when you buy propane by the tanker loads, it costs virtually nothing. We could have saved money if we just ran the place on propane. But we saved more money on natural gas and, in a company that had $50,000,000 to $60,000,000 a year in sales, that actually added over two percent to the bottom line!

With No Finish Line Your Goals Are Always In Front of You

This is an interesting statement because I believe that there is no finish line. I believe that a person should conduct his or her life and business like running the hundred yard dash with no finish line. That way, once you get ahead, it is virtually impossible for anyone to catch you. In fact, I know a lot of people who talk about setting goals and achieving goals. I don't know if I have ever achieved a goal in my life simply because every time I set a goal, once I approach that goal, I eventually look at it and say, "Well, that was too easy. That wasn't hard enough." Then I always move the goal out farther. **So I never actually accomplish any goals, but I do set my goals and that is how you get a lot of things done.** I know what I am doing tomorrow. I know what I am doing at the end of the week. I know what I am doing next month. I know what I am going to be doing a year from now. That is how you get a lot done!

WINNERS...

#75. approach goals only to reset them
to accomplish much and stay ahead

"The world has the habit of making room for the man whose words and actions show that he knows where he is going." (Napoleon Hill)

In business, just like in racing, it is nice to win and it is nice to be ahead of the competition, but that is as far as you should let it go. You should continue to strive to do better, better, and better. Once you win a race you savor the moment, but shortly after that you try to figure out how you are going to win another race, and another race, and another race. It's the same with business. You must never let up. Never say "enough is enough" unless you are prepared to retire, sell your business, or are on your death bed. If you are on your death bed, then you say, "I'm finally tired with this. I'm done. I'm done running the hundred yard dash. I'm finally going to quit and let someone else take over."

In racing, you can really relate a lot to the finish line because you are trying to get there first and be noted as the fastest. In business it's the same. You want to get where you are going first and you want to dominate the market place just like when you win the race. The bottom line is you can call it the finish line but you are never truly finished. You are never finished! There is always something else to conquer and there is always another race to win. So you can call it the finish line but you are never finished. Take the lead and maintain it!

Chapter Seven

HANDLING CRASHES AND OTHER MISHAPS

Turning the Negative into Positive
Moving On to Positive Learning Experiences
Using Ethics and Integrity as Preventive Medicine

What happens when you DNQ or "do not qualify." How do you handle premature losses and the negative things that happen to you in life and in business? Are you able to handle the crashes and other mishaps that come your way?

Turning the Negative Into Positive

There really are no negative experiences in life. Sometimes you may think they are negative. **What I have found that works best for me is to not even acknowledge that they are negative.** You may have to look at a pretty obscure angle of something to see some positive in a negative experience. But you always can! If you ever run into something that is so negative that you cannot believe it and you can't see anything positive in it, well, guess what? It was a positive learning experience. I guess you could basically say that I have eliminated the word negative from my vocabulary.

WINNERS...

**#76. are eternally optimistic by viewing negatives
as learning experiences**

"The ultimate measure of a man is not where he stands in moments of comfort and convenience, but where he stands at times of challenge and controversy."
(Martin Luther King)

Another word that I have eliminated from my vocabulary, as far as business goes, is the word "luck." **In business, luck is where opportunity meets preparation.** Now I will concede that there is luck in this world. Luck, to me, is if you happen to win the lottery. The only other luck I have ever seen is in drag racing and it is pure luck. There are by far more ways to lose a drag race by bad luck than there ever are winning outright with preparation, opportunity, and skill. I have seen just about everything in the world of drag races and I have had everything in the world happen to me from not qualifying to losing races.

WINNERS...

#77. consider luck to be where opportunity meets preparation

> "A wise man will make more opportunities than he finds." (Francis Bacon)

The year we were running top dragster was when we won all those quick eight races and the one national event. That year, the only races we lost were when the transmission failed. We were so brutal on the transmission that we rebuilt it for every race. Even then, we had them go out on us causing us to lose races.

There are a multitude of ways to lose. At the 1997 President's Cup Nationals, Angelo Alesci had the entire field covered by 0.06 of a second. There was no way in the world that national event wasn't his. He had the track figured out, he had his clutch perfect, he had perfect 330 progressive times, and he was head and shoulders above everybody in the whole field. In drag racing, the number 1 qualifier, which was Angelo, runs the number 16 qualifier. Number 2 runs 15 and so on until number 8 runs number 9. Well, number 8 and number 9, number 7 and number 10, and number 6 and number 11 are the most competitive races. When number 1 runs number 16, it's usually a lopsided race.

Well, Angelo did his burn out, hit his brakes, blew off a hydraulic, braided steel line, good for 3,000 psi (pounds per square inch), and had no brakes! He had to forfeit the first run. Just when you think you have seen everything, something will sneak up and get you and there is no way in the world to anticipate that. There is no way. You are not going to sit there and cry about it. Wake up and realize how much more you will appreciate an eventual win if you have lost a few times through a little bad luck.

We, personally, have lost qualifiers. We have missed qualifying a lot just because we will be in the field Friday at noon, Friday night, and Saturday at noon. Come Saturday night, when the air gets really good, we will make a wrong call on the clutch, it won't get down, and we have to abort the run. We have qualified well on the field Friday at noon, messed up on the clutch adjustment on Friday night, gotten bumped out of the field on Saturday at noon, and then have it rain on us Saturday night. So, when it rains, they close the fields and you are qualified where you were when it started raining. So you don't even get a chance to qualify. We have missed qualifying by, up until a few races ago, a thousandth of a second, but we have missed qualifying by no seconds, too! If the E.T. is the same, the guy who runs the faster mile an hour gets the best spot.

Literally, we have seen everything and we have had everything happen to us. We have had wheelie bars break and we have had the two step fail. A two step is what holds the motor at a certain RPM as the tree is activated. You bring the motor up against the two step, which is usually between 4600 and 5200 RPM, and then when you take your foot off the clutch, that lets the motor go to its maximum RPM level unrestricted and you take off. Well, if the two step breaks while you are trying to hold the car, no human being can hold the centrifugal clutch above 6, 7, 8,000 RPM. Then the car rolls through the lights and you red light. So you are disqualified and you lose that race. Most people would say, "That's negative." The fact that I can actually sit here and tell you about these things is simply because it is a fantastic learning experience. You are gaining knowledge upon knowledge upon knowledge, which is one of the reasons why we started racing pro-stock.

We completely dominated top dragster when we ran that class. We were the best. The only time we didn't win was when we had a mechanical failure. Life is all about tough breaks. Life is a challenge and it's no fun to beat up on people. It's just no fun! The challenge lies in seeking out a caliber of competition that is either equal to or better than what you are. Hopefully, you are looking for better. That is why we want to race pro-stock because these guys are better than we are. We are going to try to be as good as they are and when we are, we want to be better than they are. All these little "negative" experiences are positive learning experiences.

You can look at some of the problems that most race car teams have and you can say, "Well, you should have seen this," or "You should have been prepared for that." Well, you cannot prepare for everything. That is why in racing, a little bit of luck goes a long way. It is not so much luck on your part as it is bad luck on your competitor's part because sometimes their brake lines break and other times their wheelie bars bend and they might not know it. Sometimes the torsion bar that centers the rear end and holds it level breaks. There are a multitude of things that can happen to your competitor. So in that case, the competitor's bad luck is your good fortune.

There is luck in winning the lottery, and there can be a little luck in racing, but when it comes to business, there really is no such thing as luck.

You plan ahead, you think long and hard, you use strategy, and you make all the goals to know where you are going and how you are going to get there. So there are no surprises. There really isn't any luck in business. You either planned or you didn't. I have had my share of negative things happen in business and I choose to call those positive learning experiences. In fact, one of the things that I have always done, whether it was on an engineering project, cost reduction, automation project, or whatever, is when I lay something out and I design something, I always look at it and think to myself, "If this doesn't quite work the way I planned it, what can I do to turn it around to make it work?" **I always leave some side doors or some exits, so that I can turn something that is going sour around and make it right. I never stick with anything while it is sinking.** Particularly if I know it is sinking. Always do something about it. Always leave yourself a side door so that you can do something about it.

WINNERS...

#78. always assess when projects are sinking to make them right

He will not allow your foot to slip;
He who keeps you will not slumber.
(Psalm 121:3)

In fact, one thing on which I always prided myself when I was an engineer was that none of my projects ever had a birthday. By that, in engineering jargon, I mean that if you started in November and you didn't get it done until one year or more later, then it had a birthday. It's a year and a month old! **Never have a birthday on any project.** Always complete them within a year. That is how I operate.

WINNERS...

#79. complete projects within one year
to ensure efficiency of operation

Do not love sleep, lest you become poor;
Open your eyes, and you will be satisfied with food.
(Proverbs 20:13)

Moving On to Positive Learning Experiences

This is a good story as I have had some real dazzling learning experiences, too. I was working at Teledyne and we bought an eight inch Ajax upsetter over in Ohio at Canton Forge. Now what's funny about this was that no one actually knew what the thing weighed. I would say that by the size of its block of steel casting, it weighed between 600,000 to 800,000 pounds. That was what this machine weighed in my mind, but no one really knew. We bought this thing for little or nothing compared to what a new one would cost. To transport it we called the company that we always used, Martin International out of Fort Wayne, Indiana. They had hauled several hundred thousand pound hammer bases for us. This stuff was just enormous. We never had a problem with these guys and they were and still are the best.

We asked Martin International to, "Give us a quote on moving this thing." They did and said, "We're going to move it by truck." We basically said, "Well, whatever you think is best." The railroad tracks had all been removed, so there was no railroad there. They got this gargantuan trailer which had 110 tires under it. I've never seen anything like it in my life. Our machine was probably 40 feet long, 16 feet wide, maybe 10 to 12 feet tall, and was almost a solid block of casting. It was enormous. You couldn't believe it. It was like a small house. So they put it on their trailer and they took off from Canton during the winter time. You probably heard about this story already because it was the largest load ever caught by the state patrol in any state.

They had an enormous diesel tractor pulling the trailer and they had another behind pushing it. That is how heavy our machine was. So they were pushing it along, and they were running at night. They got to this little town called Lodi, Ohio, where the road might have had a one-half percent grade. Unfortunately, it started snowing. Martin International literally could not get enough traction to pull the trailer up a one-half percent grade because the load was so heavy. They pulled off behind a restaurant and parked it. Well, the local police, or sheriff, or whoever eats at this restaurant in Lodi, Ohio, was just sitting there enjoying his snack when he happened to look out the window and saw this enormous trailer with this gigantic machine on it. In the snow, the trailer had been pulled off the road into a stone lot behind the restaurant where the truckers parked. He looked this thing over and he said, "This thing must weigh 200,000 or 300,000 pounds!"

Well, now I will give you a little insight into the story. You are allowed only so many thousand pounds per tire if hauling something in Michigan. You are allowed so much gross weight per axle in Indiana. But, in Ohio, they don't care how many axles you have. They don't care! They have a weight limit. I think the weight limit is 160,000 or 180,000 pounds. That's it! Anything bigger than that has to go by rail or you can't move it. I suppose if you did it in advance you could probably get a variance on it, but I don't know.

So the local diner and the police department were looking this trailer over and a policeman said, "Man! There is no way this thing weighs 180,000 pounds or less." He called the state patrol and they staked the thing out. Well, it had stopped snowing, the road was cleared off, and Martin International came back out and hooked it back up. They had to rock it back and forth a bunch of times because it had already sunk in a few inches into the stone in the back lot of the restaurant. They finally got the thing moving and they had just pulled out onto the road and the cops jumped and pulled them over to arrest them. I don't know if they ever truly arrested anyone, but every negative story seems funny after the fact. It was somewhat amusing, even though at the time, it wasn't. So they rounded up every scale that they could get their hands on from all the state patrols in the area and they tried to pull the trailer up on these scales. They couldn't do it. If you couldn't pull this load up a one-half percent grade, there was no way on earth you could pull it up on the angle of the portable scales that the police had. It was impossible. You couldn't do it. Nothing could pull it up on the scales. So because they couldn't weigh it, the state of Ohio impounded it. When we got wind of it a couple of hours after they impounded it, we called Martin and said, "What's the problem? Didn't you show them the permit?" The guy said, "We don't have a permit for this. You can't get a permit for this load." We replied, "Oh, no!"

This was my baby! We argued back and forth with the state and finally they requested my presence, along with a representative from Martin's, in Ohio's state capitol, Columbus, at the department of motor vehicles. We showed up and there was a room full of about 15 people around this long oval table. Honestly, I had the distinct impression as I walked into the room that every one in that room thought that I was responsible for raping every one of their daughters. I knew that I had a problem here. This was not amusing to them. They were reading us the riot act and asking us how stupid we were, and I said, "Hey, I'm not a trucker. I don't know anything about loads and limits. That's why I hire professionals. It's our load and it's illegal, but we still have to have this upsetter machine. We bought it and we want it."

They finally let us go and I think there was a minimal fine. Basically, nothing was done for months and we needed the machine. We had production to run. So finally we sent them a registered letter saying, "If you don't release the upsetter to us, you can just have the thing. We don't want it anymore. You can make it a state of Ohio monument! We don't care what you do with it."

That finally got them off dead center and the ironic thing was that there was a railroad spur right across the street from where the trailer had been left. We had to jump through more hoops. They made us plate, with one inch steel plates, the very same road that the state patrol had the trailer on when trying to get it up on the portable scales. Well, now we couldn't pull it even though the state patrol had pulled it back and forth four or five times and not hurt the road. We had to put steel plates down across the road and drag it across the road. Because there was a culvert there, we had to hire someone to set a movie camera up in the ditch with flood lights and have the film running as we drove across the road. So in case we collapsed the road the police would have the film documenting what we would have to pay for to return it to normal. We finally got it on the railroad's property, stuck it on a rail car, and ran it by train to Portland, Indiana to our side spur.

Other than a slight time inconvenience, the monetary inconvenience of this was basically nothing because it was a million dollar machine for which we had paid a couple of hundred thousand dollars. So what if we had an extra 40 or 50 grand in moving it. Big deal! It made no difference to our bottom line. So now we had the machine in our possession and we even had the governor of Indiana working with the governor of Ohio because this machine was going to add quite a few jobs to Indiana. We weren't taking jobs from Ohio because the plant that we had bought the equipment from was now closed. So it was an economic development consideration, too. Martin's showed up with the same trailer used in the original haul and we took it off the train and put it on the trailer. We, too, didn't have a permit or anything. We had a state patrol escort and they closed down Route 67. They closed it just for us! We pulled out on the road and drove into town. We got a running start and pulled into the chip and seal parking lot adjacent to the building where this machine was going to go. When we got about half way across it, the trailer sunk in the pavement about eight inches. It sunk right in!

We got it on our property and went about our business moving it into place. We already had the foundation put in while it had been impounded, so we really didn't lose much time at all. The positive learning experience on this deal was to make sure you have a permit. Make sure you see the permit. If you can't get a permit, then you need to find some way to get it on a train and get it to your facility. **I guess the bottom line as far as a positive learning experience here was that you can trust all kinds of people, but you may wish to be just a little bit leery and ask to see some**

proof once in a while. If we had done that, we would have eliminated a lot of embarrassment because Teledyne didn't find it too amusing. We did get the job done, got the machine in, and got it up and running. It was a good machine.

WINNERS...

**#80. sincerely trust others but utilize controls
on a precautionary basis**

**The mind of the prudent acquires knowledge,
And the ear of the wise seeks knowledge.
(Proverbs 18:15)**

One other amusing side note of this was that the restaurant, behind which our machine was held captive, had tee-shirts printed that said, "I saw the big one at the Lodi restaurant!" So they had a successful tee-shirt concession which was a big deal. Every once in a while I'll run into a trucker or two and in conversation they will talk about the Lodi restaurant incident and I will start laughing. Then they'll ask, "Why are you laughing?" "Well, that was one of my screw-ups." But that's life and that's how you learn because if you didn't ever have any negative experiences that you could see some positive in, you really wouldn't learn much in life.

It's the same with drag racing. You need all the negative experiences so that you can correct or work around them and not have them happen again. See, there is really nothing bad with doing something wrong or having something fail. What's wrong is if it happens twice. Then there's something wrong with you. You need to seek help because there's something wrong with your brain. **You should only have one negative thing or failure happen per episode.** Never should it happen again. Never!

WINNERS...

**#81. laugh in the face of failure the first time
but cry if it happens again**

**He is on the path of life who heeds instruction,
But he who forsakes reproof goes astray.
(Proverbs 10:17)**

That's what we are doing with our racing team. That's why we are undaunted by not qualifying or by getting beat the first round or whatever. It's just one of those things where you are unhappy on the spur of the moment and only for a little while. It's only a little time before you realize what went wrong, why it went wrong, and that it will never happen again. Eventually, you will be on top of your game because you will have had everything in the world happen to you that could have possibly happened to you. Before long, you will have it all solved and that's when you will start winning races.

It's the same for business where there is actually no substitute for experience. There is none. You cannot teach the school of hard knocks to an individual in high school or college. You cannot duplicate what takes place in the real world. In Jay County, Indiana, I've been involved with a school to work program. We actually have the teachers do interns at our local businesses, called tech prep, to find out what we are doing, why we do it, and how they can teach their students what they will need to know when they get out in the work place. This really works because the teachers are training individuals who we are very comfortable employing in our businesses.

The other thing that we do is participate in an ICE (Interdisciplinary Cooperative Education) program in which industry can employ a student half time during the day. The student goes to school for half a day and works for a business the other half. The student receives job experience and the employers are able to see if they want to employ the student after they graduate from high school. I am very involved in the high school and with our youth, and would encourage others to do the same.

Using Ethics and Integrity as Preventive Medicine

Most companies have actual books on corporate ethics and how they want their managers and their execs to behave. I don't subscribe to any of that stuff. **I subscribe, as an engineer, to the philosophy that what is right is right, and what is wrong is wrong. It is black and white, end of discussion.** You don't really need a book to tell you what is right or what is wrong because believe me, deep down, you know. Next time you are contemplating a business deal, think about what you are doing. Think about, "Would I be comfortable telling my wife or children about this?" Or, "Would I be comfortable telling my minister about this?" Well, guess what? If you are not, then what you are doing is wrong.

WINNERS...

#82. know what is right to do and do it without question

**...never tire of doing what is right.
(2 Thessalonians 3:13)**

You can't buy integrity. Someone has to bestow it upon you. Someone has to say that you have integrity and for them to say that, you have to earn it. **You have to earn it by always doing the right thing.** I know that a lot of times the right thing is not always the popular way. I have had to do some very bizarre things in my day, but they were the right things to do. No matter who they hurt or what they cost me, I always knew that when I did the right thing, and my mind knew that it was right, I didn't care what anybody thought because it was the right thing. In fact, I always call it, "The Blush Factor." Believe it or not, when you tell a lie or when you do something that's a little shady, guess what? You get a little heated, your skin blushes, and you know you have done wrong. You know it's wrong and like I said, always do the right thing and that way you will earn integrity.

As a plant manager at Portec in the mid 70s, I was proposing a ceramic lined flat flame roof burner, walking beam, fossil fueled production furnace. This would be the first ceramic fiber walking beam furnace ever built. One day I was at the Golden Fox restaurant with the vice president of sales of a major furnace builder. At this point in my career I was accepting "free" lunches and dinners from vendors. This man leaned over to me and said, "We want this order and we will do anything to get it." (It would mean a sale of well over a million dollars to him!) I said, "Great! We want it to our specs, delivered on time, and to be cost competitive." The vice president laughed and said, "No, no, no, what do you want? A new car or truck? We want this order!"

Talk about the "The Blush Factor." I think my ears burned off! I was taken off guard. After I regrouped I said that is not the way I work. The meeting was over as far as I was concerned and I excused myself. They did not get the order. Salem Furnace Co. matched their bid, without a bribe, and they got the order.

That was some 20 years ago. Ever since then vendors find it very difficult to take me "out to lunch" since I won't go! I will not owe anyone anything. That way it cannot affect my decisions. If anyone out there thinks that all the graft, "freebies," gifts, and election and re-election campaign funds that filter to our elected officials does not affect their judgment, you are a fool! Everything is for sale. The only way to turn this around is for everyone to stop taking "free lunches." They are not free!

WINNERS...

#83. earn integrity by always doing what is right

**He who walks in integrity walks securely,
But he who perverts his ways will be found out.
(Proverbs 10:9)**

When you are a person of integrity, the people with whom you deal, including your wife and children, will know that you are someone they can trust. It will make your business dealings easier, your life easier, your marriage easier, and everything easier because ethics and integrity should be utilized throughout your entire life, not just with business. You will find that your life will be a joy to live and you will never have to look over your shoulder. You will never have to worry about repercussions to a bad business deal or about something that you did which was unethical. You don't even have to worry about it. What you have done is that you have saved some more time to get more done because you are not having to worry about looking over your shoulder. **You don't have to worry about what other people think.** You just do the right thing and then you forget about it. You just forget about it. "I know I did the right thing. I don't care what they think and they will eventually figure out that I did the right thing." So you don't even worry about it. You would be amazed how much more pleasant and how much more confident you will become as a manager by applying these principals of ethics, integrity, and virtue in your life.

WINNERS...

#84. have no need to worry because what they have done is right

**"If you tell the truth, you don't
have to remember anything."
(Mark Twain)**

As you go along in your life, you will find that a good manager leads by example. What I just mentioned is the kind of example that you want to present to the public and you want to present to your work force because strange things will start happening: The people that you deal with and your employees and your spouse and especially your children, will notice how you conduct your life and how you conduct your business. Guess what? They will develop integrity, a strong code of ethics, and virtue. That's the whole meaning of life. It really is.

Just think about it. If everybody in this world behaved like I just described, what a great place this would be to live. It would be far better than it is now. It just boils down to always doing the right thing. I really don't understand why people have so much trouble doing the right thing. I've talked about this before, but it seems like people are out there looking for something else. "Well, I am on top of my game. I am on top of the world. I am the best there is at shooting a basketball." Or, "I am the best at making axles." Or, "I am the best there is at making engine blocks." These people have reached the pinnacle of success and they look around and they say, "Well, there must be something else." So they start looking for other things to do and that's when they get into trouble. Whether it's infidelity, alcohol, or drugs, people, for whatever reason, can't learn to live within themselves. I know the thing that I have done in my life is to help other people. That is the something else in my life. I don't need to drink alcohol to excess. I don't need to take drugs. I don't need to chase women. **I don't need to do any of those things because I have found that the inner calm is helping other people.** It is so much fun. It is so relaxing. It is so fulfilling to actually help or give money to a total stranger and expect nothing in return. It really makes you feel good and you know that you are helping people. Sometimes you are helping people who don't even know they need help. I try to make the world a better place.

WINNERS...

#85. make the world a better place and find inner peace by helping others

"The best portion of a good man's life are his little nameless, unremembered acts of kindness and of love."
(William Wordsworth)

You actually help people who don't even know they need help because after you have helped them they will figure it out. Maybe, just maybe, it will rub off and they will help somebody else. So what you are doing is you are making the world a better place for other people by donating your time, your efforts, and your money. In turn, you are making the world a better place for yourself. Here again, not everybody can be fortunate enough to think up a way to make a lot of money. So not everybody can give money away. But it just tickles me to death to see people who coach little league and basketball and boy scouts and girl scouts. I look at all these volunteers and think, "Well, I know where the guy works. He doesn't have a lot of money. He doesn't need a lot of money because he is donating his time." So I think that the moral of the story to everyone out there is: If you don't have money, then donate your time. If you've got money then donate your time and money. Because, when you give, you will make the world a better place for everyone else, which will, in turn, make the world a better place for you.

Chapter Eight

RUNNING THE RACE TO WIN

**Being Competitive is the Start of the Game
Everyone Must Want to Win
Expectations Play an Important Role
Speed Bumps Always Slow You Down**

To me, life, business, and racing are one big game and the whole object is to win the game. Now you can all think back to when you were a child playing a game. Whether it was monopoly, tennis, croquet, or whatever, you never entered the game with the attitude that you were going to lose. Never would that have been the case! You always entered the game with the attitude that you were going to win. If you had the attitude that you were going to lose, then you shouldn't have been playing the game. Everything in life is about winning. You want to win the game.

Being Competitive is the Start of the Game

Everything is a game. When you become very competitive, whether in your business or in drag racing, you are on top of your game. You may have thought that you were in the game, you may have thought that you were dominating the world, or you may have thought that, "I've got it made now," but you haven't even started to play the game because once you are very competitive and on top of your game, that's when the game really starts.

It's like a professional athlete or a professional team that wins a world championship the prior year. They are now the target of every team. They are the team to beat. Once you become very competitive in your company, your racing, yourself, or whatever, you are now the business, the team, or the person to beat. This means that you really have to get your act together! That's why I made this statement, "The game has only now begun. The game has really started once you have become very competitive." Now you have to do what almost no one else can do, and that is to keep your business climbing up on the bell curve. Just keep going up, up, up, and up because once you flatten out, there is no way to go but down. So, running the race to win by being very competitive is very important to discuss.

Trying to maintain your growth can be very difficult even in racing.

In the pro-stock that we run, it is probably the most technologically advanced class known to man and everybody is spending every waking moment on the dyno picking up more horsepower, trying to think up ways to save horsepower through frictional loss gains, through trickery and transmissions, lightweight trick components, aerodynamics, and looking at every way possible to pick up a thousandth or two of a second in E.T. That's what it takes to stay competitive and you can't stop. I know there are several race teams out there, like Calvin and Tim Neighbors, who got behind on their dyno work and their engine technology and in a matter of one year, only one year, they went from being the national record holder to not even remotely being able to qualify. This was in one year! That's hard to believe, but it's true. The same is true in business. Racing is just a mirror of business. **Once you're competitive, the trick is to stay competitive.** Whether you do it through cost reductions, man-hour efficiencies, selling more product, diversifying, adding new products, or adding what I call "value added products" to your existing line, you have to do whatever it takes to keep your business growing. If you are not growing, that means the competition is growing which means you are falling behind.

WINNERS...
#86. stay competitive through all possible means to win

*"Success is the maximum utilization of
the ability that you have."*
(Zig Ziglar)

It is really interesting where cost reductions can come. Here is an interesting little story. With the majority of axles on my product line, I have always bought the blanks pre-drilled. We bought the blanks with a Chevy bolt pattern and a Ford bolt pattern and both patterns were in the axles which saved us a lot of time and hassle because 90% of your customers bought one or the other pattern. Well, just recently I designed and built two computer controlled automatic drilling machines. The floor-to-floor time on both of these identical machines is 27 seconds. As I said previously, the machinist picks the part up, loads it in the machine, and punches the start button. The machine, then, rapids it in, drills indexes, completes whatever holes that were programmed into it, pops the part back out, and sets it back down on the floor in just 27 seconds. An interesting thing about these machines is that I have built them out of old manual horizontal mills, so that I have no more than $14,000 in each machine. They actually will do the work of a $100,000 CNC mill, but twice as fast. Now with these particular machines, we have found that we get 3,000 holes on a $20 insert. Three thousand holes on a $20 insert and one man can run both machines. It is physically impossible for someone to manually drill all the axles that we sell because we typically sell over 40,000 axles a year. At one time we had Spencer Manufacturing pre-drill most of our blanks and what they didn't drill, we drilled manually. One guy running both machines for a shift can now do what used to take two guys 16 hours to do. That is how much of a cost savings there is here. But what is really unbelievable is that we are finding out that very few people want two bolt patterns on the axles. In fact, maybe only one or two percent of them do. So I went back and did some figuring. Spencer used to charge us 25 cents a hole to drill these holes. Well, in the last five years, we have spent over $125,000 on holes that most people didn't really need or want. That's how much money we have paid Spencer to drill holes that, for the most part, didn't need to be drilled. That's what you would call a heck of a cost reduction. **There are always situations like that where you just have to look at your operation, I mean really look at it, and look at what your people are doing and listen to them.** When someone says, "Boy, this is a pain to do," or, "This takes a lot of time," or, "This is hard to do," or, whatever, take a look at it! Look at it and see what you can actually do to make the job better. Once you have isolated what you have brought to light, or what can be done to speed up the operation, or to make it more efficient, or to save money, then follow through with it and do it because that is how you stay on top of the world. You stay competitive because it is very difficult for somebody to catch you when you are at the top and running hard. It is very difficult! The more cost reductions you can come up with and the more efficiencies you can come up with, the healthier your company is going to be, and you will stay competitive.

WINNERS...

#87. listen to their employees to change situations which need attention

The way of a fool is right in his own eyes,
But a wise man is he who listens to counsel.
(Proverbs 12:15)

The same holds true in drag racing. Ron Miller spends basically night and day thinking up ways to increase horsepower through cylinder head technology and intake manifolds, different specifications, and different spacer plates. I do a lot of the machine work so nobody knows what we are doing. The opportunities are endless such as making dyno pulls. That's how you say the game starts now. The game actually starts after you are on top because the trick of the game is to stay on top. That's the hardest part of it all.

Everyone Must Want to Win

In my business, it is really easy to have phenomenal growth and you need it. If you are actually making a product that is better than the competition, that is cheaper than the competition, and that you actually deliver 20 times quicker than the competition, well, your product is going to sell. It has to sell. You start in the market with a zero share because you weren't in business before, and the business has to grow. It will grow like crazy. My business grew from '87 and it doubled every year up until '92. The sales actually doubled. In fact, it's kind of ironic that in '87 as a part-time job in my garage at home, the business had $75,000 in sales that year. Ten years later in 1997, the business has $7,500,000 in sales. The business has grown 100 times and I have no intention to stop growing it. That's the game and what a game it is!

The pre-game is to get the business to the top, but then the real game starts in keeping it there. When you are on top, you have everybody shooting at you. That is when it gets interesting and when you really have to use your brain. **That's when you must guide your work force to make sure everyone wants to win. You must work together to innovate and recreate to achieve victory.**

WINNERS...

#88. achieve victory by guiding their work force to innovate together

**Where there is no guidance, the people fall,
But in abundance of counselors there is victory.
(Proverbs 11:14)**

Someone who runs a company in our town was in the other day to look at my facility to see if he might be interested in purchasing it from the Jay County Development Corporation which is building me a new plant. I showed him around and we looked at things including the insulation, air conditioning, and how things were laid out. He asked the standard stuff but was particularly interested in the reason why my shop is air-conditioned.

There are a lot of reasons why the whole thing is air conditioned, but the big one is that I spent most of my life in rolling mills and forge shops where the temperature gets 90 to 100 degrees in the summer and productivity stops. Your employees go home because it's too hot to work. Since I had the luxury of starting my business from scratch, it's all air conditioned. **Since it is a nice working temperature year around, you lose zero productivity.**

WINNERS...

**#89. increase productivity by creating
a comfortable work environment**

**Just as I also please all men in all things,
not seeking my own profit, but the profit of the many,
that they may be saved.
(1 Corinthians 10:33)**

After we were finished with the tour, this individual was getting ready to walk out the door and he said, "Can I ask you a question?" I said, "Yes, of course. Anything you want to ask." He said, "Where do you find your people?" Now you have to know a little bit about my people to understand his question. As a member of the Portland Chamber of Commerce, we have an industrial committee that meets every other month. The CEO's, plant managers, and the owners of all the plants in Jay County get together and talk about what is happening with their businesses. They discuss what's happening with the personnel, wage hikes, benefits, things that have happened to the plants, things that they see, trends, or whatever, and we share all this information together. It is a unique setting. I have been asked before in these meetings about absenteeism and I say when it gets around to me, "Well, I don't have any absenteeism." The first thing stated in response is, "What do mean?" "Well, I don't have any." They say, "How many sick days did you have last year?" Frequently, I will say, "None." They say, "That's impossible." "Oh, no it's not. Nobody gets sick."

That is where the question, "Where do you find these people?" came from. Keep in mind that I had the luxury of starting my company from scratch. I had the luxury of working for a lot of major corporations which means I found what didn't work and I also found what would work and that is how I set up my plant. The very first job I had to do after our move from a two car garage behind my home to the industrial park was to hire an employee. Getting tired of doing this all in the evenings, I started looking for a helper. I couldn't find anybody who would suit me. By pure coincidence, I met an individual by the name of Russell Jordan who installed a satellite dish for me. He was working on it while I was working in the shop, and he said, "Man, don't you get tired of doing this?" I said, "Well, yeah, but I am just trying to find that right person to hire." He said, "I have someone for you."

"Oh naturally!", you say to yourself. "Yeah, right, sure. Everybody knows somebody who is a super employee." He said, "This is a good employee. He's my nephew. He has been working at this truck stop and they hardly pay him anything. He works around 60 hours a week to make a livable wage, and I think he has been there about seven or eight years. To the best of my knowledge, I don't think he has ever missed a day."

Well, that rang a bell with me right there. **So I checked the guy out and found that he had never missed a day and that he was also mechanically inclined and trainable.** So I spent quite a bit of time interviewing him and talking with him and just seeing what he wanted to do and why he would want to do it and how he would fit into what I wanted him to do. I hired him and immediately told him, "This is how I want to run my business. I want to set it up so that whoever orders something today or whatever comes in UPS today, we are going to unbox it, make it tomorrow, box it up tomorrow evening, and ship it out the next day. That is how I want to run this business. A maximum of a two day turn around." **I continued, "Now what this means is, since you are my only employee, first, it is your responsibility to do the work correctly and second, it is your responsibility to get it done the day it is supposed to be done."**

WINNERS...

#90. know who they need, what they want done, and how to do it

"Success depends on three things:
who says it, what he says, how he says it;
and of these three things, what he says is the least important."
(John Viscount Morley of Blackburn)

Right off I started by telling Greg Imel, my first employee, how it was going to work and that he would get a minimum of eight hours each day. I would guarantee him eight hours but he needed to be prepared to work whatever time it would take to get the job done. If there were enough orders which required him to work 16 hours, well, he would be expected to work 16 hours. Basically, I told him, and I continue to tell people this when I hire them, "If you get tired of working overtime, and we have enough overtime so that we can employ another person, that's your call. If you want me to hire someone, then I will hire someone. If you want to work the overtime, and you don't want me to hire someone, fine. Whatever you want."

So now with the ground work set, we have a healthy employee who never gets sick, who knows why he is there, and who knows he is your only employee. He knows the job has to get done and has to be done correctly. He wants to win, and together, we set a course to win. I proceed to train him how to do all this stuff and he turns out to be everything that his uncle, Russell, said he was. He is prompt, he is intelligent, he is mechanically inclined, he is healthy, and he works until the job gets done. He is what you would call "the perfect employee!" This is how to run the race and win.

The second employee I hired was Chad Franks. I looked for everything that I had looked for when I hired Greg. **We sat down and I told him exactly what I expected of him and what he could expect from me.** There is no guess work here, such as, "Well, I think this is what he wants," or "Maybe I will do this." There is none of that. You know where you stand and you know what I want you to do. The fact that we only hire enough people to get the job done means just that. That is all we hire.

WINNERS...

#91. communicate precisely what it takes to make a winning team

**My son, keep my words,
and treasure my commandments within you.
(Proverbs 7:1)**

In the last couple of years we have reached 23 employees and they don't ever want me to hire anybody. They all have the overtime money spent and, with the way benefits cost, it is a savings for me to pay them overtime rather than to hire someone new and pay the benefits. This gets back to what this individual was asking; about how I find my people. It's kind of a self-fulfilling prophecy. **I have so many good people now that if I thought that I was hiring the world's best employee only to find out that he wasn't, believe me, he would conform to the way my employees think or they would run him off.** They would hassle him to the point where he would have to be prompt and he would have to be there all the time. He would have to make quality parts. He would not call in sick because you can't call in sick. There is no one to do your job. I have to go into the shop and do the job if someone calls in sick. It has only happened a couple of times in the last ten years and usually, the people are so contagious we don't want them at the plant anyway. If they are that sick, they can't come into work. They are contagious and we don't want them. We have had to send some people home half days. They are so sick and throwing up that they can hardly stand up and we don't want them to get hurt running the machines so we have sent some people home. But we have gone years without one lost sick hour. Not one.

WINNERS...

#92. build a motivated team that regulates itself toward winning every time

**Plans fail for lack of counsel,
But with many advisors they succeed.
(Proverbs 15:22)**

Expectations Play an Important Role

In most companies, it is expected that you are going to get sick. **Believe me, if you expect somebody to do something, they are going to do it.** If you tell them that they are going to screw something up, they will screw it up. If you tell them they are going to do it right, they will do it right.

WINNERS...

#93. have high expectations of employees resulting in a winning team

**"Get in, sit down, buckle up, shut up, and hold on."
(Unknown)**

At one large corporation of 400 employees, they hired 30 to 40 extras and that was their job title. Thirty to 40 extras hired to do what? Well, if that isn't a self-fulfilling prophecy, I don't know what is. They have

40 people there just to take the sick person's place because historically they know how many people are going to call in sick and be on vacation and they have all these extras to get the job done. So what have they promoted? They have created an atmosphere where people can take off since the company is willing to pay the salaries and the benefits of 40 extra people. Well, of course, people are going to call in sick. You have just made it convenient for them to do so. Now let's consider my business. Let's say in my little plant of 23 people that I will employ 400 people 20 years from now. I'll tell you what, if I employ 400 people, there will not be one of them classified as an extra. Not one! All 400 will be expected to be at work every day, on time, and produce quality parts. My employees have absolutely no thought whatsoever about calling in sick. When you have those kind of expectations, believe it or not, people fulfill them. I don't know why companies can't see that.

There are some companies that give people a week off for perfect attendance. Now if that isn't the craziest thing that I have ever heard of in my entire life. The reason you encourage them to have perfect attendance is to save the company money. So then you give them a week off? Then you need to hire somebody to replace them while they are off. That's crazy! What you want to do is give them a week's pay, not time off. They get enough time off with the vacation time you have scheduled for them.

All I know is that because I have high expectations, I have probably the world's finest group of employees assembled. They all know their job, they all know how to get their job done, and they all know everybody else's job. That's why they all get done at the same time and they all work the same overtime. They all know they are expected to be at work, expected to produce quality parts, and expected to put out an adequate number of quality parts. In fact, enough stuff is set out everyday to keep them all busy eight hours and they all get it done. Every Monday is the busiest sales day which makes Tuesday the busiest machine work day. On a busy day, there will be 250 pair of axles needing to be done. That is 500 axles that will need to be done in 12, 13, or 14 hours on Tuesday. They stay until the job gets done, and they all get done at the same time. This is what I have told them, "I want you all to help each other and I want you all out of here at the same time. I want everybody to have equal overtime and I don't want any complaining about somebody else getting more overtime." We don't have that. The job gets done. Everybody comes into work, nobody calls in sick, the job gets done, it gets done correctly, and it gets shipped out the next day. We have had the luxury of starting from scratch to accomplish this. **I don't know how you could turn another company around other than to just be flat honest with employees and lay your cards on the table and say,**

"This is what we are planning on doing and this is how we are going to do it. This is what we are going to expect from you guys." It is just like when I was talking about ethics and what's right is right, and what is wrong is wrong. If you do the right thing, you will have a good bunch of employees.

WINNERS...

#94. are honest and direct when needing to implement change

...speaking the truth in love...
(Ephesians 4:15)

When my expectations are met, and they usually are, we do all kinds of fun things. We have a company canoe trip. We go drag racing with our employees. We take them to various places for Christmas like the Bahamas, Las Vegas, Chicago, Detroit, and we have a pretty good time. My employees know what they can expect from me. I tell them what I am going to do. I also tell them what I expect them to do. Believe it or not, no one has ever let me down. That is why this individual came to me and asked, "Where do you find these employees?" Well, I look long and hard for them and I even hire students out of high school. I call their counselors and find out what their attendance was in school. That is a strong indicator of what their attendance will be when they work for you. In fact, a lot of times when I am asked to speak to the high school students in entrepreneurial classes, classes on business and ethics, or whatever, that is one of the things I always discuss. **Employers are looking for attendance records.** They are looking for intelligent people who come to work.

WINNERS...

#95. hire intelligent, as well as dependable, individuals to build their team

Unless the Lord builds the house,
They labor in vain who build it...
(Proverbs 127:1)

Speed Bumps Always Slow You Down

One thing that really blows my mind with all the politicians passing all these "feel good laws" is that they have completely lost sight of why industry hires people. We hire people to work. We don't hire people to give them time off. If an employee wants time off then evidently he doesn't need a job. It is the craziest thing I have ever seen.

An example of the craziest law I have ever had to follow is unpaid family leave. An employee can take off so many weeks unpaid for adopting a baby, having a baby, caring for a sick parent, or whatever. Now, don't get me wrong, I agree that if a good employee needs time off he or she should be able to take time off. But I believe it is an agreement between an employer and an employee. No where should the government have any rights whatsoever to tell an employer what he has to do for an employee. That may sound a little harsh but let me throw some facts at you. When I am talking about a good employee, I am talking about a responsible citizen. I am talking about an employee who has a home, cars, and children he is trying to raise to be responsible citizens. He has bills, debts, and credit cards. He is a responsible citizen. He has never been late on his payments and he knows what he is doing, where he is going, and he knows how he is going to get there. No good employee who fits what I have just said, in your wildest dreams, would take 14 weeks off from work without pay. It's not going to happen. It will never happen. He is too responsible to miss a paycheck for 14 weeks. If he has a problem, he will find a way to take care of it and it doesn't involve taking time off from work.

Now, if you want to turn that around, only a substandard employee would like to take off 14 weeks. This is an employee who would just as soon not be working, which means you would just as soon fire him, but you can't fire him because he shows up for work and he does just enough work to prevent his being fired. I am not talking about my plant but I am talking about other places where I have worked. He does just enough to get by so you can't fire him. He is not a desirable employee, he is not competent, he doesn't own anything, nor does he ever want to own anything. The problem is that he is the only employee that will take the 14 weeks off without pay because he doesn't own anything and he can't lose anything. If he doesn't make any money, so what?

The federal government says that if you have over 50 employees hired, you have to give this employee 14 weeks off. As an employer, to whom would you want to give this time off? Would you want to give it off to your best employee or your worst employee? It should be your best employee, but that wouldn't happen. A good employee won't take the time off, so the only employee who you have that will take the time off is the substandard employee. Now the substandard gets the perk of getting 14 weeks off and you, as the employer, get the "privilege" of maintaining this clown's insurance while he is off. Yes, you have to pay his insurance premium while he is not working. That is 400 bucks a month for 14 weeks! The sheer lunacy of this law is that if you have a 50 man shop and you have no extras, you are going to have to employ an individual to cover this guy's job while he is off the 14 weeks. When he comes back, you get to lay off the person you hired to fill in for those 14 weeks. If your replacement employee has worked long enough for someone else prior to working the 14 weeks for you, he gets to collect unemployment. Since you are the last place at which he worked, guess who gets to pay for the unemployment? You do! Like I said, if this isn't the stupidest "feel good law" that has ever been passed, I don't know what is. I am sure there are multitudes of other idiotic laws being passed, but this isn't a law to protect or to help the employee, it is a "feel good law" that does nothing but hurt the employer. A good employee wouldn't take the time off, regardless. The thing of it is that if the worker is a good employee, he or she could go in and talk to you and you probably would give him the time off anyway. It is the principle that you have to give the time off to all the employees. Think of the concept, all employees regardless of worth, input, value to company, absenteeism, work record, etc. are <u>guaranteed</u> the same <u>benefits</u>. Isn't that why communism failed? What has happened to the concept that you have to work for what you want? **That's what is wrong with the law and I consider it a speed bump that is unnecessary and could prevent the race from being won by some.**

WINNERS...

#96. agree that good employees are worthy of their wage

For even when we were with you, we used to give you this order: if anyone will not work, neither let him eat.
(2 Thessalonians 3:10)

Again the federal government has lost sight of the reason we employ people. We employ people to work, not to give them time off. If they don't want to work, then they should go find a part time job somewhere so as not to screw up the industrial system. True wealth is generated from industrial employment, manufacturing products, or mining something out of the ground. These jobs are what make the world go. Anybody who thinks any differently does not have the applicable knowledge.

Our company is at the point now where we have so many good people that I could hire a bad one and they would make him or her conform to how we operate. It is like the old adage: if you take four good kids and put a bad one with them, within a day or two, all five will be bad. That is not the way it works at my facility. You could throw one in with my people and within a couple of weeks he or she would conform to being a good employee or would be forced to leave. So your business has to be started correctly and it has to be managed correctly and that is how you get everybody going in the right direction. You just let them go. Because it has been my experience that people want to do a good job, that people want to be responsible, and that people want to be held accountable. That is the beauty of a happy work force. You are not telling them what to do because they know what to do. You don't have to harp at them to get it done since they know how to get it done. They know that it takes just as much time to do something correctly as it does to screw it up. So why screw it up?

Do the job right, make the part correctly, and everybody is better off. Your customer is happier, the company makes more money, which, in turn, means you are going to get more money. I'll tell you right now that we pay the highest wage in Jay County. We pay 100% of the benefits, life insurance, holiday pay, vacation pay, and we typically give each employee a fabulous Christmas getaway for a company meeting. Plus, we give every employee about $3,000 for Christmas. I've been doing it ever since I have been in business. **I have learned that when you give, it all comes back to you.** Because of the kind of employees that I have, I know that I can leave my company and know that when I get back it will be running correctly and everybody will be doing a good job.

WINNERS...

#97. give and, in turn, receive much

**Give, and it will be given to you, good measure,
pressed down, shaken together and running over
they will pour into your lap.
For whatever measure you deal out to others,
it will be dealt to you in return.
(Luke 6:38)**

The number one thing that you will never hear in my plant is, "That's not my job," because it is everybody's job. You know you have a great work force when everybody does what is necessary to get the job done and do it correctly. I know that we have a wonderful work force. That is why people ask me where I find my employees. I don't know where I find them, I just know how I got them and how I got to where I am today. You can emulate what I have done, and I wish you all the luck in the world, because if you do, you are going to have a trouble-free, happy work force to win the race. That is how you make money, that is how you are competitive in the market place, and that is just another reason why it is going to be very difficult for someone to catch me because we are running flat out and we don't intend to even stop and take a breath. We intend to continue running flat out and it would be interesting to see if anyone ever catches us. I intend to only be caught when I want to be caught. Some day I might decide to say, "This is enough. I am done working this hard. I am done trying to expand the business." I will probably be on my death bed. But then again, who knows. My son may want to run it just the way I run it and I hope he does, because if he does, it is going to be that much more difficult for anyone to ever catch my company because we're running the race to win!

Chapter Nine

ACCELERATING BEYOND TOP SPEED

Helping Others is the Best Way to Accelerate
In the Fast Lane Every Second Counts
At These Speeds Anything Can Happen
Other Speeding Stories

Until about the age of 33 or 34 I maintained a fatalist view of the world. By that I mean I always felt that everything was meant to be and what is going to happen is going to happen. Most high school students and teenagers think they are going to live forever. They think nothing can hurt them. Death or being killed doing something is the farthest thing from their mind. Like I said, I was 33 or 34 years old before I realized that maybe I could get killed doing some of the crazy things that I was doing.

When I was in high school and in college, the group of friends with whom I ran around had elevated our thrill level to the point that we wouldn't do something unless there was a good chance that you would be killed doing it because it just wasn't any fun otherwise. That's where our thrill level had evolved. I never really gave it any thought at the time. But after my father passed away, I thought it was a little dangerous doing things like this. Earlier I had figured, "Well, I am going to die and there is nothing I can do about it." But after you get older, you realize that there really is no sense in doing something stupid and getting killed to prematurely end your life. So I really wised up in later years after doing some crazy things.

Helping Others is The Best Way to Accelerate

Doing crazy things started at day one. We used to go up and ride dirt bikes at Manastee National Park in Michigan. I know of one time when a friend, Dewy Sanderson, and I were up there racing, and we wanted to win at everything we did. We picked up some different riders and we were racing them down fire trails. I remember I was hot on this guy's heels. I was just getting ready to pass him and all of a sudden the guy hit the brakes and I blew by him. There was a cliff right there and I rode my dirt bike off this cliff! The ravine was caused by a glacier in prehistoric times. I don't know what the depth of this ravine was, but it was deep enough that before I hit the dirt bottom, I had plenty of time to kick the bike away so I wouldn't run into it or it wouldn't run over me. I remember to this day how Dewy said, "I could hear you laughing because you were flying over this cliff." There was never any thought of dying. No thought whatsoever. We have done so many crazy things in pursuit of the win.

In fact, when I look back on my teenage years, I am lucky to have lived through them. I have been darn lucky! I used to think what is meant to be is meant to be. Today I believe you can enhance what is meant to be in life by a lot of hard work. For example, I know that my philanthropic ways have helped me considerably. **I have had opportunities that probably wouldn't have come my way if I had not been involved in the community helping people.**

WINNERS...

#98. recognize the value of giving and in turn receive rich blessings

**He who is generous will be blessed,
For he gives some of his food to the poor.
(Proverbs 22:9)**

When I started my business, we were at home in a two car garage. At the time, I was doing some work at Portland Forge where we thought we had some water problems. The city of Portland was helping us work on them so, one day, I found myself speaking with Mayor Jim Luginbill and after finishing my Portland Forge business I told him that I was looking around for some three-phase power close to potential building sights. He said, "Hey! We have the perfect place for you!" The outcome of our conversation was that we got a two and a half acre lot that would normally be too small for most industry needs. It is in the industrial park, right off of US 27, and visible from the highway. It has a nice cul-de-sac in front of it with city water, gas, and a sewer, all right there. I think it was $2,500 an acre. I bought it and I moved out of the garage. As the business grew, we added on 6,000 square feet to our initial building and later added on another 10,000 square feet. Our original building was 3,000 square feet, so we eventually grew to 19,000 square feet.

We have outgrown it all and the next logical step is to add on again. With the kind of unique business I have, there are eight sales people, seven machinists, and two welders. There are nine people in the shop then who can make everything that those eight people can sell. The office that I am in is 2,000 square feet with no more space. In fact, we have everybody packed into little bitty offices, with my business in 1997, literally, stagnant because of lack of sales people and lack of office space. We have added on new products and value added things to our race axle line. I wanted to build an office in front of my existing plant so I called up the Jay County Development Corporation, spoke to its Executive Director, Bob Quadrozzi, and said, "What kind of covenants and restrictions are on the property out here? How close to the road can I build? What's my setback if I can get a variance or whatever?" He asked, "What are you doing?" I said, "Well, I want to build about a 6,000 or 7,000 square foot office addition for my facility." "Oh," he said, "That's interesting. I'll talk to you at Rotary."

So the next Tuesday night he cornered me and he said, "I have thought about it and you don't want to add on there. We could get you a variance and you could put your office in front of your existing building, but you don't want to do that." I said, "I don't?" He said, "No. What you want to do, first of all, is consider this brand new industrial park where we basically have no one. It needs an industry out there to get it kick started. Secondly, Jay County Development Corporation needs a spec building in this industrial park so it is easier to attract a potential company, whether your building suits them or not. Once you have got them here, you can sell them on the County. I said, "What does that mean to me?" He said, "Well, I'll tell you what. You get your plant appraised at the fair market value and we will buy it from you. Secondly, we will take your land and we will trade it for the land out there in our new industrial park. Basically, what you will have in this new facility is what you would have had in the office that you were going to build, plus more space in a new plant!"

This is one of those "too good to be true" deals. But it is true! So I have to believe that my involvement in the community, my involvement with the city, and my involvement with the Jay County Development Corporation, has once again paid off. My new facility is a 9,000 square foot office and a 20,000 square foot manufacturing plant, so I have almost 30,000 square feet. It's a thing of beauty.

Somehow things always work out and if they don't work out quickly, just be patient and don't get excited. They will eventually work out for you. **Patience and hard work will always cause things to work out for you.** In business, there is no such thing as luck. You can say, "Aw, you're lucky. You have Jay County Development to do this and do that." It has nothing to do with luck. An opportunity arose and I was prepared to take advantage of it because of blessings that are returned to you if you help others.

WINNERS...

#99. rejoice when challenges arise because they know that patience and hard work will accelerate them beyond top speed

Consider it all joy, my brethren, when you encounter various trials,
knowing that the testing of your faith
produces endurance (patience).
(James 1:2-3)

In the Fast Lane Every Second Counts

As a teenager, I always had the need for speed. **I was fearless and I have carried this trait into the business world. You have to be fearless to venture out and do things. You have to have absolutely no fear of failure to lead. That is how you get ahead.** It was instituted at an early age because even then I had the need for speed. It was not uncommon for me to go fast whenever possible. Not only were we drag racers, but we liked to do a lot of high speed running. I have literally been over 200 miles an hour in a car and over 160 miles an hour on a motorcycle. I am not talking just high speed for a few minutes but for a lot of miles. We would literally hold motorcycles flat out for a 20 mile stretch. Absolutely no fear whatsoever! At that kind of speed, at 160 miles an hour on a motorcycle, if you hit a ground hog, you would disintegrate. But that's how we operated. We had absolutely no fear whatsoever. In fact, I have been clocked by state patrol at 150 miles an hour and I have actually been let go with a warning. You could probably attribute that to a little bit of luck, too. My whole life has ended up revolving around speed. Whether racing cars or making high speed runs, the question is how many seconds are clocked? **That is how I operate my business. How many seconds does it take to do something? It is speed. It's not wasting seconds, it's utilizing all the time you have today for you do not know what tomorrow will afford you.**

WINNERS...

#100. are fearless leading others to accomplish the impossible

WINNERS...

#101. are efficient in organizing work for today since tomorrow is unknown

Do not boast about tomorrow,
For you do not know what a day may bring forth.
(Proverbs 27:1)

If you enjoy a good high speed story, I have one for you. We were in Germany looking at the latest technologically advanced equipment to buy for Teledyne's brand new Lebanon, Ohio, facility. They said that they knew I raced cars so they rented me a BMW to enjoy. We were driving on the autobahn in this BMW and ran straight out at 150 miles an hour. Flat out at red line on every gauge! I have never had so much fun in my entire life. It was really funny, too, because it had been a few years since I had run a whole tank full of gas through a car at top speed flat out. I drove with this German, who was riding shotgun, and believe me, at 150 miles an hour, it helps to have somebody riding with you. At the very first auto plaza that we pulled into, there was an on and off ramp. We pulled in there and I think I slowed down to 100 miles an hour, locked up the brakes, slid past the pumps, went out the other side, came to a stop, backed way up, and I thought, "Hum, maybe we better start slowing down a little sooner." It was extreme. It was a lot of fun. Some people would think that driving 150 miles an hour or 200 miles an hour is frightfully fast. Well, it really isn't if you know what you are doing and if you know how to do it. **You have to have total, supreme confidence in your ability. You must have no doubt. You must have no doubts whether you are driving a race car or running a business.** That is how you manage people and that is how people will follow you. They will follow you into doing anything as long as you display that confidence. If they know that you are that confident, then they know that you know what you are doing, and they know that whatever you are thinking up will work because of your confidence. That is how you accelerate beyond top speed. We drove over 2,000 miles and it was during a week that the autobahn wasn't clogged up. We ran it flat out. I know our first exit off the autobahn we missed because we didn't slow down soon enough. We were going too fast and we blew by the exit. Then and only then did we start slowing down.

WINNERS...

#102. exhibit unusual confidence, do not doubt, and believe in what they say they will do

Truly I say to you, whoever says to this mountain, "Be taken up and cast into the sea," and does not doubt in his heart, but believes in that which he says is going to happen, it shall be granted him.
(Mark 11:23)

Two cars passed me that whole week. What was ironic was that when it started to rain, we passed them back. They had no guts. They slowed down because it started to rain. We were running 150 miles an hour in the rain! One thing I did discover, and this is good information for some people, you don't need windshield wipers at 150 miles an hour. The rain hits the windshield so hard that it explodes and you can see right through it. That may be worthwhile to know if you are ever driving in a downpour and your windshield wipers don't work. No big deal, just drive faster. We drove the whole week that way. We ran tanks full of gas out of this BMW at ultra high speeds and it had to be one of the highlights of my life.

My co-pilot, who lived in Germany, had never driven at speeds like that. At the end of the week he said, "I'm impressed. I have never driven that fast. I have always thought that it was totally unsafe. You are one fine driver!" It all has to do with confidence and my confidence wore off on him. Your confidence should wear off on your employees and the people with whom you deal. It will definitely help you in life to have supreme confidence. Now, I don't know about the fatalist view of things, but I do believe that what's going to happen is going to happen as long as you don't do something stupid to short change yourself in life. If you are able to improve your situation by working hard, rather than by being stupid, you can basically change what is going to happen for the better. I do know that someday you are going to die and that you have no choice about it. That is one reason why I do so much. **I am involved in so much because someday, if I die in my sleep, I want to be able to look back on my life and say, "Well, there was nothing else that I could have possibly done. I did everything I wanted to do, I did everything that I could think to do, and I did it everyday of my life. I will know that I have done a good job and God will know that I have done a good job."** No person could ask for more!

WINNERS...

#103. do all they can, when they can, knowing rich results are the reward

**Those who trust in the Lord
Are as Mount Zion, which cannot be moved, but abides forever.
(Psalm 125:1)**

At These Speeds Anything Can Happen

    In attempting to tie in some of this fatalist outlook over my life, I have been involved in numerous accidents with interesting results. I can think of four times that these have happened to me. The first time I think was in '68 when I had a friend stop over and he had a Fiat Sportspyder. He was bragging about how fast this thing would take curves and corners. I was in high school at the time and was pumping gas on the weekends at a Sohio station. He picked me up at closing time and took us out on Route 111 which has some really vicious curves on it. He just kept going faster and faster and finally, on one of the curves in front of an old county home, we broke traction and slid off the road. We slid down a unique kind of ditch on the side of the road which took a 90 degree turn at the end of its length. We hit the embankment of the ditch at about 70 miles an hour and our vehicle stopped dead right there.

    Keep in mind that a Fiat Sportspyder is tiny. This friend who was driving ripped the steering wheel off, knocked out the windshield, and ended up on the ground in front of the vehicle. I know there were two hand prints in the dash about six inches deep where I had braced myself for the impact. The strange thing that happened while this accident was taking place was that everything seemed to slow down. You could see everything perfectly clear. It seemed like it took forever for this to happen and during the crash, in slow motion, I actually saw things in my life before my eyes. My grandparents flashed before my eyes as did my parents. It was really neat. I didn't think much about it at the time, but then several years later when we were dirt bike riding in Michigan, I rode off a cliff and the same thing happened, only this time the images were even more vivid. You see your life flash before your eyes as everything actually slows way down. As I said previously, it was like I had all kinds of time to kick the motorcycle out of the way so I wouldn't hit it on the way down. These are totally unique experiences.

The third time that this happened to me was when we had just turbo charged a tow vehicle so that we could tow faster and get to the races sooner. We were heading to Rockingham, North Carolina, to a national event and we were flying as we towed our race car in a 30 foot tag trailer. I had a friend who went along and after I had driven for five or six hours I asked if he wanted to take a turn driving. He said, "Yes." So he was driving just as fast as I was and we rounded a curve on a mountain side just out of Knoxville, Tennessee. There were a string of semi-trucks that we had just passed and as we flew by them at an excessive speed, we also cleared the side of the mountain. Just beyond this point, a gust of wind hit our tag trailer blowing it to a 90 degree angle to our van. Then the tag whipped back to the right 90 degrees, whipped back again to the left 90 degrees, and then on the fourth whip, it literally pulled the van around backwards. Now here we were looking at a row of five plus semi-trucks we had just passed as we were going backwards down the mountain with a big ravine on one side of the interstate. What was really neat about this experience was the fact that it was all in super slow motion. I could see all kinds of relatives and events in my life, but it was in such slow motion that, even though we were going backwards at an excessive rate of speed down the mountain, I was able to get out of my van seat, go over to my friend, who was driving and frozen stiff, and get his foot off of the accelerator so he could hit the emergency electric brakes to lock the trailer brakes. He couldn't reach them though because they were down underneath the dash! This whole time we were going backwards. I had enough time to get back in my seat, fasten my seat belt, yell to him to put his hands on the ceiling of the van, and, "Brace for impact!"

About that time we barrel-rolled down the interstate. The crash literally destroyed everything, but we walked away from the scene and didn't have a scratch on us. This van was beaten to death. All the glass was shattered and broken out and everything inside was destroyed. The enclosed aluminum trailer was a flat bed and was completely disintegrated. I had been racing with this trailer since '82 and the accident took place in '86 so it had four years of parts packed into it that were scattered up and down the interstate for about a mile. The turbo charged diesel van was lying upside down and idling so we shut it off, crawled outside, and looked at each other saying, "Are you all right?" "Yeah. Are you all right?" "Yeah." The doors were all jammed and after we looked the situation over we said, "Well, we are not going to get to the race, but we have to get out of here." The four wheeler that we towed the race car with to the track had come out of the tag, and was down the road with only its handle bars bent and that is about it. We got it, got it started, and were actually able to pull the van over with it.

Of course, the windows on the van were broken out and the top was smashed in, but it still ran because it had been idling when we had climbed out of it.

At about that time the state patrol arrived. He didn't really say a word, but he did look at the race car which was beaten to death. The body was smashed, the wheels were smashed, the intake manifold was smashed, and the scoop was smashed. It was a total wreck! He eventually said, "Man, this happens a lot here. The wind comes around that mountain and it catches the trailers." So, anyway, we loaded everything up on our "new" flat bed trailer. It took us all afternoon. They called the wrecker which came and towed the trailer in and then another wrecker towed the van in and we parked everything at a garage. We got to talking to a few people and found out that they wanted a small fortune to tow everything back home. So I looked the situation over and thought, "Well, we will just drive home what we can ourselves." They said, "Are you nuts?" "No, I am not paying that kind of money and I am not waiting until Tuesday to get back home. I have to be at work on Monday." **At this time, I was working at Teledyne as an engineer and my first responsibility was to be back on the job on time where I was needed.**

So we bought a piece of Plexiglas, held it over the front of the van, bought a few rolls of duct tape, and duct taped the Plexiglas over the front windshield. We also had to straighten a few wheels on the van. Everything seemed to run all right then. We got everything loaded up on the flat bed race car trailer and discovered the tongue had twisted about 270 degrees. I took it to the weld shop and borrowed a torch. The mechanic and I had to twist the tongue another 90 degrees to make the full 360 degrees. We were about to leave when he said, "Man, you are nuts. You are never going to get this home." I just looked at him and laughed and I said, "Nah, there isn't a state patrolman in the world who is going to stop me. See, my entire racing operation is temporarily ruined. They will never stop me."

They didn't and we drove everything all the way home. That was a fantastic crash. **I always laugh when I see these crash videos for sale. They always say, "And they walked away."** Well, of course, they walk away. **If you know what you are doing, you can survive any crash.**

WINNERS...

#104. in accelerating to win, handle mishaps as best as they can to survive

The fourth accident, of which I spoke in an earlier chapter, was on a race track at the sport's national when my alter got away from me. It got into a high speed bounce and I pulled the parachute just as I hit a bump in a shut down area. It turned sideways on me. I was running at probably 120 or 140 miles an hour. I finally got it back straight the only way possible; I accelerated out of the high speed bounce. Ron Miller's parachute was right in front of me and I hit him square in the back. The impact knocked us both over the guard rail. The entire sequence moved into slow motion, as I have previously described, and I saw my family, my wife, and everything flash in front of me.

These are totally unique experiences! **Once you have had them happen to you, from then on you don't get excited even when you get in a life-threatening situation. You just take it calmly, see what is going on, and look around you. It's really amazing. Don't get excited, yell, scream, or holler. It may be a life-threatening experience, but there is no reason to get excited.** It's just incredible how things slow down and how things always manage to work out.

WINNERS...

#105. learn to stay calm even when the going gets rough

**Since then these are undeniable facts,
you ought to keep calm and to do nothing rash.
(Acts 19:36)**

Other Speeding Stories

In conclusion, I know I drive way too fast when I go places, but it's ironic because I'm a very careful driver. I look in front of me, I look behind me, I look to my sides, I am constantly looking in my mirrors to see who is coming up from behind me. I drive like I am crazy, but I am also very courteous. I absolutely will not pull out in front of someone if I can't get up to their speed before they get close enough to me to have to kick it off cruise control. I just wish the rest of the world would drive that way. People pull out in front of you, and you need to lock up the brakes to keep from hitting them. It's like, are you blind? Do you have no depth perception? What is your problem? You only pass in the left lane and when you are not passing, you get back in the right lane. It is just common courtesy. But everywhere we go, I drive fast.

The ironic thing is that, with the exception of a 58 miles per hour speeding ticket in a 55 miles per hour zone, I have never had a speeding ticket! That one time, which just drove me crazy, I thought, "My goodness! You caught me going 58 in a 55. It was really bizarre! That is not speeding. The car speedometer can stray off that far." Well, anyway, I drive like I'm nuts and I have never gotten an excessive speeding ticket. I have been clocked twice at over 150 miles an hour and have been let go. I won't relate to you the details of that story, but twice that has happened to me. I drive fast!

Now, I want you to know that I am not the only person who drives fast. Here is a good story that involved a friend who was the vice president of IFSI Furnace Company, located in Cleveland, Ohio. This guy, Pete McHenry, races BMW's in auto crosses and he also builds high performance motors for them in his basement. I remember years ago I visited IFSI because they were building a new furnace for Teledyne. I had to inspect it before they shipped it. I flew into the Cleveland airport and Pete met me at the gate.

We walked out, got into this new company car that had a new quad four motor, pulled up to the parking attendant, and paid for the parking. It was at this point that Pete whipped out a stop watch from his pocket. I didn't have a clue what was going to happen next, but I like to drive fast and I am comfortable even riding shotgun with somebody who is driving fast as long as I know that he knows what he is doing. Anyway, he whipped this stop watch out and as soon as the gate came up, he hit the stop watch, nailed this car, and just fried rubber. Away we flew! We took off, whipped around the airport, got out on the interstate, and he drove in and out and around, on the left, on the right, and was driving a lot crazier than I ever drive. We were just flying! We screamed around the off-ramp, went through town, where I think we hit every stop light green, came screaming into IFSI Furnace Company's parking lot, locked the brakes, slid into his parking place, and as soon as the car stopped moving, he punched the stop watch, looked at me, smiled, and said, "How 'bout that? Knocked seven seconds off my best time!" He had the need for speed, too. He drives that way and to the best of my knowledge, he has never had a ticket either. That is a speed story and I think everybody's got it in them. I am thoroughly convinced you can drive fast and safe. I think the games that I play with my mind when I am driving, like watching the other drivers and calculating how fast I am catching them or how fast they are catching me, is what keeps me awake. That is what keeps you alert when you are driving long distances and I can drive a long distance.

It's like the time I rode a motorcycle 950 miles in one day. I have taken my bike from Paulding, Ohio, to Pensacola, Florida, nonstop in one day. I have driven other vehicles long distances too; I had to pick up a new

Harley soft tail springer last year and only one place in the world had it on the floor, in stock, and that was Barnett's Harley Davidson in El Paso, Texas. That was 3,300 miles and I drove it in 3 days. I drove something like 17 hours one day, 19 hours the next, and 18 hours the last and averaged 61 mph, that's including gas stops, fast food on the run, and three and one-half hours at Barnett's going over the new Harley and loading it up. I did it so I could get home in a hurry. I think I left Thursday morning and got back Saturday evening. The reason that was important was so that I could ride it with Marianne the next day. We like to go bike riding every Sunday.

Another great speed story during this trip was when I was traveling through Arkansas. I picked up someone behind me and we caught up to someone else in front, each of us driving 80-85 mph. We were approximately one-eighth of a mile apart. We passed two Arkansas patrolmen in the southbound lane giving someone a ticket. We didn't slow down. About 30 minutes later my radar detector went crazy. I looked up in the rear view mirror and one of the patrolmen had pulled the guy behind me over and the other drove up next to me. I didn't even slow down! What was the point? I was busted or so I thought. The patrolman looked right at me and the new Harley. I looked back at him with both of us still going 85 mph. He passed me and pulled over the guy in front of me! I kept right on driving 85 mph. The only thing I can figure is that both patrolmen ride Harleys!

Interstate highways are made for one reason and that is to get you from point A to point B in the shortest time possible. I guess my belief is that if you are not interested in using them for that, then you should stay off of them, so that people who have places to go and things to do can get there. That is kind of a bold, rash statement, but it is true! How many times have you been held up by some fool driving 45 miles an hour in a 55 miles an hour speed zone? They are not getting anywhere. All they are doing is holding you up from getting somewhere and preventing you from doing something constructive. All of us need to be more sensitive to the needs of other drivers by paying attention to the flow of traffic, staying alert, and being courteous while driving.

Chapter Ten

WINNING IS IN SIGHT

**Service Helps, Strikes Don't
Clear Vision Must Continue No Matter What
Doing the Right Thing Pays Off
Take Risks to Give the Masses What They Need
Quality Customer Service Says It All**

As a successful business is built, winning is in sight. A successful business depends upon having a product that someone needs to purchase. In my little business we started out manufacturing OEM differential parts in a way that no one else had ever done. No one had ever advertised that they could actually do this. I basically invented some machinery, then built it to quickly modify OEM components. So what we did was to actually create something that no one else had ever done before. We started advertising that we could do this and slowly built the business.

Service Helps, Strikes Don't

My business, from the years of working with other corporations, was totally based upon customer service. When you are dealing with race car people, show car people, and street rod people, they want service quickly. **They don't want it tomorrow, they want it now.** So we devised a method by which someone would send something in, we would remanufacture it the next day, and we would ship it back the next day. That is our two-day turn around which is the slowest service that we offer. If someone is in a big hurry, we can do it the same day that we get it and ship it back that day. Another way we operate is to do the work tomorrow and ship it on that same day. So we actually offer a no-day service, a one-day service, and our normal two-day service. The only possible problem with the no-day and the one-day service is that we can only do two or three no-days and maybe ten next-days. We can do everybody else's in two days.

**WINNERS...
#106. realize that being first is all about
the speed and quality of service**

> "When a man feels throbbing within him the power to do
> what he undertakes as well as it can possibly be done,
> this is happiness, this is success."
> (Orison Swett Marden)

So actually, it was really easy to dominate the market because, being a drag racer, I knew what my customer needed. **They need a good product, they want it now, and they don't want to pay very much for it. So by figuring out how to do that, I generated a good business from day one.** Total customer service can become very challenging, especially when, for example, UPS (United Parcel Service) went on strike in the middle of August '97. This is one of the few things that has ever happened to me in my entire life over which I really had no control. We could have been shipping RPS (Roadway Package Systems) and if we had been shipping with them, they would have continued to ship what we had been shipping with them. So, prior to the strike, say, three to six months before, we could have given our business over to RPS and they would be shipping for us now. We did not do that for two reasons. The first reason is that UPS has never been on strike in the 90 years that they have been in business. The second reason is that UPS provides better service because they have been delivering packages longer than RPS. Sometimes RPS is unable to track your product, so you don't know where your product is in the system. Another problem is that sometimes they don't deliver on time. These are a couple of reasons why we did not switch over to RPS prior to the strike. RPS is a new start-up company and as time has gone by it has been getting better. So we used Federal Express (FedEx, as they are called), which took only ten packages a day while UPS was on strike.

WINNERS...

#107. know what their customers need and how to give it to them

> "When a man has done his best, has given his all, and in the process
> supplied the needs of his family and his society,
> that man has succeeded."
> (Mack Douglas)

It became very evident to me just how important customer service is to what I do. We are the fastest on the earth as far as manufacturing or making products for race car people. Using UPS, they are the fastest delivery service on the planet. So you combine those two things, us with them, and we have what I call "instant axles." They are instant! You need them, you have them. When UPS was on strike, we had a big problem. I lost 50% of my speed and I had no control over it. We shipped parcel post, and at least they took the stuff. The only problem was that there was no guarantee when it would be delivered, and there was no way to track the product while it was being delivered, so it was difficult to find out if it had, in fact, been signed for and received.

When you sell something to race car people, the order for the product is taken and you tell them you are going to do it tomorrow and ship it the next day. Usually, they call the day after and say, "Well, did it get shipped?" "Yeah, it got shipped. We told you it would get shipped and it got shipped." Then, the day that it is supposed to be delivered, if any UPS truck drives by the guy's business, even if it is not his UPS truck, the guy is on the phone saying, "Hey! The guy didn't stop! I didn't get my stuff! Where is it at?" Well, you can imagine just what kind of problem we have shipping products through the postal service. I can't track it, I can't tell you where it is, and I can't tell you when it is going to be delivered. I can't do any of those things which are the key elements of my business.

Another thing that we did with UPS is to structure our business so that UPS is the collection agency. This is why I have absolutely no argument with what they pay UPS drivers because they are worth every penny of their salary to me. They also send me documented computerized read-outs of what they collect and we use that for our bookkeeping. **So they are actually my bookkeeper, my collection agency, and they basically never lose any money for us.** We typically do $7,000,000 to $8,000,000 worth of business each year. Fifty percent of that goes on a credit card and the other 50% UPS collects. So UPS collects between $3,500,000 to $4,000,000 of my money each year. They don't lose a penny of it. It is a wonderful service.

WINNERS...

#108. organize their finances making it easy to control money handling

"The mold of a man's fortune is in his own hands."
(Francis Bacon)

Another problem with the UPS strike was that you really couldn't effectively send anything C.O.D. through the post office. They're not good at that. Sometimes they don't collect the money since there is no record of the product being delivered. Your customer can simply call up and say, "I never got my order." No one can prove if they ever got it or not. If the post office fails to collect, they just shrug their shoulders and say, "Oh, well." If UPS fails to collect, UPS reimburses you for what the amount was on the C.O.D. tag. So, as you can see, this was one big mess due to the fact that we couldn't ship with any kind of certainty through the post office. We could only ship ten things a day with FedEx and people weren't willing to ship red or blue label with UPS. During the strike, even the UPS management staff delivered air packages. We temporarily lost 40% of my business. We did a lot of drive-ins over a five state area with people willing to drive-in to get their product. During August of '97, we should have been shipping 700 pair of axles a week and the first week of the strike we shipped 430 pair and in a later week, we shipped 401 pair. We were basically at 60%. So that just shows you how important service is to my customers. They want it right, they want it quickly, they don't want to pay much for it, and they want to know where it is at all times. When I lost that ability while UPS was on strike, my business suffered, and I had no control over it. Because of my high standards of customer service, it was very frustrating.

Clear Vision Must Continue No Matter What

Because of the UPS strike and the way I am structured, even though I was still making a profit, I was just not where I wanted to be. I knew exactly what I was doing, how I was going to do it, how I was going to get there, and how I was going to accomplish it at all times. So I was just kind of floating and doing the back stroke. I wasn't going forwards or backwards because I couldn't do what I wanted to get done. This was the worst possible time for this to happen because we were about to move into a new 30,000 square foot, $1,300,000 manufacturing facility with all new furniture, all new computer software/hardware, and all kinds of new equipment which I was building.

So much has been automated in the new plant that it is really an easy place to work. I now have seven people in total, including five machinists and two welders, who produce $7,000,000 to $8,000,000 worth of saleable product each year. You can pick up any entrepreneurial magazine or business newspaper and read about other people's successful businesses, but there is not one, unless it is a telemarketing scheme, that can generate that kind of sales dollars with so few manufacturing people. Nobody can do it!

WINNERS...

#109. must have vision beyond present circumstances in order to be first

"You learn that, whatever you are doing in life, obstacles don't matter very much. Pain or other circumstances can be there, but if you want to do a job bad enough, you'll find a way to get it done."
(Jack Youngblood)

What we did once UPS was back to work was to pull probably 30% to 40% of the items that were shipped UPS and ship them one-day, two-day, and three-day FedEx. We also took 20% of the market that we gave to UPS and we placed it with RPS. That way, if this ever happens again, then we can ship 20% of our product RPS, 30% FedEx, and 50% UPS. If one of those delivery services goes on strike, the post office can pick up the slack. The shipping companies' policies are that if you shipped x number of packages with them before the strike, then during the strike they will ship that number of packages. It is just that no shipping company on the face of this earth can pick up UPS's slack. UPS ships 80% of all packages shipped in the United States. No one can pick up the slack of 80%. They can pick them up but they just sit there because they do not have the man power or the equipment or the network to move that many packages. So the UPS strike really calls attention to what my customers are after and that is total service. Total customer service means that every one of your sales people has to know everything about a differential drive train component that a customer could possibly ask about over the phone because that is what you are selling. You are selling service and that's what people want. We have seven phone lines with seven sales people working eight to nine hours each day and I have written down everything that I know in what we call the "Little Black Bible," and everybody has a copy. It takes years for my sales people to actually know everything. It takes years! Maybe they never will know it, but there are enough people who know enough about what I know and what my wife knows that we can basically answer any question anybody would want to ask. Now that's customer service. **Basically, you have to know what the individual needs when he calls you, even when he doesn't even know what he needs, because what I have found in life and in this business is that human beings want to agree with you.** They want to agree with you whether you are right or they are wrong or whatever. When someone asks you a question about their differential or about a part that they want to purchase, and you think that you know exactly what they are talking about and you relate to them and say, "Yeah, this is what you need. You need it that long and this is what you need for backspacing because you told me you are running Ford brakes." Whether the sales person is right or not, the customer will agree with you. They will say, "Yeah, that's right. That's right." It's like, wait a minute, we are making a custom part here for you and you are agreeing too easily. It is the hardest thing to train our sales people to really listen to what the customer is saying because even then, you get stung an awful lot and I guess as far as customer service goes, we are unique in the fact that we can remanufacture product. Once my competitors make you a custom axle, that's it. The way they design and build their axle, it cannot be remanufactured. The flange is too hard to change, the bolt pattern or the shaft is tapered so you can't cut it down and make a different axle or a different length axle out of it. The stuff is junk! Well, the beauty of my business is that with a little bit of additional labor, we can modify something that someone erroneously ordered. If we took a wrong order, or we took the wrong specs and delivered to the wrong customer, we can make it right if she or he sends it back to us. Since my flange isn't hardened, we can change the bolt pattern, and we can build a lot to get a customer moving. In fact, that is probably the greatest thing that we do well, and that is customer service. We know it and our customers know it.

WINNERS...

#110. find their responsibility increasing as others are willing to be led

"Success on any major scale requires you to accept responsibility...In the final analysis, the one quality that all successful people have... is the ability to take on responsibility." (Michael Korda)

When someone totally screws up, though, the customer tells us and we will look at it. If the one complaining is nice on the phone, and that is the key, Moser Engineering will do about anything to assist. **The customer needs to be civil and needs to be nice on the phone because we are only human, so we can make mistakes. Our customers are only human, too, and they can also make mistakes.** So there is no sense in getting angry because you get more things in this world using honey than you do using anything else.

WINNERS...

#111. encourage civility and do not allow anger to rage among their ranks

Cease from anger, and forsake wrath;
Fret not yourself, it leads only to evildoing.
(Psalm 37:8)

Actually, as a company, we are too nice and I honestly believe that a lot of our customers view that as an admission of guilt or wrong doing on our part. When someone calls up and says, "I told you housing width of the bare differential housing differential," and we say, "Well, actually you told us axle flange to axle flange," there are only five inches difference between the two. We read back all instructions to everyone before we hang up the phone and we put a check mark beside their name so that we know that we read it back to them. "You said this is where your wheels bolt on, well, now you are telling me it is the housing." "Well, they are five inches too short..."

Maybe we are too easy on the phone. If the axles that are too short for the customer are something that we can very easily sell to someone else, we will take those axles back and charge them a recut fee of 45 bucks. So here you have a $300 pair of axles that we will take back and we will make a new pair of axles for 45 bucks. Believe it or not, there are people that take that as, "Well, if they are doing that for so little money, they are obviously wrong." These guys will argue about even paying the 45 bucks! If they had bought this product from my competitor for $500 for the pair of axles, guess what? They would eat that $500 and if they wanted another pair of axles it would cost them another 500 bucks. It is the difference between $345 for two pair of axles or $1000 for two pair of axles. So in all reality, sometimes in my customer service we're too nice to the customer, too forgiving, and I can't say whether that is good or bad. I really can't. **All I know is that what I do for my customers is what I feel is right.**

WINNERS...

#112. treat others like they would want to be treated

> **Therefore whatever you want others to do for you,
> do so for them...
> (Matthew 7:12)**

Doing the Right Thing Pays Off

My son, Rob, who is a sales manager, takes care of all problems including all situations needing customer service. When he runs into something that he can't handle, I take care of it. **I totally believe that what is right is right and what is wrong is wrong. I base my decisions on this philosophy. I also like to think that we maintain humility in our business.** But no matter what, even if the customer is foul mouthed, totally mean, poor spirited, non-compromising, and a real jerk on the phone, we have never, ever, ever charged anyone full price for their mistake on a second pair of axles. Even the real jerks, we will make them another pair for 50% of what the first pair cost.

WINNERS...

#113. do what is right with humility

> **When pride comes, then comes dishonor,
> But with the humble is wisdom.
> (Proverbs 11:2)**

Our customer service must be working because our business has grown 100 times in ten years. It has to be totally based upon customer service. What people want is what you give them, and that's the reason my business is successful.

We know who our customers are, and we know what they need. We know what they like and that is what we give them. We are constantly working to give them even better service. I have just completed two computer controlled drilling machines that drill the bolt pattern and the flanges. We are holding our bolt patterns to within one-thousandths. We just completed a machine to rifle drill axles which is something that we had done but were not good at doing. I just built an automatic machine to drill the access and lighting holes in the flanges. We are constantly building new equipment to make things quicker, better, and cheaper. In turn, we pass the savings on to our customers. We just redesigned our tool line and we are going to be lowering the pricing on some of our products. How's that? In the last ten years, other than on products that I have bought from another manufacturer and marked up, I have never raised a price on something that I actually manufacture. The only thing that we have done steadily is lower prices. We have lowered prices through the years and that has been the right thing to do.

You would think that building all of our equipment and doing whatever it takes to improve our products would involve a lot of risk. Others may disagree, but my personal feeling is that there is no risk whatsoever in this world. It is not even remotely in my mind that I am taking a risk as an entrepreneur. The reason I can say that and the reason people should believe me is simply because of what I had when I started my business. Did I have nothing? I was a plant engineer making $60,000 to $70,000 a year. I had a really good job. I started this business, but what risk was I taking? None. I was a plant engineer in a forge shop. You can get a job there any day of the week if your business fails. It's a no brainer and it's no big deal. To me, there is absolutely no risk in starting a business! There is no risk in building equipment. You just build it. It works, saves you money, lowers your prices, and gets more customers. It's a no brainer to me. **I basically do not acknowledge that there is any risk whatsoever in anything you do in life. Just do it!**

WINNERS...

#114. just do things rather than finding the reasons why not to do them

**The desires of the sluggard puts him to death,
For his hands refuse to work...
(Proverbs 21:25)**

Some of the things that you engineer work and maybe some don't work. But a person who is in my position or is in an engineering type position cannot look at failures as a negative. **There is no such thing as failure. There is no such thing as a negative. Everything is a learning experience and that is how you should consider the negative. You want your people to think like you think. If something fails, it was a learning experience.** Let's not do that again. You want your people to think like you think and that is that everything and anything is possible. If they are afraid that the boss is going to yell at them for their failures, I can assure you that they will not be trying anything new. No way! Where will the innovation come from, the new thinking, the better equipment and processes? Nothing in this world is impossible. The impossible just takes a little longer. Let your people think creatively and definitely not have the fear that someone will say they failed!

WINNERS...

#115. believe that it is better to have failed than to not have tried at all

*Failure is only the opportunity to
more intelligently begin again.
(Henry Ford)*

What you are going to find is that people will look to you, and your business will take on your persona. People will act like you act, people will perform like you perform, and that is what makes a successful business. In fact, that is what is going to get your business out of the entrepreneurial stage and actually get it to where you say, "Wow, maybe I have a business now." It has just been in the last year or two that I have actually leaned back and looked at my business and said, "Yes, I guess we do have a business." Up until then, it was just a hobby, a very big hobby.

Take Risks to Give the Masses What They Need

As far as having failures as a person, you have to be able to laugh at yourself. You have to be able to tolerate other people and enjoy a laugh over your failures. Believe me, there are so many things in this world that can go wrong. To give you an example, even when the roof fell in when I was working at Portland Forge, when things got really bad, you could always find me smiling. Why? Well, people either thought I was crazy or they thought that I knew something that they didn't know, meaning it was all going to work out anyway. People feel better when you keep your cool in the midst of difficulty and that is what moving forward involves. Do the job to the best of your ability, but if it doesn't work out, laugh at yourself and get on with life!

WINNERS...

#116. enjoy life to the fullest by laughing in the face of failure

> **"The successful man will profit from his mistakes
> and try again in a different way."**
> **(Dale Carnegie)**

We actually tailor what our customer needs, not what our customer wants. I really believe that is why we are so successful. You see, it is hard to believe, but most of the people who call and buy products (hundreds of thousands of them do this, or perhaps millions of them) really don't know what they need. That is why so much training must be given to my salespeople. They must try to discover exactly what the customer really needs because they often don't know. Fortunately, we do know what they need and that is one reason why our product is so good. Other companies charge a lot more for their product, take a lot longer to build their product, and have a product that has a poorer guarantee than our product. **Our competition makes their products out of a material that needs to be micro polished on the surface so that is doesn't create stress risers when it is used in a torsional twist application.** They use this as a selling point by saying, "Look at this beautiful piece of material, it is just beautiful." Well, it is beautiful and they have a pretty little emblem on the end of the axle, whereas we do not. Our axle is machined and doesn't need to be micro polished. Therefore I don't add any more cost in doing that. We do not put a cute little sticker on the end of the axle. We forge "M" and "E" on it, for "Moser Engineering," the name of my company. It looks a little crude and is not beautiful, but I don't have any money in a sticker which means I do not have to bill my customer for it. We make an axle that my customer actually needs. Maybe it is not what he wants, but that is not my business. **My business is to do my best to make an indestructible axle, sell it cheap, and deliver it quick, because that is what my customer needs!**

WINNERS...
#117. succeed by meeting the needs, not the wants, of others

> **"I do the very best I know how -- the very best I can;
> and I mean to keep on doing so until the end."**
> **(Abraham Lincoln)**

Always keep your eyes on the competition. In my business, though, the competition is basically clueless with no common sense. They don't really know what the customer needs. They don't make what the customer needs. They make a lot of high dollar trick stuff that might sell one or two times each week. Well, we are not into that business. **We are in the** business for the multitudes. When you drive by a local drag strip or a circle track race and see all the trailers, dually trucks, and all this, you will see hundreds and hundreds of people racing and they are my clientele. Money is to be made from the masses.

WINNERS...

#118. know the value of marketing to the masses over a select few

"Rather have good common sense than brains any day."
(Unknown)

The money is not earned from trick parts. I guess you could say that I am a very fortunate individual to actually have competitors who are clueless. They think designing all this trick stuff and selling them a couple times each week will help them sell their product to the sportsman racers. "We make professional stuff and that will help me sell to sportsman racers," as they say. They are so far off base, they are clueless. That is not what the sportsman needs to buy. **What the sportsman is looking for is something quick, something cheap, and something that works. That is all the sportsman is looking for and he doesn't even care if the product looks crude.** I have no intentions of ever making my product look beautiful. Why should I? By my estimations, I have 60% to 70% of the market in the known world for race car axles. One of my competitors only sells 1000 axles a year (I sell 50,000 axles a year) and he puts in his ads negative comments like, "One of my competitors does this and that and makes short cuts to make a cheaper axle." Yes, and I pass the cheaper price on to my customers, but not a cheaper quality. It is like he is trying to knock me by saying I am efficient, I am automated, and I can make a cheaper product. My competition is oblivious to the fact that I pass product savings on to my customer. So thank you for helping me to advertise! You couldn't wish for poorer competition or for more clueless competitors than I have. Everybody in business would love to have the kind of competition that I have because they are not competitors. They are clueless at what I am doing, they are clueless as to how I do it, and they are basically no threat to me whatsoever. They have lost the market share that I have gained and they will never get it back because even though I sit here and tell you how clueless they are, I keep an eye on them.

WINNERS...

#119. distribute products quickly that have perceived value and work

"Everyone will experience the consequences of his own acts. If his acts are right, he'll get good consequences; if they're not, he'll suffer for it."
(Harry Browne)

Quality Customer Service Says It All

    The other group I keep my eyes on is my clientele. Never, and I repeat, never, take your eyes off your customer. It is like a ball. Keep your eye on the ball. Whether it is a football, basketball, or whatever, do not take you eye off that ball. Do not take your eye off your customers. Keep an eye on what they are doing and remember that marketing to what the masses need will sell product because they have to have it. Wants, on the other hand, can always be put on a Christmas wish list for the customer to buy someday or when they have the money. Needs must be purchased today! It's like razor blades vs. an electric razor. Every man needs new razor blades on a regular basis. Some men want an electric razor, but even those who want one almost never buy one.

WINNERS...

#120. keep their eyes on the customer identifying their needs continuously

"We don't need more strength or more ability or greater opportunity. What we need is to use what we have."
(Basil S. Walsh)

    We have created perfection in what we do. We offer our customers perfection and we go beyond that in solving their problems. We inexpensively solve their problems. People think they have a problem, but they really don't because we will take care of that problem. Whether it is their mistake or our mistake, we take care of all problems. Like I said, if it is our mistake, it won't cost them a cent. I think the only thing that we have really done with our customers, as far as spoiling them, is that we literally ship stuff in two days. Prior to that, people would order early because they knew it would take six to eight weeks to get a pair of axles made and delivered. Well, now that we have the whole world convinced that we can do it in two days, all of my customers wait until the last minute to order their product. If there is something wrong with the product, they are really mad because, as they say, "We were planning to go racing this weekend." All I can do is say, "Oh well, I can't help that because I cannot back up the clock." If I could tell my customers anything, it would be, "You shouldn't wait until the last day to order your axles. You should order them at least a couple of days in advance, and that way if there is a problem it can be taken care of before you plan to go racing."

Customer service is trying to determine what your customer needs, when the customer needs it, and what he or she is willing to pay for it. Try to keep an ear open so that you can change if the customer changes. It boils down to keeping your ear to the ground, seeing what trends are happening in the industry, and keeping on top of them. The beauty that you have when you are a small organization like mine is that you can change almost instantly. If you see a product that needs to be made, you can decide to do it today. You can react quickly. In most larger companies, by the time someone comes up with a good idea, they are not even at the stage of discussing it in a meeting. The small company already has the product made and on the market. That is the beauty of a small company.

My goal is for our company to get as large as possible, but not too large. I guess I would say that when I have 50 employees, doing $15,000,000 in sales, possibly $20,000,000, I will be satisfied. But I really don't know that I ever want to get any larger than that because it is very difficult to keep your perspective when the company gets that large. It is very difficult to keep your eye on what your customer needs. It's also very difficult to keep your eye on your competitors and I really think that probably $20,000,000 and a 50 man operation is probably as large as I ever want to get. On the other hand, as winning is in sight and my goal is about to be reached, who knows – I may set a new target of dollar volume and number of employees working and apply the principles detailed here to surpass even my own success formula.

Whatever the case, my business philosophies have to filter through my sales people to my customers. That is what I want. What it all boils down to is customer service. Even though you think you have what the customer needs and you think you have it quicker and cheaper, it is still the customer who is buying your product to make your business successful, so customer service is everything!

Chapter Eleven

BEING RECOGNIZED AS THE LEADER

**Communicate Clearly
Set the Example
Trust Others to Do Their Job
Recognize the Leader and Win
Entertain Fresh and New Ideas
Realize Knowledge is Power
Practice What You Preach
Be Mentally and Physically Fit**

What does it take to be a leader? I guess I have really never stopped to think about it, but throughout my life, I have always led people every place I have worked. It requires dedication, stamina, integrity, honesty, a lot of hard work, and it involves making decisions. I have always thought that a quick decision is the best decision. **No decision at all has everybody worried about what is going to happen next. Procrastination just puts things off and I have always believed that any decision, right or wrong, is better than no decision at all.** When you have a crisis, like the UPS strike, how you react is a key to what your employees think of you. Leadership is demonstrated as you handle adversity and run your business.

WINNERS...

#121. realize that procrastination only leads to poor performance

"Any decision is better than no decision at all."
(Unknown)

Communicate Clearly

When I was working in New York at the Portec Corporation for Bob Treinen, I was the plant engineer. I discussed with my plant superintendent what I wanted him to do and what I wanted to see done. Unfortunately, it would never quite be done like I would want it. I was in talking to Bob about this man one day and said, "You know, I just don't understand this. I explicitly told him exactly what I wanted him to do, but it just doesn't quite get done." Bob laughed and he said, "I'm going to tell you what your problem is." Realize I was probably 22 or 23 years old at the time when Bob advised, "Next time you tell him what you want him to do, wait about a half hour and go back and ask him what you told him to do and listen to what he tells you." So I did just that and what I found out was something that all management needs to understand. I had assumed that people knew what I knew and what I wanted. I just assumed that everybody had the same mechanical gifts that I had. When I would tell this fellow worker what I wanted done, I would unintentionally leave out the details necessary for him to understand. So he couldn't do what I wanted him to do. **My advice to individuals who are working with others in trying to get something accomplished is that they must make sure they are on the same wavelength as the people who are instructed in the task.** Don't talk under their level or over their level. Sometimes it is impossible to tell where that level is, but after you have given instructions, ask them to tell you what it is that needs to be done. Then determine if they understand what is expected to be accomplished from your instructions.

WINNERS...

#122. know to reconfirm all important communications with others to be certain that what has been stated is well understood

> And we urge you, brethren, admonish the unruly,
> encourage the fainthearted,
> help the weak, be patient with all men.
> (1 Thessalonians 5:14)

Set the Example

The one thing that I have always enjoyed about leading people is that it is a self-motivating experience for me. I am motivated within myself. I do not need recognition from anyone. In fact, I delight in building, engineering, and accomplishing things for myself without recognition. It makes me feel good since I am the only person I really want to please. It sometimes embarrasses me when I receive awards for my accomplishments because that is not why I did them. I did them for me, to make me feel better inside, and to motivate me to do things even better the next time I do them. I really find it amusing when people talk about dreaming about doing this and doing that. I have a simple solution. Don't dream. Don't dream about what someone else has and don't dream, "Boy that would be nice," or, "It would be great to live like this or to do that." Don't waste your time dreaming about things like that. Spend your time accomplishing what you want done.

In speaking with the principal of Portland High School in Portland, Indiana, Ms. Jodie Gibson, and the superintendent of the Jay County School Corporation, Dr. Tom Little, I said to them, "I didn't realize it until now, but up until 1992, I have worked a minimum of two jobs for 35 years of my life. From the age of nine years old until about 24, I worked three jobs. Then, from 24 to 40, I worked a minimum of two jobs." I have always done that! Why? Well, people don't realize that if you really want something, you go out and you do it. You make the money to do what you want to do. If you don't have a job that supports you with enough money to do what you want to do, then get another job. Work two jobs. **There is no excuse for anyone in this day and age in this world to not have everything that they want. Just do it! Don't dream about what other people have, just do it.** I have said this before to people, "I don't consider myself very smart, but I do think I have an above average amount of common sense. I have the ability to spot a good deal when I see one and I have got the intestinal fortitude to jump on it before it gets away.

In fact, the funny thing I do is that I have trained my brain to think about projects when I sleep. I don't dream about wanting this or doing that. My dreams consist of solving problems and figuring out what I am going to do tomorrow, and that is how I get so much done. I actually plot out in my brain while I am sleeping what I am going to do tomorrow. I am sure my employees, my plant manager, and my sales manager really wonder why I am bummed out when I come in and find that I have a broken machine. The reason I am bummed out is because I have spent all night dreaming about what I was going to accomplish and then I come into work to find that my plans have been totally disrupted. When something breaks down that I have built, it means that I have to fix it because I really don't want anybody else messing with what I have engineered. That is why I say, "What!?" Now I can't get done what I wanted to get done. I can get some of it done, but not all of it. That is how I plot out my day and decide what I am going to do, how I am going to do it, when I am going to do it, and how I am going to get things accomplished. This sets a fine example for everyone else: to be organized and to accomplish what needs to be done on any one day.

WINNERS...

#123. please themselves and set the example by doing rather than dreaming

The sluggard buries his hand in the dish,
And will not even bring it back to his mouth.
(Proverbs 20:4)

Trust Others to Do Their Job

Basically, I give everybody the benefit of the doubt or enough rope to hang themselves. Sometimes you make good decisions and sometimes you make bad ones. Another Portec story will illustrate that. I will tell you the punch line before I tell you the story. Bob Treinen told me that I am probably the worst judge of character of anyone that he has ever met in his entire life. Here is the way the story went. We had an old blacksmith, a genuine blacksmith, who made the tongs for the steel mill and forged them all. He was a true artist. The guy was around 70 years old and wanting to retire. So I found him an apprentice since one of the welders was interested in learning the trade. We started training him and it took a long time. He was a pretty nice kid.

Well, one day he didn't show up for work so I went out and asked his fellow welders what was going on and where he was. They said, "He's in jail." So I asked, "What for?"

"He is in jail because he didn't pay his back child support."

So I called the judge up and said, "He works for Portec, has got a good job, and makes a lot of money. If you let him out of jail, I will give him enough overtime each week to pay his child support." Well, eventually they let him out of jail.

A couple of weeks went by and everything was working out just fine. We went out to dig a trench on Wednesday morning. We had a lot of equipment there including high lifts, cranes, bulldozers, and back hoes. We had all kinds of neat toys. We had to dig this trench and put a new sewer line in and one of the millwrights said, "I can't find the back hoe." So we were looking around this rather large facility with a lot of square footage and a lot of acreage. We couldn't find the back hoe. The old blacksmith came up to me and said, "Hey, where is my apprentice?"

"Well, he didn't come in today."

"No?"

So we continued to look around for this back hoe and the crane operator came down out of the crane and said, "I saw a blacksmith dragging the back hoe down the railroad tracks this morning."

We did some investigating and found out that the apprentice stole our back hoe, drove it down the railroad tracks, took it to a salvage yard, sold the thing for $5,000, stuck the money in his pocket, and left the country!

Now you can see why Bob Treinen told me that I am absolutely no judge of human character whatsoever. Would I do it again? Of course I would do it again. I truly believe that to get the most out of your people, you have to explicitly trust them or empower them. **You have to give them the ability to make their own decisions, right or wrong, and not to crucify them if they make the wrong decision. Most importantly, you must praise them when they make a right decision.** That way you will get the most out of them and they will do the best job that they can possibly do for you.

WINNERS...

#124. trust others, congratulating them
when they make the right decisions

"To measure the man measure the heart."
(Malcolm S. Forbes)

Recognize the Leader and Win

Once you are successful at leading, everybody wants you to be successful, wants you to handle their project, and wants you to do things for them. In other words, recognize who the leader is and win every time. **If it is perceived that you are successful at what you are doing, then others think that if you do something for them, it will be successful also.** It has been amusing to me that people actually think, "Because you are so successful in business, you can be successful in my project." The funny thing is, you are! It is like a self-fulfilling prophecy. Your reputation proceeds you in getting things done and doing things right. That is why I have been involved in so many projects, such as volunteering my services, time, money, and energy, because I wanted to see projects happen. I knew that they were right to do and I knew that if I did them, they would get done. Miraculously, they do get done!

Greg Moser at age two was already thinking aerodynamically to gain some speed in life.

By the time he was three, Greg was already learning values from his mother and work ethics from his father by training on his new tractor.

Joan and Paul Moser were Greg's parents.

Greg's new bike would travel
30,000 miles helping him to d(
three paper routes over a sev(
year period.

John and Edith Montgomery.

Frank and Eva Moser.

Grandfather and Grandmother Montgomery at the Toledo Zoo with Greg and Connie.

Greg rebuilt this Norton and added it to his collection.

This Norton was bought by Greg when he was 15. His grandmother found it at Heniser's Motor Sales where someone had traded it in on a car.

Greg's Harley Davidson Sportster was built by him after he bought it for $1.00 because it had been destroyed in a fire. All that was left was the frame, motor, and the headerpipes. The wheels, drums, magneto and carb had melted, and it was a lot of hard work to rebuild it. The year was 1971-72. It was well worth the effort!

John Griffith Young. Mr. Young is Chairman of The Jay Garment Corporation, Portland, Indiana. He is a great grandson of Isaac Griffith, the eldest brother of Greg's great, great grandmother, Sarah Malvena Griffith.

The original two car garage where Moser Engineering had its start.

The original shop built in the industrial park in Portland, Indiana. It was 3,000 square feet.

Connie Burns, D.D.S., on the day she graduated from Case University in Cleveland with her degree in dentistry.

Going 170 to 180 miles an hour, Greg pulls the parachute as he crosses the finish line.

Moser Engineering was expanded by 6,000 square feet of manufacturing space.

Greg's son, Rob, mans the display for Moser Engineering at one of the NHRA national events.

The Christmas Tree helps the racer to be alert and ready for the beginning of business.

Employees, with Greg, prepare to scuba dive in the Bahamas during their annual Christmas meeting there.

Moser Engineering after its last 10,000 square foot addition.

New Moser Engineering plant.

When Greg's sister, Connie (left), Greg himself (center), and their father, Paul (right), each bought a Corvette from H and K Motors in Continental, Ohio on the same day in 1980, this picture was taken and made Chevrolet's *Friends Magazine*.

The theater room in Greg's home features tiered seating and a 104 inch television screen surrounded by four 30 inch monitors.

Greg's home pool is indoors and features a water slide from the balcony!

Greg and Marianne designed each room to be unique. The fireman's pole surrounded by glass is spectacular!

All woodwork is done in cherry as seen on this magnificent stairwell and living room balcony banister.

The bar area is graced with a 150 gallon salt water live coral reef tank.

Greg and Marianne purchased 50 acres adjacent to their home to build a lake on which to water ski.

Greg takes the employees of Portland's First National Bank to a national racing event at which each of them sports a Moser Engineering T-shirt.

Greg and his controller, Bruce Hedges, set up this race arch to help raise money for the new library. The Great Race Pit Stop Competition was won by Greg's community. Looks pretty good, doesn't it?

The community of Portland, Indiana is proud of its new library.

Arts Council Building.

Moser Engineering displays locally at the Jay County Expo.

Directors of the First National Bank.

First National Bank employees always like to support the races.

First National Bank President and CEO, Barry Hudson, at the races.

Bob Quadrozzi.

Vicki Tague.

Ron Miller working on the engine.

Jeff Bickel.

Greg at the races.

This is a typical "Altered" Drag Race Car.

This is the '94 pro-stock Camaro built by Rick Jones, driven by Ron, and sponsored by Greg. It started the black/red paint scheme that is run on all of the Moser Engineering cars.

The '96 Olds pro-stocker.

The dragster that won 12 of 14 quick eights and one national event with two runner-ups. It is the top dragster in which Greg sponsored Ron Miller and runs consistent 6.80s at 199 in the quarter mile.

The dyno facility above is used to test and build engines as seen in the picture to the right.

Robert Read, Ph.D.

WINNERS...

#125. are asked to lead projects because success breeds success

"To be what we are, and to become what we are capable of becoming, is the only end of life."
(Robert Louis Stevenson)

  It tickles me that when I am in a meeting, I can instantly determine who the leaders are. In fact, frequently, I know who the leader is when he or she walks into the room. I know who means what he says and I know who does what he says. But then again, I'm also in meetings where the one leading it is not a leader and it is obvious that nothing is ever going to get accomplished because they don't know what they are doing. They think they know what they are doing, but everybody who is trying to follow them doesn't think that they know what they are doing and so it is a reverse self-fulfilling prophecy. What they are doing is dealing with failure. In such a scenario, a leader needs to evolve from the group to make things happen or nothing ever does.

WINNERS...

#126. know who the leaders are and appreciate that they get the job done

"All successful employers are stalking men who will do the unusual, men who think, men who attract attention by performing more than is expected of them."
(Charles M. Schwab)

  Portec frequently saw me in a leadership position, like the time when I was a plant engineer. We had a large shipment that needed to be sent by rail. We had a local transportation rail engine pull some product out of the plant the day before and the train derailed. Our track rolled on one side so a repair company came in with a big crane and got our train back on the track. The company representative left saying that they wouldn't come back until we got the track repaired.
  So we went to inspect the track and all the millwrights and the welders were standing around looking at it saying, "This is impossible." Every spike in it was ripped out. The train had derailed for 100 feet and had just destroyed everything. I asked, "Has anybody here ever driven spikes?"

"Well, no."

"Well, I haven't either," I said.

A welder said, "We have a couple of spike sledge hammers here."

They are a funny looking hammer and weigh quite a bit. They have a long nose on them about ten inches long, and they are double headed so that when you hit the spike the handle doesn't hit the side of the rail. We had to get started because it looked like it was about an eight hour job. So I put some old clothes on, went out, and started driving spikes. They thought that was funny, but I could actually drive a spike as well as anyone. We worked for six or seven hours straight, respiked the whole track, and regauged it. We gauged it with tape measures and the entire job was a lot of fun.

About half way through this I said, "If we get this done by dark, we'll all go to the tavern and I will buy you all beer for the rest of the night." That is what we did! We had unbelievable camaraderie. This is what leadership is all about. **You lead by example. When you tell someone you are going to do something, you do it. When you tell them how you are going to do it, that is how you do it. When it is all done, if you promised them something, you do that.** I think from that moment on, I had quite a rapport with all the maintenance people because they knew that I knew what I was talking about and they knew that I could actually do the job if I had to do the job.

WINNERS...

#127. lead by example, sharing their expertise by assisting where necessary

And the Lord's bond-servant must not be quarrelsome, but be kind to all, able to teach, patient when wronged...
(2 Timothy 2:24)

Entertain Fresh and New Ideas

The other thing that I learned by being a leader early on, particularly when I was a young man in my early 20s, was to never discount a young person. It was easy to say back then, but even today, I never discount a young person. Such an individual doesn't know that something won't work, so they can look at a problem from a fresh perspective and maybe find a solution.

When managers advertise for an engineer, they want someone who has done it all and has had a lot of experience. If the engineer has had 30 years experience, then the managers think that he has gained all of his valuable knowledge at the plants where he has worked his entire life. That may be all well and good, but there is a possible drawback. Maybe this knowledge is not what is best for the new job. It may be a debatable statement, but it's one of the drawbacks in hiring older engineers. He may not be open minded. He may see things as he has seen them work before, and I can tell you that what has worked before isn't necessarily the best way to do something now. It is not necessarily the quickest, the cheapest, or the best way to do something. But someone with a young mind can look at something and say, "I wonder why you have always done it this way?" They can look at it and say, "That is a dumb way to do it. Let's do it this way." He doesn't know that what he is proposing, the older engineer would look at and say, "Well, that is not going to work because once upon a time..."

Times are continually changing. How do you know it won't work? Maybe it wouldn't have worked 20 years ago, but guess what? It might work now with different materials, different applications, new computers, and everything else that we have. What didn't work 20 years ago may work just fine right now. **So there are advantages to giving youth an opportunity and employing them. They have fresh, new ideas with no preconceived notions that this won't work or that can't work. They actually have no fear that it won't work, so in trying, it may work.** If you don't attempt something, you will never accomplish it or even begin the process of change for the better.

WINNERS...

#128. encourage fresh thinking by involving youth in problem solving

Therefore encourage one another, and build up one another, just as you also are doing.
(1 Thessalonians 5:11)

Let no one look down on your youthfulness...
(1 Timothy 4:12)

Another thought about youth and leadership is that you never stop learning. You never complete your education. With the same enthusiasm and reckless abandon that you use to solve problems, to invent things, and to engineer and reengineer things, you need to recognize that someone else might have a better idea than you do. You need to realize when someone else knows something that you don't know. **It is really nice to hire youth because of their thought process and the fact that they don't entertain the idea that something won't work. But when you get an older person who thinks the same way as these youth do, that is, they realize that they can continue to learn, then you really have an excellent employee.** This is why life, until you die, is a total learning experience, and if you are unwilling to acknowledge that someone else has a better idea or knows different things than you do, you will never go anywhere in this world. So your lifetime education is exactly that. You never stop learning! You never stop saying, "What if? What if I do it this way? What if I did this? What if I did that?" Never stop trying to raise the standard. Never stop pursuing excellence. Never stop trying to make something quicker, better, cheaper.

WINNERS...

#129. look to others for better ideas and knowledge
which they don't have

"The young man knows the rules,
but the old man knows the exceptions."
(Oliver Wendell Holmes)

Realize Knowledge is Power

One thing that I tell young people when I talk to them is just how important knowledge is. The following is one of my recent speeches to those attending an academic achievement awards banquet at the Jay County High School, Portland, Indiana, where I said that "knowledge is power." The more knowledge that you have, the more power you have. I believe that the students in attendance were extremely intelligent and hard working because they had to have a 3.8 or higher grade point average to be at this ceremony.

"Good evening students, parents, teachers, and administrators. I would like to share some of my real world knowledge that I have gained through my own experiences with you this evening. There are several things that I wish to talk about with you. I want to talk about eliminating several words from your vocabulary. I want to talk about education. I want to talk about work. I want to talk about time management in your life – AND I want to talk about success.

You look around and you wonder how some people can manage to get so many things accomplished. They always have time to help, they are always there when something needs to be done, and they still manage to get everything done. Well, chances are that those people have eliminated the word "procrastinate" from their vocabulary. Never put off doing something today 'til tomorrow. You see, life is an opportunity and you want to be caught up on your daily activities so that you are free to spot and grab an opportunity. If you are always behind and playing catch up by putting things off, you are going to be busy playing catch up when an opportunity arises. Believe me, it is easy to spot an opportunity, but hard to take advantage of it. If you are busy playing catch up, you cannot take advantage of it.

When I talk to young people, I often ask them how old they hope to live. The answer is usually 80. Now most of you students out there are 15, 16, 17 years old. You have basically lived one-fifth of your life and you think you have all kinds of time. Well, you have four-fifths of your life left, but I am here to tell you that you don't have all the time in the world. You do not have a minute to waste. In fact, you do not have a second to waste. Someday, you will wish you had that second back or that minute back or that day back that you wasted. If you hope to live to be 80, well, when you hit 40, your life is half over. If you are an optimist you are going to say, "Well, I have half of my life to live," and if you are a pessimist you will say, "Wow, my life is half over." Something that I do not want you students to do when you turn the magic number 40 is to say, "Boy, I have wasted all this time in my life and I have to get in gear and get things accomplished." The reason I do not want you to say that is because, believe me, your life may be half over but your gas tank only has about a quarter tank of fuel left in it.

Trust me, you can get a lot more done from 0 to 40 than you will ever get done from 40 to 80 because you are basically running out of gas.

Like myself, I have spent most of my life operating on four or five hours sleep a night. Well, right now I need six to seven hours sleep. I am going to waste several years in the next 40 years sleeping because my life has reached that half way mark.

The next thing I want to talk about is education. You students have my admiration for your success in your academics. I can personally tell you from my own experience in high school and college that I should have paid attention and received better grades. But before I get into talking about education and advanced courses and things like that, I want to talk a little bit about the lack of education.

No doubt you have all heard stories of very, very successful people like Sam Walton and other people who barely made it to the eighth grade. Very successful, very wealthy, and you look at someone like that and you think to yourself, "How can this be?" Well, it was easy. The people who make it in this world without a formal education know how to work hard, know how to work smart, and have a total grasp of the obvious. But guess what? If you can do those three things and combine them with your knowledge, and then gain more knowledge, the world is yours! Education is the foundation for the rest of your lives. It is the building block that you will continue to build on because education is knowledge and power.

Now, speaking of the rest of your lives, I sincerely hope that everyone in here realizes that you are going to have to work the rest of your lives. I hope you realize that is why you are here. You are here getting an education and knowledge so that you can work the rest of your life. If you have to work the rest of your life, you want a fun job and you want to make an above average wage so that you can live an above average standard of living. I sincerely hope that someday after you have worked a lot of your life you will be able to say what I have said. I have not actually "worked" for over 25 years. I have loved what I have done so much that I would not call it "work" and I would basically do it for free. In fact, I used to come home from Teledyne, get paid once a month, throw the check on the table and say, "Can you believe this, Marianne (my wife)? They actually pay me to do this." I hope that I hear some of you say that someday. That means that you are having fun, that you are a benefit to society, a benefit to yourself, and a benefit to your boss.

Another word I would like for you to eliminate from your vocabulary is the word, "luck." Luck only applies to winning the lottery. Success in business comes when preparation meets opportunity and that is not luck.

Now what is opportunity? Opportunity is working smart. This is my own percentage that I have come up with but I believe that about 95% of the world wants to follow. Only about 5% want to lead. Why is this? Well, to follow is safe. If something goes wrong with an engineering project or whatever you are working on and you are in a group, they are not going to fire the whole bunch of you. But what is the inverse of that? Well, if it goes right, you are not all going to get promoted. The person leading and who is in charge is the one who is going to get promoted. You can look at the negative side of that and say, "Yeah, but if it goes wrong, the guy leading is going to lose his job." Well, that is true but that is another word to eliminate from your vocabulary. The word "negative." I don't acknowledge that "negative" even exists.

Almost anything in this world that is said to be negative can be viewed at an acute or an obtuse enough angle to see some good in it. Even if you absolutely cannot find any good in a negative experience, guess what? It is a totally positive learning experience. So you do not look at what can happen if it goes wrong. It's like a self-fulfilling prophecy. You look at everything positively and it will make everything in your life positive. People will follow a positive thinking individual.

Another thing about success and business is that I fully believe that 75% of all promotions in this world go to the person who is in the right place at the right time. That is what you would call working smart. You put yourself in the right place at the right time so that when a promotion becomes available, you are right for the job, but if you work smart, you are the only person for the job.

One thing I have found is that I like to relate to life as a game. It is a big game. All you have to do is have confidence in what you are doing, do what you know is right, and things will go your way.

Now let's talk about success. How do you know you are successful? Well, somebody will probably tell you that. Somebody will say, "Yeah, you are successful." Well, trust me, take it with a grain of salt. I subscribe to the theory that you can never actually think that you are successful. About the time that you think you are successful is about the time you become complacent. It is like Lee Iacocca said on the Chrysler advertisement years ago, "You either lead, follow, or get out of the way."

When you become complacent is about the time you get run over by somebody leaner, meaner, and hungrier than you ever were. When you are at the top of the bell curve and not going up, the only way is down. I like to think that you need to conduct your life like you are running the 100 yard dash and there is no finish line. That way, with enough of a head start, you keep running and even a Michael Jordan couldn't catch you. Now, from everything I have just told you, you want to be current, you want to help people, you want to volunteer your time, you want to get everything done, and you want to do everything that you want to do so that if you should pass away in your sleep tonight, you know and God will know that you did your very best. If you are fortunate enough to wake up tomorrow morning, then you have the opportunity to do an even better job tomorrow than you did today.

In closing, I want to congratulate each of you students on your awards this evening and I wish you all success in your future. Thank you and good night."

Practice What You Preach

Speaking to a group of students in my home town can be a challenge. Not so much because I have to write the speech, but because I have to live by the words I say. Do you realize that everything that you say indicates whether you are a leader or a loser? Whether planned or off the cuff, your choice of words, gestures, and tone tells the world who you are.

The language you use tells everyone about your personality, your attitude, and your potential for success. It determines not only how other people view you, but also how you feel about yourself.

What you see in your mind is what you say from your mouth. What you sow is what you reap. What you speak is who you are. The question is whether you wish to be a leader or something else. By not making a choice, I can assure you how others will view you and, unfortunately, how people view you is often how you actually become.

In general, losers complain, say they will try, and generally give the impression that they will do what needs to be done if forced to do so. **Leaders, on the other hand, keep any negative thoughts to themselves, say they will do the job, and they do it. They keep a positive outlook toward everything knowing that they can work things out eventually.**

The term "failure" is not a part of the leader's vocabulary. He or she will learn new ways to accomplish a task by turning "I can't," "I don't," or "I won't," into "I will," "I'll do my best," or "I haven't up until now, but I..." Problems are looked at as opportunities, and challenges as ways to improve one's future.

Losers say, "It's not my job." Leaders say "Yes, I will assist as I have time." The difference is in the sincerity of heart to do the best you can. Positive thinking and speaking will build your mental well being and change your outlook on life. A smile and warm welcome to greet individuals is indicative of a leader, but an "always too busy attitude" in response to other people's needs moves a person away from leading and toward losing. The key is to always be sincere in your reactions to others so that they can sense your desire to meet their needs. The best way to lose is to play like you're sincere and not be. For example, you may be sitting with a colleague and appear that you are listening, but when a question is asked of you by that person, you do not have any idea what has been said. You were hearing the words spoken but not listening to them. Not listening is indicative of the loser who appears to be interested in what another has to say, but really is not.

Begin to listen to yourself. Be sensitive as to who you would like to be and work on being where you would like to be. The process is not difficult but the attitude change may be. Start practicing today by saying how great you wish to be, thinking positive thoughts, and smiling sincerely at those who pass your way. It won't be long before others will recognize you as a leader!

WINNERS...

#130. are leaders planting good seed to harvest a plentiful crop

So then you will know them by their fruits.
(Matthew 7:20)

Be Mentally and Physically Fit

Mental and physical fitness go together. Every night that I am home, I try to swim a mile just to stay physically fit and mentally alert. This is so I have the stamina to do everything that I am trying to accomplish. I exercise daily and have to really be careful when I am swimming 50 laps because I will get so engrossed in thinking about projects and how to solve problems, which are nothing more than opportunities to succeed, that I have nearly knocked myself out hitting the end of the pool with my head. I am concentrating on fixing something or reengineering this or designing that for the business or for someone else.

WINNERS...

#131. desire to stay fit in order to have the stamina
to lead and help others

Do you not know that you are a temple of God,
and that the Spirit of God dwells in you?
If any man destroys the temple of God, God will destroy him,
for the temple of God is holy, and that is what you are.
(1 Corinthians 3:16-17)

It is really ironic that there are so many things out there in this world that need to be fixed. For example, Bill Davis, president of the Portland Country Club, called me one day and said "I have a slight problem. Could I come and talk to you?" So he showed up with a print of a new bridge they wanted to build across one of the little streams on the golf course. It was an elaborate structure. I mean elaborate with all kinds of trusses and braces. He said, "I have priced this out and the engineering firms have quoted a price that is totally outrageous! Can you figure the stresses on this structure?" I responded enthusiastically, "Boy, yeah, I can do that."

So he left and I started to look at the print and thought, "Oh, boy!

This looks like a lot of fun." I got out my engineering books and my college dynamics book, and spent all afternoon calculating this project. I figured how many golf carts you could line up on the bridge loaded with two people and two sets of golf clubs and figured out what the forces were. Then I called him up and said, "This is what you want to do and this is how you want to do it."

The bridge is working just fine. There are so many ways in this world to help people, and I not only view it as something a person should want to do to make the world a better place for everyone else, but I think it should be mandatory. It is very difficult for me to say "no" to anyone for any project whether it is for my time, money, advice, or whatever. **I firmly believe that it is every person's responsibility to make the world a better place for everyone in their community, if not the whole world. By making your community or your county or your state a better place for other people to live, you, in turn, make it a better place for you to live.**

With my community service, volunteerism, and work, I am just as tired at night when I go to bed now as I was the first 40 years of my life. Every once in a while I will go have a complete physical. I will get on the treadmill and run my guts out for two reasons. First, I have had several people in my family die from cancer so, if there is anything wrong with me, I would like to know. The second reason I do this is to see how far I can push myself. I want to know what my point of exhaustion is so I can push myself right up to that limit.

By staying physically and mentally fit, I am constantly exercising my brain and my body so that I can handle anything that comes along. In fact, it is quite a game I play with myself as to just how much I can handle. I have never reached the end point yet. People keep asking me to assist on projects. I keep building things at work, reengineering products, and figuring out better ways to do things. You would think you would get your mind full, but it's impossible! Your mind can do anything. All you have to do is do it and it gets done. It is an interesting scenario that you would think you could overload your brain, but you really can't. Physical and mental well being are important to me and should be to every leader and winner.

Chapter Twelve

WINNER'S CIRCLE

**Building Our Home
Enjoying Our Home
Making the World a Better Place
Volunteering to Help Others**

Whether we are racing cars, designing and building things, or starting a business, Marianne and I have decided it is all a game. **It is fun to play games and once you begin to achieve whatever goal you set, it is time to move the goal out farther or the target higher just to keep moving forward.** Each game is basically something to keep our brains occupied and then it is on to the next project. As we approach the winner's circle, or goal accomplished, in any game, it is a joy to experience the rewards or satisfaction of completing that game successfully.

WINNERS...

#132. move from project to project viewing them as games played with a purpose

"A man without a purpose is like a ship without a rudder."
(Thomas Carlyle)

Building our Home

One of the projects that my wife and I have done to occupy our time and keep active has been to build a large home. We wanted it to be totally unique and different from anything anyone else has ever built. We decided that the exotic should be incorporated into the design and furnishings. I came to find out, though, that there was no one who could make those things or provide them for us. Marianne and I spent five years planning every detail. The home took four years to complete, so it was a nine year project!

Even though nine years may seem like a long time, we have the innate ability to look at everything, break it down, and determine what it is going to take. We basically created a light at the end of the tunnel and went for it. You could say that it would have taken a lot of patience, but it really didn't. Because the project was so enormous and massive, we were moving along briskly to get the thing done in nine years!

The home is over 15,000 square feet. The shop or garage area is 12,000 square feet. It has five bedrooms, ten bathrooms, four kitchens, a sunken living room that is two and a half stories high with an imported marble fireplace, a den, a grand piano room, a lot of hall space with balconies, and a basement having a theater room with tiered seating and a 104 inch television screen surrounded by four 30 inch monitors.

The viewing area has all the latest trickery including digital viewing disk and laser disk. We also have a total home sound system so every room can have up to eight different modes of music. Our 150 gallon salt water live coral reef tank graces the entrance to a bar that was designed to be a replica of anything you would find in a fancy lounge. There are two pool tables, a gun-room, since I like to shoot rifles and pistols, an exercise room, and a family room with a fire place. The other fire place is in the master bedroom where the master bath features a heated floor, two person hot tub, 27 shower head J-Dream, and a door opening onto a deck where we have a ten person hot tub. The in-ground, arch roof enclosed, 20 ft. by 50 ft., twelve foot deep pool has an outdoor waterpark slide from the bedroom balcony into the deep end and a one meter board for diving.

One exciting touch to the home is a fireman's pole that goes from one story to the next. It has a solid brass and glass surround that I had to personally build myself because I couldn't find anyone who could even remotely construct it. All of the wrought iron and brass railing outside is custom built and the rocks were imported from Arizona. The entire house is a wood worker's dream with the first and second floor finished in solid cherry. Even the doors are solid cherry! The main large spiral staircases, handrails, and banisters are cherry. We have two spiral stairways that run for three stories that are solid cherry. Nothing like this, with everything in solid cherry, has ever been built according to the manufacturer. The downstairs is solid oak. The pool is surrounded by oak and cedar. The exterior of the home is cedar. We have miles and miles and miles of copper in the ground and the house is very well insulated to make total use of its direct conversion geo thermal heat. For anyone who does not know what direct conversion is, you pump a Freon-like substance directly into the coils that are in the soil so that it is converted energy when it comes back into your heating unit. Before that, the most efficient method was to pump the antifreeze or ethylene substance through the coils and that would come back and change the Freon to create heating and cooling in the system. We keep the pool (which is 55,000 gallons) at 86 degrees and the outdoor hot tub at 101 degrees. We air condition and heat all 27,000 square feet and the typical dead-of-the-winter heat bill is only 900 bucks. If you figure that out for a typical 2,000 square foot home, it is almost free electricity. The design of the house keeps the cost down.

We spent five years engineering our home. We took the time for every room, whether it was the bathroom, the grand piano room, the barrel vault, or dining room, to create something unusual and unique. Our whole goal with the house was to create something in each room so that a person would walk in and say, "This is unbelievable. I have never seen anything like this before." Whether it is the bathroom or the pool, the pool tables, the bar, the salt water aquarium, the theater room, the spiral stairway, or the fireman's pole, we wanted each room to be a "WOW!" We have an H.O. layout table that is incorporated into the downstairs, on which my daughter and I are building a 180 foot H.O. train layout. Anyone who would walk into the train area or one of the other rooms in the house would just stand there and say, "This is unbelievable." The house was designed and engineered so that you could select just one room, look at it, and say, "I have never seen anything like this before in my life." This was our goal, and I know we achieved it.

The garage, in which I keep my collection of cars, has hot-water floor heat as does the basement. The floor is segregated into three sections and has the drain grid floor system like you would find in a Chevy or a Ford dealership. It is all paneled with fluorescent lights everywhere, electrical outlets with 220V and 110V every eight feet, and compressed air lines around the whole circumference. The home and the garage were built with steel beams hidden by wood. In fact, there are 36 inch beams in the ceiling of the garage so that we can store cars on the second story. You wonder how the cars get up there? Well, we have a car elevator that I engineered and built that raises the cars from the first to the second floor. The garage also has a fully automatic touchless car wash system. Totally engineered and built by myself, this enclosed system is all aluminum and stainless steel and after you drive in you punch a remote button and the car gets washed. It is all automatic and you do not touch anything!

Another unusual feature of the house is that the exterior is either copper, rock, or cedar. We have a large hospital type caterpillar diesel generator that will run the entire operation for one week at a time. We also have a basketball court and a tennis court. We spent a fortune on landscaping and the home was actually built and engineered with a foundation having twice as much concrete in it as what a normal engineer would put in a project like this. Also, it has four times the rebar in the foundation. In fact, my criteria when the home was built was to see it standing 500 years from now. Believe me, it will be! What my wife and I are setting up is a trust fund so our home can be maintained forever after we die and so that the kids will have a guest house for the plant and a vacation home for family members should they wish to visit.

The wiring on the landscape lighting was completed by myself. Most of the stuff I did myself because I just couldn't find someone to do the quality of craftsmanship that I demanded. Even if I could have found the workers, they would have been too busy to do the work for me so I would have ended up doing it all myself anyway. That is the joy of a project like this. If you do it yourself, you know it is perfect and you know it is done right. In fact, my home was probably a builder's dream. When my builders, Neil and Karen Whitner from Hiedel Burg homes out of Fort Wayne, Indiana, were working on the project, they would say, "Well, this is the way this ought to be done and this is the way someone else would do it." I would say, "Well, if this were your home and you really didn't care what it cost, how would you do it?" They would say, "Well, I would do it this way." So I said, "Then that's how I want you to do it." I wanted the place to be immaculate and I wanted it to last forever and that is what I got. I am pleased with the results. Very few people could build a project that is as enormous as this is and still be friends with the builders. In fact, we try to go out to dinner every two or three months with them. We gained lifelong friends. They do quality work and I appreciate quality work. We get along really well.

Our home is built on 80 acres and my next year's project is to buy a bulldozer to carve out a 40 acre lake on which to water ski. This project should be interesting and I want to do it myself. It will be fun!

Enjoying our Home

You are probably wondering, "Why on earth would somebody build a lake?" Well, we spend most of our time away from home. We are usually off racing and when we come home, we want something to come home to so that we don't have to go anywhere else. So everything that we like to do is at our home. Everything! We also like to entertain and we wanted a home that was comfortable for entertaining. We have parties for our employees. New Year's Eve parties and things like that are some of our favorites and we wanted a home large enough in which to entertain with enough activities to do so that people would feel comfortable and have a good time.

One of the reasons why we built our home was to help out the community. We have had House of Representative candidates use our home for fund-raisers and we have used it several times for United Way fund-raisers. We have had fund-raisers for the American Red Cross, as well as for the Jay County Arts Council, and we have also used our home for weddings. The home has been used to raise a lot of money for the Jay County community and we have been happy to use it for that purpose. It is unusual and totally hidden in the woods. You cannot see it from the road and to get to it you go back a lane, cross over a little creek on a bridge that I engineered, and arrive at the entrance in fine fashion. It is designed so that nobody can really see what is going on unless you are invited back there. The home was built to entertain and to help the community. It is someplace for Marianne and me to crash, and it serves that purpose well. It was also built to occupy our minds as one of our multiple projects.

We recently completed a brand new Moser Engineering facility at a cost of $1,300,000. This 30,000 square foot manufacturing plant is located in the industrial park near our home. Once we are done with one project, we go on to the next project, then to another, and so on. In fact, one of my goals is that when my company reaches $10,000,000 in sales, I want to buy my own plane. I want my own Citation jet so I can travel more quickly and efficiently and then be able to spend more time doing what I want to do at home. Everything we do revolves around a goal, but we never quite obtain those goals because we are always moving the target out when we get close. **We might seem to be in the winner's circle, but we really think of that circle as being comprised of our family, friends, and community who all enjoy the rewards of our blessed lives.**

WINNERS...

#133. consider success to be the sharing of their rewards with others

**And do not neglect doing good and sharing;
for with such sacrifices God is pleased.
(Hebrews 13:16)**

Making the World a Better Place

Speaking about the winner's circle, what do you do after you have won the race? If it has to do with racing, the satisfaction of winning a race is short lived because you always find something that you could have done better or should have done better. It is just like in golf where you are trying to better your last score. So, too, in racing, you always wish to improve upon the last time. In business, many consider the winner's circle to be success and dollars in the bank. **My thought on perceived success and money, and I truly believe what I am about to say, is that you have to learn to live within yourself.** You have to define happiness for yourself and recognize where you have been and where you are going.

WINNERS...

#134. continually reach for new goals
but have inner peace at all times

"And the Lord is the one who goes ahead of you
He will be with you. He will not fail you or forsake you.
Do not fear, or be dismayed."
(Deuteronomy 31:8)

Most people seem to think that there is something else out there. That the grass is greener on the other side of the fence. **They never reach happiness because they have never defined it for themselves in the first place.** You take a "so-called" highly successful man in our society, for instance, who after his wife works for years to help put him through college, easily dumps her and marries some sweet, cute little thing in his search for happiness. A lot of business people can't live within themselves and they do crazy things. They seem to think that there is something else out there. I have seen so many careers ruined by successful men chasing women because they think there is something better out there.

WINNERS...

#135. know what happiness is and will focus
on what it takes to achieve it

When you shall eat of the fruit of your hands,
you will be happy and it will be well with you.
(Psalm 128:2)

Drugs are rampant in our society. We see their use in professional sports. Many players in professional sports should thank their lucky stars that I am not the commissioner of the league in which they are playing. If I were the commissioner, any person caught doing drugs who had been elevated to superstar, idol, or hero status would be out of sports for the rest of their lives. You say, "Man, that's pretty drastic. These guys are only human." I say, "Management is at fault, too." The people who own these teams are so hungry to win that they actually employ these drug users! They shouldn't even be allowed to play, but more than that, the owners obviously have no morals either. They could care less about what they are doing to today's youth. All they are concerned about is winning and they line up to rehire these guys. So, it's everyone's fault. The same is true with business people when observers say, "They are only human when they go a little off the deep end and look for something else. They are only looking for a little something to somehow satisfy their lives."

What I am about to say is going to hit home. Children learn by example. You can tell them to do this. You can tell them not to do that. But they are going to learn by example. What example is being set by a hero or an idol or a superstar who gets caught doing drugs, gets a year suspension, gets back into the sport, gets caught again doing drugs, gets some more suspension, and is back in the game again? What message is that sending to our young people? These people are actually helping the moral decay of our entire society. **When someone reaches the hero, superstar, or idol status, they are beyond being human. There is no room for error. It is their responsibility to behave correctly, to be someone for a young person to idolize and to want to be like, and it is their total responsibility to lead a straight life. Period.**

Now, for all of you people out there who are saying, "There has to be something else out there to do once I've been successful," I have these thoughts for you. Business is just like sports. **When you are on top of your game, you are a mentor. You are a hero to somebody because of your success and it is your responsibility to behave accordingly.** You must set an example for young children and adults, colleagues and associates, and anyone else who might want to emulate you. That is just one of the many responsibilities of receiving a higher salary, better benefits, and an appropriate title for the job you do!

WINNERS...

**#136. are mentors to society and must live the part
by setting the example**

> **Let no one look down on your youthfulness,
> but rather in speech, conduct, love, faith and purity,
> show yourself an example of those who believe.
> (1 Timothy 4:12)**

Remember, if you are perceived as being a success, then somebody is looking at you. You are somebody's hero and you must conduct your life such that those observing you will use you as an example of the correct way to conduct their business and lives. Using impeccable ethics, virtue, and integrity, you will help raise a new generation of young people who will be an asset to this world, which will, in turn, make this world a better place for you and the generations to come.

So what do you do when you are looking for something else out there? **Well, the thing that I have found, and if it works for me, I know it will work for you, is to help other people.** While there is much satisfaction in getting ahead and being successful, there is just as much satisfaction in helping other people be successful. This can be done in many different areas. I know I get great satisfaction when people call me up and say, "I've got this invention. Would you look at it and tell me what you think?" I not only tell them what I think, but if I think it's a good idea, I'll tell them how to manufacture it and how to market it. I do not want anything in return for doing this. It is my responsibility to help other people, especially having reached the comfort level I have in my life. It goes beyond helping your family and it goes beyond helping your employees. **You will find that by helping anyone and everyone, you will make the world a better place for them, which will, in turn, make the world a better place for you.**

WINNERS...

#137. return what they can to the world to make it a better place for all

> *So then, while we have opportunity, let us do good to all men...*
> *(Galatians 6:10)*

Volunteering to Help Others

By not procrastinating, by not putting anything off, by doing everything when it needs to be done, and by doing it on time, you would be amazed at what you can actually accomplish. You'd also be amazed at what your expertise will actually do to help a community. Because you have been perceived successful in business, people will want you to help them in projects and community projects. My involvement in the community really took off when my sister became ill with cancer. **It became apparent to me that God really smiled upon me by allowing me to live. I still have not figured out why He took my beautiful sister, but it may have been to encourage me to help others.** She's gone and there is nothing I can do about it but to make the best of it and do my best, so that someday I can see her again in heaven. So I do a lot of work for the community. A lot of people have made the comment, "This guy does the volunteer work of two people." Well, I should, because my sister is no longer here to do her part and I wish to do it in her memory.

WINNERS...

#138. respond to God's calling not by questioning but by doing

Little children, let us not love with word or with tongue, but in deed and truth. (1 John 3:18)

Two years ago, I was the general chair person for the United Way Fund Drive. We set a record for the campaign that year. At the same time, I was the president of the Portland Chamber of Commerce, vice-chair of a local emergency planning committee, director of the east central Indiana Advisory Council, and director of the First National Bank Board of Trustees. This latter position is for life and affords me an opportunity to take bank employees to the races on occasion.

As the president of Rotary and present director, I have applied the Rotarian's four-way test whenever possible in my life. **Is it the truth? Is it fair to all concerned? Will it be beneficial to all concerned? Will it build good will and better friendships? These are four questions to ask in everything you do in life.** I believe in Rotary, in what a Rotarian should stand for, and in the four-way test.

WINNERS...

#139. seek the truth

You shall know the truth, and the truth shall make you free. (John 8:32)

Over the years, I have been a chair of just about every department in the United Way. As the chair for the United Way's dollar a week campaign, I spoke before 560 teachers from the Jay county School Corporation. Trying to get everyone to contribute to the United Way is an endless task. It just never ends! **You get done with one project or one party or one fund-raiser, and you have another one. I guess that is how fund-raising goes. A true statement is, "If you want something done, ask a busy person to do it."** There is always a way to get something else done.

WINNERS...

#140. lead in the spirit of giving to help others

**He who gives to the poor will never want,
But he who shuts his eyes will have many curses.
(Proverbs 28:27)**

A group of volunteers including Phil France, who is the leadership chair of the United Way, Gary Huber, who is the overall chair, John Coldren, and I, all showed up to give our spiel to the high school teachers. I am sure we will gain a few extra dollars from it. In fact, every year we have a record United Way campaign. Last year, we had 1,800 people give $161,000. One hundred and four of those people gave $56,000. Those are our "Patriot Brigade" givers and they are phenomenal. In our community, with its 21,800 residents of which 12,600 are employed, if every one gave a dollar each week, we would collect over $650,000. There is a totally untapped potential in Jay County. That is one reason why I like to tackle the dollar a week campaign. I will be talking to every business owner, every industry person, the high school teachers, and professional people. **I am going to talk to everyone who employs someone in Jay County to promote my dollar a week campaign because a dollar a week by itself is nothing, but multiply it by 12,600 times 52 weeks and you have $650,000.00.** It's just a candy bar. If I can get everybody to do that, think of what a wonderful place Jay County will be.

WINNERS...

#141. know that if all do their part in giving
a lot more can be done

"In every thing I showed you that by working hard
in this manner you must help the weak and
remember the words of the Lord Jesus, that He Himself said,
'It is more blessed to give than to receive.'"
(Acts 20:35)

Chapter Thirteen

SHARING THE WEALTH

The Library Fund-raiser
The Arts Council Project
The Arts Council Speech
Philanthropy

From my committee work to helping others, I believe in sharing the wealth. This is a natural progression from the winner's circle and should be the goal of every successful person. Over the past few chapters, you have seen what it takes to be a winner and now I will tell you how to maintain your status as a winner.

The Library Fund-raiser

A new library was proposed for the 21,800 people in Jay County during the same time I was busy in the community. The library's Board of Directors had put together the plans and had proposed a state bond to fund it. You have to have so many signatures for the bond issue. They went out, obtained 950 signatures, filed all the paperwork, and, at that point, allowed anyone in the community a chance to remonstrate against the bond issue. Quite a few people got heavily involved and obtained over 1,000 signatures against the library. In other words, the remonstrance was successful. One of the big concerns was that the remonstrators didn't want their taxes to go up much. On a $3,000,000 project, they only wanted to have a $1,600,000 tax burden.

Reading about this in the papers, I looked at it and didn't think any more about it until the remonstrance was successful. **It really bothered me. I sat down and talked to Marianne about it, and, in fact, I sat down and wrote a letter to the editor of the newspaper describing my displeasure with the citizens of Jay County for their remonstrance against the library.** I hadn't even known who our librarian was so I told Marianne, "I wrote a letter but didn't mail it." Then I asked Marianne, "Who is our librarian?" She said, "Rosalie Clamme." So I called Rosie, as she calls herself, and said, "What is going on? Why on earth would anyone be against such a worthwhile project for this community?" I just ranted and raved and said that these people were crazy. Libraries are the second most important structure for our children with the school being number one. It's just beyond my comprehension.

WINNERS...

#142. release ill feelings immediately so appropriate action may be taken

"Work joyfully and peacefully, knowing that right thoughts and right efforts will inevitably bring about right results."
(James Allen)

A few months later I got a phone call and Rosie said, "Would you be interested in serving on a committee to review what the Library Board did right and what they did wrong to cause this remonstrance?" I said, "Certainly!" Dean Jetter of Fort Recovery Industries, Inc. was the chairperson of the committee and we became very involved. We reviewed everything that the Library Board had done. We reviewed the size of the library, the cost of everything in the library, and we visited other libraries to review the construction, cost, and the size of their library in comparison with the circulation of our library and its book usage. We put together a lot of recommendations and we talked to the architect quite a few times. We basically took our jobs very seriously. We probably spent eight or nine months reviewing everything that the Library Board had done.

During the time we were putting our conclusions together, it became apparent that the structure which the Library Board had submitted was not possible to build. It was a $2,600,000 structure and the library had saved only $500,000 over the years in the library fund. So the new library would still require a $2,200,000 bond. Dean had asked some remonstrators to speak to our committee so we could get them on our side. What we were told was that the bond could be no more than $1,700,000. At that point, we realized that if we wanted to get these people on our side we would have to find a new way to build this library. So we cut the project back to its bare bones and figured out how much we would have to raise. We took everything out, including the kitchen sink, and presented it to the Board and said, "This is what you are going to have to do to get this thing to fly." We found out what had gone wrong and we found out what we could do to make it right because you have to wait a year after a successful remonstrance before you can repetition the state for another bond issue.

Now, like I said, Rosie had saved about $500,000 in the library fund and we submitted all this to the Library Board. Based on the library fund, a possible state grant, and a $1,700,000 bond, we were going to have to raise around $375,000. Most of the people on the review committee thought, "That is just not possible. There is no way in the world we can raise that kind of money." I thought about it and I knew how important the library had been to me and my family and basically said, "If we can't raise that kind of money, we shouldn't even be here. I see no problem whatsoever." So as we concluded our review committee, I received a phone call within a week and the Board asked me if I would volunteer to head up a fund drive. Even though I was involved with everything I previously described, serving on ten committees, I volunteered and said I would chair the fund drive!

My committee consisted of seven people including Rosie Clamme, Bill Hinkle, Ramon Loucks, Phil France, Donna Haggenjos, and Gary Huber. We thought about our strategy for raising this $375,000. Our first thought was, "Well, we need to take a couple of the rooms in the library and put price tags on them and tell people if they were to give 'x' amount of money, they would have a plaque naming them as the room's donor." So we planned to have three $50,000 rooms, several $25,000 rooms, a couple of 15's and a couple of 10's. We put together a list of the people in town who might be interested in our high dollar rooms and contacted them first so that they would have an opportunity to say "yes" or "no" to the room before anyone else.

Within the first few hours I signed up for a major room as did the First National Bank and the Portland Foundation. So in the span of one day, we had sold three of the major rooms. Barry Hudson from the First National Bank then had a board meeting with Mutual Securities and brought our project to their attention. We had carefully laid this out and he took the information that we had given to him to this board meeting and they looked it over and said, "We will take this $10,000 room here." This was a group that we didn't even have on our list to contact for a $10,000 room. So I had a little emergency meeting and got my gang back together and said, "We have a problem. We don't have enough rooms!" So we spent the next couple of hours finding 20 areas in the library on which we could put a price tag. We ended up selling every one of them. We also had etched glass windows that described donors names and then last, but not least, we put bricks on the paved walk in front of the library priced at $125. People bought these to contribute to a worthy cause and get recognition.

When our fund-raising was complete, the committee had privately raised $605,000. Rosie wrote the grant requests again and we received a federal grant, a state grant, and we even had a fund-raising race that went through Portland. This was a cross-country race which also had a pit stop competition visiting various cities with the winner to receive $3,000 worth of software and $5,000 for their local library. **So the entire town went wild on this competition. I spent quite a bit of time making an entrance arch through which we could welcome the racers.**

A local company called Art Craft did signs for recognition. The First National Bank sprung for some money to finish the decorations. Hunt's Emporium donated the balloons and I built the arch with my employees helping to paint it. We set this all up with checker board mat, balloons, a "Welcome Great Racers" sign, and won the contest hands down. We had the best pit stop in the whole United States. That put $5,000 in our hands for the library!

WINNERS...
#143. work behind the scene to ensure that all parties are participating

"Most successful men have not achieved their distinction by having some new talent or opportunity presented to them. They have developed the opportunity that was at hand." (Bruce Barton)

With the success in fund-raising, it meant that we not only could put everything back in the library that we had taken out, but we could use better materials, better furniture, and better woodwork. We had chandeliers installed and this library is something that you will never see in a community of 7,000 people in Portland proper and, as I said previously, 21,800 people living in the entire county. We ended up with about $3,300,000 in our library. It is beautiful. Also, we actually raised enough money that the bond that was needed came in less than we had anticipated. So not only did we not have a remonstrance, but we actually had remonstrators get on our side and actually make donations to the library!

In the end, I had a lot of help on this project, especially from my six committee members. The friends of the library awarded me Citizen of the Year and the Chamber of Commerce awarded me its Citizen of the Year. Also, the Indiana Federation of Libraries awarded me its Citizen of the Year and when I received the award, I found out that people like Bobby Knight of Indiana basketball fame had also won it. That was exciting for me. That is how I got involved in the library project. **I am a firm believer that you should put your efforts and money where your mouth is.**

When we were in the library review committee meeting and I made the statement, "If we can't raise that kind of money, we shouldn't even be here. I see no problem whatsoever," I was thinking of what is important for

Jay County. So when I was asked to head the fund drive, I did it. **I am a firm believer in action.**

On the other hand, if you ever see me at one of my children's basketball games or little league games, I never, ever yell at a referee. My children are all grown up, except for Danielle and she is still at home, but you will never see me yell! Why? Well, because I don't want that job. I don't want to have anything to do with what the referee is doing. **I do not want to do the job and there is no way that I can do the job any better than it is being done.** So I am absolutely not going to belittle someone or yell at them or holler at them because they are doing the best they can and I don't want to be asked to try to do a better job. **This is a matter of choosing not to take action.**

WINNERS...

#144. speak to implement change or keep their thoughts to themselves

...let everyone be quick to hear, slow to speak, and slow to anger.
(James 1:19)

Begin today to volunteer your time and help your community People want someone who has perceived success to head up campaigns. Any business person who is thinking, "I've got it made and I'm on top of the world," and who is trying to figure out what else there is in life, do what I have done. I really got wrapped up in the fund drive and with good members on my board, we built one of the finest libraries that you will ever see on the face of the earth in one of the smallest communities. It is just beautiful!

The library was an interesting project as far as raising funds because 2/3 of it was paid for by tax dollars. I didn't realize that until we actually pulled it off. It is really hard to do when there are tax dollars involved!

This is what people should do with their time after they've been successful and are looking for that something extra. So if you're out there and you're looking for something better or you're looking for something and you don't know what it is, volunteer for your community. Volunteer to help others. You will find that acknowledged expertise and involvement in projects will be a self-fulfilling prophecy. Everybody will assume that what you are doing is going to work, and it does work, because you have everybody on your side. If everybody is saying this is really going to work, well, it has a lot better chance of working, and you will have returned something to the community in which you live, resulting in greater happiness for everyone. Sometimes that happiness is the result of letters written about you and an award given to you. Such is the happiness I now enjoy from the following letters attesting to the great job we all did in building our community a new library!

THE GREG MOSER STORY

Jay County Public Library

131 E. WALNUT ST.
PORTLAND, IN 47371
AC 219-726-7890

December 27, 1995

Awards and Honors Committee
Indiana Library Federation
6408 Carrollton Avenue
Indianapolis, IN 46220

    Re: Achievements of Greg Moser

Dear Committee Members:

    In May of 1994 the news broke that a remonstrance was being waged against the bond issue of the Jay County Public Library. I received an unexpected call shortly thereafter from Greg Moser, a local businessman. He wanted to talk about the building project, as he was puzzled as to why anyone could be so against it.

    The remonstrance petition was successful. Believing a new building was still needed, the Library Board appointed a nine-member, independent Review Committee to re-examine the library's needs and the Board's proposed solution. Knowing of Greg's interest in the project, the Board President asked him to serve on the Committee. Greg readily accepted.

    The Review Committee met numerous times over the next five months, turning to experts in a variety of fields for advice, touring other libraries and crunching numbers. The ultimate decision: build it, but reduce the dependency on property taxes. In other words, go raise money.

    Throughout the review process, Greg looked for facts and figures from a businessman's perspective and continued to be enthusiastic about the project. Needing a fund raising chair person, the Board President again looked to Greg. Greg readily accepted. A minimum of $170,000 was needed to finish the basic structure. Additional funds would be needed to restore options cut by cost reductions.

    Over the next many months, Greg worked with a core committee and a wide range of community solicitors. He spoke at meetings, made innumerable phone calls, personally called on individuals, and regularly energized committee members and solicitors. To date more than $538,000 has been raised.

Awards and Honors Committee
December 27, 1995
Page 2

    You might imagine that Greg is a community elder, a retiree with lots of time on his hands. Far from it. Though prematurely gray-haired, Greg is the young president of a young, rapidly growing manufacturing company.

    During the more than seventeen months he has been involved with the library in the review and fund raising processes, Greg has been President of the Chamber of Commerce, President of the Rotary Club, Campaign Chair for the United Way, and a member of the First National Bank Board of Trustees, as well as overseeing the construction of his family's dream home and spending many long weekends traveling with his auto racing team. He had to <u>make</u> time to complete his committment to the library, and he never shorted us. He openly enjoyed the challenge.

    Greg, in working on economic development committees, the Chamber of Commerce and the Jay County Leadership Academy, has stated his hope that no Jay County High School graduate will have to leave the community to find meaningful employment, with and without a college degree. He nourishes that hope with his own entrepreneurial business and by volunteering his time to work with students in school settings.

    The Friends of the Jay County Public Library recently recognized Greg, not only as a member of the Fund Raising Steering Committee, but also with an individual award for Outstanding Service. At the group's prior award ceremonies, Greg received honors along with other members of the Building Project Review Committee.

    When our new library building is complete, it will be a giant relief. But I will miss the phone ringing and hearing a delighted voice say, "I've got more money for the library."

    This nomination is accompanied by twelve letters of support, although I surreptitiously solicited only ten. Good news travels fast.

                                 Sincerely,

                                   Rosalie Clamme
                                   Director

RGC/slf

The Greg Moser Story

LAW OFFICES
HINKLE, RACSTER & LOPEZ
PROFESSIONAL CORPORATION
121 W. HIGH STREET
P.O. BOX 806
PORTLAND, INDIANA 47371
TELEPHONE (219) 726-8104
FACSIMILE (219) 726-9113

LON R. RACSTER
WILLIAM W. HINKLE
GEORGE O. LOPEZ

WAYNE W. HINKLE
(RETIRED)

December 12, 1995

Awards & Honors Committee
Indiana Library Federation
6408 Carrollton Avenue
Indianapolis, Indiana 46220

Re: Nomination for Citizen's Award

Gentlemen:

I am pleased to offer the name of Greg Moser of Moser Engineering, 1616 North Franklin Street, Portland, Indiana 47371, as a nominee for your annual Citizen's Award.

I have known Greg personally for more than ten years. I see him weekly at the Portland Rotary Club where he is currently serving as President. He has always been a very active member of the Rotary Club and the Portland Rotary Foundation which he serves as a director.

As a past president and campaign chairman of the Jay County United Way, I am well acquainted with this organization and the time and dedication which is required to assure a successful fund raising effort. Greg has served actively in this organization, leading the advanced gifts campaign in 1994 and assuming the position of campaign chairman in 1995. Through his leadership over $150,000.00 was raised which exceeded the 1994 fund raising effort and set a United Fund record.

Greg has also served as president of the Portland Chamber of Commerce. As a former two term director, I am again familiar with this organization and the skill which is required to work with the directors who come from the retail, financial, industrial and professional segments of the community. Greg has a unique ability to "get the most out of everyone" in an easy going manner and in leading by example.

However, the best example of Greg's commitment to the community was his willingness to serve as campaign chairman to raise funds for the construction of a new Jay County Public Library. I have had the honor and responsibility of serving as president of the board of trustees for the past two years during which time the board was faced with a successful remonstrance against the

Page -2- December 12, 1995

building project. The board worked with the remonstrators to reach a funding agreement which limited the size of the general obligation bond issue to approximately 60% of the total building cost. Therefore, it was necessary to raise at least $350,000.00 from private donations.

Greg was quick to accept this challenge and at the first fund raising committee meeting, he stated "If we can't raise $500,000.00, we shouldn't be here!"

In following his practice of leading by example, Greg personally pledged the largest individual contribution and he then inspired, without any pressure, each member of the committee to meet and exceed his goal of $500,000.00. I can state unequivocally that Greg's positive attitude, self-assurance and personal fund raising skill was the primary reason for the success of the fund raising effort which has raised over $550,000.00 to date! This success greatly exceeded my initial expectations but Greg never had any doubt about the response by the Jay County community.

I can think of no person more deserving of the Citizen's Award than Greg Moser and I am happy to support his nomination.

Very truly yours,

HINKLE, RACSTER & LOPEZ

By William W. Hinkle

WmH/wrm
library\citizltr

THE GREG MOSER STORY

Fort Recovery Industries, Inc.

2440 STATE ROUTE 49, FORT RECOVERY, OHIO 45846

PHONE: (419) 375-4121
FAX: (419) 375-4194

December 6, 1995

Awards & Honors Committee
Indiana Library Federation
6408 Carrollton Avenue
Indianapolis, IN 46220

Dear Committee Members:

Greg Moser is truly a special individual. I have had the privilege of getting to know Greg by working with him on various professional and community projects. He is very deserving of recognition for his outstanding service to not only the library but to many other community projects as well.

Greg served as a key member on the library review committee which I chaired. He was a very optimistic member and did much to help the committee find an agreeable conclusion. After the review committee's work, Greg immediately moved on to the next phase - fund raising. Greg has chaired this campaign with over $500,000 raised in our relatively small community.

While Greg was doing the above, he also served as a chamber president, United Way Chairman, and he successfully managed his manufacturing company.

First, Greg is a gentleman and a family man. Secondly, he is a tremendous asset to this community and has played a major role in our successful library project. I wish I could convey to you what Greg has meant to the library and to Portland. You would have to spend time in our community to really understand how much positive influence Greg has had in the last year and a half.

Sincerely,

Dean Jetter
Chairperson
Library Review Committee

tb

MANUFACTURERS OF DIE CAST HARDWARE AND BLOW MOLDED CONTAINERS

439 W. North Street
Portland, IN 47371
December 5, 1995

Awards and Honors Committee
Indiana Library Federation
6408 Carrollton Avenue
Indianapolis, IN 46220

Dear Committee Members:

    I would like to recommend Greg Moser be given the Indiana Library Federation's Citizen's Award this year. As a trustee of the Jay County Public Library, I served with Greg on the Building Review Committee which helped us build support for a new library after the successful remonstrance last year. At this minute, steel for that new building is being set with a giant crane. Greg Moser is a large part of the reason that is happening. He helped build consensus within the building committee because of the respect people have for his business success. His voluntary chairing of the fund raising committee helped us raise more money than anyone (except Greg) thought would be possible, both because of his tireless efforts and his personal generosity. I really could think of no better reasons to give the Citizen's Award to anyone. Greg truly deserves it.
    Thank you.

Sincerely,

Ingrid Saxman

Ingrid Saxman, Secretary
Board of Trustees
Jay County Public Library

THE GREG MOSER STORY

Eric R. Rogers
Executive Director

Dale Widman
President

Jordan Rodden
First Vice President

Connie Ronald
Second Vice President

Ann Ledet
Treasurer

Vicki Tague
Corporate Secretary

December 14, 1995

Awards and Honors Committee
Indiana Library Federation
6408 Carrollton Avenue
Indianapolis, IN 46220

Ladies and Gentlemen:

I am writing to support the nomination of Greg Moser for the Citizen's Award. Greg is an exemplary community leader and is deserving of this honor.

Jay County Arts Council has greatly benefited from Greg's philanthropic spirit. Several years ago, one of our volunteer solicitors approached Greg to ask for a corporate contribution from Moser Engineering. Greg not only met our request but contributed double the amount we had asked.

Greg and his wife, Marianne, continue to make generous corporate and individual gifts to the Arts Council. For the past two years, Moser Engineering has provided our largest annual corporate contribution.

Yet, Greg's support for the Arts Council has not been limited to financial assistance. He has consistently given of his time as a volunteer whenever asked.

The Arts Council is only one of many projects in which Greg Moser has played an important role. This year, Greg astonished many of us in the community by taking on the leadership of two aggressive fund raising campaigns. In the space of less than a year, Greg has chaired the local United Way campaign and the Jay County Public Library's building campaign. As well, Greg has served in a number of other important community roles, including a year as President of the Portland Area Chamber of Commerce.

According to an old Danish proverb, "A willing helper does not wait until he is asked." Greg Moser is one of the truly willing helpers of this world and I heartily endorse him for the Citizen's Award.

Sincerely,

Eric R. Rogers
Executive Director

Jay County Arts Council • 138 East Main • P.O. Box 804 • Portland, IN 47371 • (219) 726-4809

WINNING THE RACE

THE JAY GARMENT COMPANY
December 11, 1995

Awards & Honors Committee
Indiana Library Committee
Indiana Library Federation
6408 Carrollton Ave.
Indianapolis, IN 46220

Dear Sirs:

I have been made aware that Greg Moser is being nominated for the "Citizen's Award" that is presented by your organization. I would like to comment about this nomination and feel qualified to do so in light of the extensive contact that I have had with Greg over the past few years. In a nutshell, I cannot imagine anyone who is more qualified for such an award if service to the community is any measure of the recipient.

To begin with, Greg has made the American dream come true by using his skills and ingenuity to bring to market a successful product that has made it possible for him to be very generous personally to all kinds of causes in our community. His business also provides meaningful employment to 40+ people.

I first became well acquainted with Greg when he served as one of my team captains when I headed the 1994 United Way Campaign. His efforts enabled us to set a new United Way record in 1994. As a result of his successes in 1994, he was asked to head up the 1995 United Way Campaign. He lead the campaign to another record, at the same time that he was heading up the successful Library campaign.

I have also gotten to know Greg well through Rotary. We are both members of the Portland Club. In spite of the heavy loads of business, The United Way and Library campaigns, Greg has served this year as an outstanding President of the local Rotary Club. "Service above self" is the Rotary motto, and, if anyone in our community exemplifies that it is Greg Moser.

I have recently learned that Jay County has the highest per capita giving record of any Indiana County. There are many reasons for that and Greg Moser is an important one.

Sincerely yours,

John G. Young
Chairman & CEO
The Jay Garment Co.

CORPORATE OFFICE:
South Meridian & 5th St. P.O. Box 907
Portland, Indiana 47371
Telephone 219-726-7151
FAX 219-726-4228

TEXAS OFFICE:
One Preston Park
2301 Ohio Drive – Suite 110
Plano, Texas 75093
Telephone 214-612-6235
FAX 214-612-6236

The Greg Moser Story

Donna W. Haggenjos
R.R. # 2 Box 240A
Portland, IN 47371

December 23, 1995

Awards and Honors Committee
Indiana Library Federation
6408 Carrollton Avenue
Indianapolis, IN 46220

Re: Mr. Greg Moser

To Whom it May Concern:

It has been my privilege to work with Mr. Greg Moser on two funding raising committees. He brings knowledge, diligence and a huge commitment of time to the task at hand. Greg was the Chairman of the Jay County Library Steering Committee. It is his time and leadership that prove to be invaluable in challenging others to meet lofty goals. The Jay County Library in progress now is testament to his abilities to inspire.

While chairing the library fund raising committee, he was also chairman of the United Way campaign. The United Way realized the highest pledge total in the history of Jay County.

He is the President of the Portland Rotary. He is a founding board member for the Jay County Health Care Plan. Loving fireworks, he donates so the whole community can enjoy a really nice display. He sponsors all sorts of local sports teams. When the Junior High School Christmas program was canceled due to snow and ice, Greg financed the broadcast of the program on the local radio station so working parents could listen. These are but a few examples of his commitment to the community.

He is a fine corporate citizen, family man and neighbor.

Many people made our new library a reality. Greg Moser lead the way for our community to take ownership of it. Often people of means give, Greg is a significant donor of <u>time</u> and money.

Greg Moser meets the criteria for the Indiana Library Federation's Citizen's Award and then some!

Sincerely,

Donna W. Haggenjos

MOSER ENGINEERING

1616 N. FRANKLIN ST.   PORTLAND, IN 47371   PH# 219-726-6689 FAX# 219-726-4159

December 7, 1995

Awards & Honors Committee
Indiana Library Federation
6408 Carrollton Avenue
Indianapolis, IN 46220

Dear Committee Members:

As employees of Greg we are keenly aware of the concern and devotion Greg has for the Jay County community. We have experienced, first hand, the time, effort, and financial support Greg is willing to share with others.

Greg, in the last few months, has either given or is currently giving his time and effort to the following organizations: President of Rotary, President of Chamber of Commerce, Member of the Emergency Preparedness Planning Committee, Chairman of Fund Raising for the United Way of Jay County, Member of East Central Indiana Private Industry Council, Member of the Jay County Library Building Review Committee, and Chairman of the Fund Raising Committee to Build a New Jay County Public Library. This is devotion to our community!!!!

Greg not only gives of his time but also of his financial resources. Greg is a major contributor to the Jay County community whether it be continuous funding of the Jay County Arts Council, United Way, or the Fourth of July Celebration, or whether it be a major one time contribution for the betterment of the community such as the new Jay County Public Library.

We believe Greg to be the right person for "Citizens Award".

Sincerely,

THE GREG MOSER STORY

CHARLES H. MILLER, JR., D.D.S.
120 West Votaw Street
Portland, Indiana 47371
Telephone 219-726-4710

Awards & Honors Committee
Indiana Library Federation
6408 Carrollton Avenue
Indianapolis, IN 46220

Re: Greg Moser

December 1, 1995

Dear Sirs:

In 1994, the building of a new Jay County Library was abruptly halted by those opposed. It definitely looked like it was not going to happen! In order to keep the project alive a committee was formed.

Greg Moser (a member of the committee) assured those opposed that private funds could be raised which would substantially reduce the cost to taxpayers. Greg then personally pledged a substantial donation and agreed to head up a fundraising committee.

Since then, that committee has raised nearly one-half million dollars.

This could not have been accomplished without the outstanding leadership of Greg Moser.

Sincerely,

Charles H. Miller, DDS
Charles H. Miller, D.D.S.

 # THE FIRST NATIONAL BANK

Awards & Honors Committee
Indiana Library Federation
6408 Carrollton Avenue
Indianapolis, IN 46220

Dear Sir or Madame:

It is truly a privilege to be able to discuss knowing Greg Moser. I am on two Boards of Directors with Greg; one is the Board of Directors of First National Bank and the second is the Portland Area Chamber of Commerce Board.

I have two short stories which help show what makes up Greg Moser. During a Board of Directors meeting for the Chamber of Commerce, Greg was approached about how he was doing in obtaining the goal for the Juffy Fund Drive. After he told the person how the fund drive was doing, Greg's quote was "Oh, I want you to know this is not a final goal, because the total targeted amount will increase each year. Because we are successful in bringing in more money this year, has no relationship with what we are going to do next year."

Greg is truly a positive person who does not stand still for today's ideas, he is always reaching into the future to see what tomorrow will bring.

Another story is when my wife and I asked Greg and his wife, Marianne, to attend a local play, Greg said "We would be glad to, and oh by the way I also want to take my 12 year old daughter to dinner and the play." Through this story we see he is not only community minded, but he is family oriented.

When you put all of this together, I believe Greg Moser needs to be honored for all he has done for our community.

Sincerely,

Barry Hudson,
President/Chairman of the Board

BH/jma

P.O. Box 1089 • Portland, IN 47371 • (219) 726-7158

The Greg Moser Story

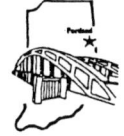

**THE
PORTLAND AREA
CHAMBER OF COMMERCE**

"Promoting Progress for Portland"

411 North Meridian Street   Portland, Indiana 47371   Phone/Fax (219) 726-4481

November 30, 1995

Awards and Honors Committee
Indiana Library Federation
6408 Carrollton Avenue
Indianapolis, IN 46220

Dear Committee Members:

I was pleased to learn that Greg Moser was being nominated for the Indiana Library Federation "Citizen's Award" by Jay County Public Library Director, Rosalie Clamme.

Mr. Moser would be very deserving of the recognition. Not only has he given endless hours to the Jay County Library's building project and fund raising efforts, Mr. Moser has also been an active community volunteer through the Portland Area Chamber of Commerce. He served a three year term as a director, during which time he served as president. As the immediate past president, he is currently serving as an honorary member of the board of directors. During the four years Greg served as a director, he has provided leadership to several key committees such as our Government Affairs Committee, the Industrial Committee and the county-wide Housing Task Force.

Mr. Moser is committed to the Jay County community as an exemplary employer, a dedicated volunteer and a leader with a vision for the progress of the greater Portland area.

Sincerely,

Vicki L. Tague

Vicki L. Tague,
Executive Director

WINNING THE RACE

 JAY COUNTY DEVELOPMENT

BOB QUADROZZI
EXECUTIVE DIRECTOR

November 29, 1995

Awards and Honors Committee
Indiana Library Federation
6408 Carrollton Avenue
Indianapolis, IN 46220

Dear Committee Members:

I have had the distinct pleasure of knowing Mr. Greg Moser as a person and as a "corporate citizen" for over four (4) years. It has been just that . . . . . a pleasure!

He is without a doubt the best example this community has of someone that puts his time, his effort, and his financial support where his mouth is.

His concern and generosity to the employees of Moser Engineering is unparalleled in Jay County. His interest and devoted efforts to this community's Fourth of July activities, Chairman of the 1995 Library Fund Raiser, and the current President of the Rotary Club are only a few examples of his giving back to the community in many ways.

Greg is someone that anyone in this community with a worthwhile cause can go to and likely receive good support.

I would strongly recommend that this committee give serious consideration to Greg for the **"Citizen's Award"** for outstanding service to his community.

Sincerely,

Bob Quadrozzi
Executive Director

BQ/tjl

121 WEST MAIN STREET • SUITE A
PORTLAND, IN 47371
(219) 726-9311
FAX (219) 726-4477

The Greg Moser Story

GRAPHIC PRINTING

309 W. Main St., P.O. Box 1049, Portland, Indiana 47371
(219) 726-8141   FAX (219) 726-8143

In the historic Hood building

December 22, 1995

To whom it may concern:

Would it have happened without him? Maybe.

Jay County is a generous community. It has a history of supporting key institutions — the hospital, the community foundation, the United Way, schools, and churches — and it probably would have supported the effort to build a new Jay County Public Library as well.

But there's also a chance that without Greg Moser's drive, it never would have happened.

Greg became involved in the library building project after a taxpayer remonstrance had sidetracked construction for a year. Library board president Bill Hinkle appointed an independent study committee to review the board's earlier decisions and help build community consensus that building a new facility was the best course of action.

Greg Moser was not only an integral part of that committee; when it made its final report, validating the board's earlier decision to build, Greg surfaced as the leader in a drive for private funds.

Private funding was important because it helped keep the bond issue at a cap insisted upon by those who had pushed for the initial remonstrance and still allowed the board to build the size and quality of library necessary for the community's future.

In classic "put your money where your mouth is" style, Greg was among the first to make a pledge for the library project. He then directed the fund-raising campaign, even though he had already agreed to be United Way campaign chairman and was running his own growing business.

To no one's surprise, he was successful with both the library and the United Way. The library pledges are well past the half million dollar mark, and the United Way simultaneously had a record campaign.

So effective was Greg's approach to the library fund drive that when he made corporate calls seeking donations in the $5,000 and up range, the question never seemed to be whether the donor would give. It was only a question of how much.

Would it have all happened without him? Maybe. But I don't think so.

Sincerely,

Jack Ronald
Editor and Publisher
The Commercial Review

The Commercial Review
BOODLE.

Publishers of
CoverSTORY

The News and Sun
The Guide

The Arts Council Project

It has been a couple of years now since the library fund drive. The Jay County Arts Council, which is probably one of the finest arts facilities in a ten or twenty county area, is too small for the amount of people who use it. The number of children who take courses there, take music lessons there, and study theater there is constantly growing. The building is too small, not easily accessible, and there is limited practice space. The room for productions with sets and whatever you need has become too crowded. A summer program for children of all ages has been so successful that it is having to turn people away. It is part of our arts park.

Thus, my latest fund-raiser is for the Jay County Arts Council and we are proposing to renovate and connect a couple buildings for a total drive of $1,750,000. Marianne and I have already made a substantial commitment ourselves to fund that. I'm going to use my perceived success in business, once again, to head another fund raiser and worthwhile project.

Marianne actually got involved in the project early on and it was determined that we needed about a $3,000,000 structure. We also needed to fund operating money to run the building after it was in operation. So it's about a $4,000,000 project, but that is way too much, so it was scaled back to raising $1,750,000 by using an existing building. Actually, we will use the old library which is located adjacent to the Arts Council. That old building was auctioned off and Barry and Elizabeth Hudson from the First National Bank and my wife and I bought it at the auction. We are going to donate it to the Arts Council.

So a plan has been devised to connect the old library with the Arts Council building by renovating both through a vacant alley that runs between them. The new structure will be beautiful. My wife and I, since we are very supportive of the Arts Council, were asked what we thought and how much money we might be willing to donate toward the new project. We have been supporting the string program yearly by donating $12,500, and we told them that we would pledge $150,000 toward the new project. All kinds of questions were then raised and one was, "Who do you think should head this new fund drive?"

A few months after that I received a telephone call from Eric Rogers, the executive director of the Jay County Arts Council, and he said, "We would like to ask you to chair our fund drive." He basically said that my name came up on almost all of the questionnaires individuals had completed. Once again, since I believe in the Arts Council, just like I did the library, I agreed to do it. This is going to be quite a fund-raiser. It is going to be very, very interesting because we are talking about raising

$1,750,000 from totally private funds and I guess I have already made the statement, "I don't think it is a problem. We can do this." So we are off and running. In fact, we kicked off the fund drive September 12, 1997, at which time I gave the following speech. It will probably take a year of hard work. But, if you want nice things in your community, if you want things of which everybody is proud, if you want things that help keep our children off the streets, and if you wish those youth to be involved in worthwhile and fun endeavors, then, if it takes a year of my time and hard work by my steering committee to raise these funds, then we are going to do it! It is going to get done, we are going to do it right, and the end result is that we will probably have for our small community the finest arts facility in the world, end of discussion!

The Arts Council Speech

"Thank you very much. It's a great pleasure for me to be here tonight with so many of my friends and so many friends of the Jay County Arts Council. What I want to tell you is very exciting, not only for me personally but for our community.

When the Center opened 14 years ago, no one really foresaw just how successful it would be. Music Works, Arts in the Parks, Arts Shops--these are just a few of the unique efforts which have generated such strong interest that the Center has become overloaded in its present facility. The Board saw this coming, and five years ago began to look strategically toward the future, to find a way that the Center could continue to provide the kinds of programs and the level of service required by its rapidly increasing audiences.

What became quickly apparent was the need to expand this building, especially those areas related to our all-important educational programs. The multiple uses of this building really are now in conflict with each other and we have only one room designed for music instruction. Gaining use of the old library has eased this situation temporarily, but we can already see that we will not be able to meet the growing demand for more instruction within a very short time. Our group lessons, ensembles, and the new children's choir also provide a real challenge as they cannot take place at times when the theater is in use. In addition to the 35 or more events put on in the theater each year, rehearsals for music ensembles and community theater groups occupy the theater on more than 140 days each year. Our Exhibition Program brings thousands of people each month to the Gallery, because of the popularity of shows like the "Harvest Biennial Exhibition" whose awards are being presented this evening.

It will come as no surprise that we have decided to move forward to create a new and enlarged Center for the Arts, which will assure not only that we can meet the requirements of our mission today, but for many years to come. I have accepted the Board's invitation to serve as Chairman of the Campaign which will make this happen. Let me quickly acknowledge that efforts like this take a lot of hard work, time, intelligence, and energy, and I am joined on the Campaign Steering Committee by some wonderful people whom I would like to introduce now, beginning with the Honorary Chairman of the Campaign, Betty Starbuck (ask her to stand). Other members of the Steering Committee whom I also ask to stand are Phil Frantz, Mark Haggenjos, Dean Jetter, Bonnie Maitlen, Gordon Meeker, Julie Myron, Jordan Rodden, Chuck Huffman--and last but far from least, my wife, Marianne. Thank you all for accepting this challenge.

At this point I'd like to share some of our excitement with you. Eric Rogers also serves on the Campaign Steering Committee, and in a moment I'd like to ask him to take a few minutes to show you the plans for our new facility--"Arts Place," a unique name for a unique facility--a place that steps into the future, building upon the past to create a sound architectural foundation for the future. A gallery, theater, art studios, music studios, rehearsal rooms, offices, and park will offer a unique setting for learning and the enrichment of lives. "Arts Place" steps into the future on a solid path of growth towards the premier community arts institution of the region.

(Introduce Eric, who does his slide show and talk describing the new facility, how the two old buildings are going to be merged, the park, etc.--Introduce you to "Arts Place--it's more than a building."

(Eric finishes and reintroduces Greg to complete his remarks.)

Thank you, Eric.

This is not going to be cheap!!! What we need to make this vision a reality will be $1,750,000, which divides out this way:

--to build the facility and to take care of the
  renovations $1,275,000
--to provide endowment support for expanded facility
      in the short-term future   400,000
--to ensure campaign costs are met, and to allow for contingencies   75,000
--in other words, a total of $1,750,000

One million dollars more than has been raised on any other project. This will not be an easy task, indeed it is a monumental task, but we know that it **can** and I know it **will** be done. This is an extraordinary community, one which my family and I are proud to call home, one which has always provided its residents with the best possible opportunities for health, education, and quality of life. Nourishing the spirit through the arts is a vital part of this mixture, and we are truly fortunate to have the Arts Council here to make this possible.

Over the next few months it will be up to each and every one of us who cherishes the Arts Council and all that it represents to make sure that this campaign--the "Campaign for Arts Place"--is a success. Let me tell you, however, that we are already on our way.

First, though, I want to acknowledge the foresight and generosity of one of our very best friends and a friend of mine over the years, Lee Hall. Five years ago he left the Arts Council a generous bequest of $250,000 with the intention that it be used in part to help us undertake this project. One hundred thousand dollars of this amount was set up as an endowment with The Portland Foundation and $150,000 was set aside for this project. His enduring kindness has enabled us to meet the cost of planning this Campaign, and of undertaking the architectural work that Eric showed you a few minutes ago. Lee's bequest is separate from our campaign goal and has enabled us to come this far. To him we shall always remain eternally and enormously grateful.

Secondly, it is my great pleasure to tell you tonight that we have already raised $417,250 toward our goal of $1,750,000...that takes us 23.8% of the way to success and the Campaign really hasn't begun yet. These pledges represent the commitment of a few lead gifts from board and steering committee members. I want to especially acknowledge these important lead gifts:

--First National Bank--commitment and pledge totals $80,000.
--Betty Starbuck our Honorary Chair has provided a very generous gift.

Betty's gift typifies the spirit of generosity and commitment which, like that of Lee Hall, has long marked this community as such a special place to live and raise a family.

Over the course of the next few months you will be hearing much more about the Campaign and about Arts Place. Your own turn will come to join with us in this important endeavor, and when it does, I know you will respond as generously as you possibly can. We're well on our way, and we are all very happy to have you here tonight to share our delight and our great hope for the future. Thank you!"

Philanthropy

Somewhere in your life, you will reach a level of comfort , a monetary position, at which you have the possessions you wish and you are satisfied materially and monetarily. This point may very well be when you say, "Enough is enough." I know several years ago I reached that point and one of the greatest joys in my life now is literally giving money away. I give hundreds of thousands of dollars away every year. We don't throw it away. It has to be a good cause and there has to be a good reason behind our giving. **But we totally believe in helping the community and we also feel so very blessed with our life that we want to make other peoples' lives happy. We want them to have things**. This is why we make our presence known in the community at such events as the Jay County Expo. We have made huge donations to the library as well as to other special projects. For any worthwhile cause that comes in the door we will usually give at least a hundred bucks. It's just the right thing to do as we try to help people. If you are blessed with the ability to make money and you are satisfied with the money you are making and you are comfortable, then why not give it away?

WINNERS...

#145. find ultimate happiness in making others happy

Now this I say, he who sows sparingly shall also reap sparingly; and he who sows bountifully shall also reap bountifully.
(2 Corinthians 9:6)

Philanthropy is not giving money to your relatives. It is not even giving money to your employees or giving them bonuses. That's just the right thing to do. **Philanthropy is giving money to a total stranger and expecting nothing in return.** When you reach that point in your life, you will find that it will give you total satisfaction knowing that you are giving somebody something and expecting nothing in return. You are simply giving it to them to make their world a little happier.

WINNERS...

#146. know that philanthropy is giving money expecting nothing in return

"You cannot live a perfect day without doing something for someone who will never be able to repay you."
(John Wooden)

Concluding my thoughts on sharing the wealth, the real beauty in having perceived success in business is the fact that there is no problem in giving money away and helping other people because you can always make more money. People who inherit money tend to hang onto it. They don't wish to give it away because, if the money was not earned, there would be no way to replenish it. Thus, they are not as likely to give it away. In fact, in line with these thoughts, any proceeds that are derived from this book, will be given to the Jay County Arts Council and the Portland Foundation. These two things will do more good for more people than anything I can possibly imagine.

The following lists suggest how I have given of my time and money:

Director of Boards with underlined being current

<u>First National Bank</u>, <u>United Way</u>, <u>Red Cross</u>, <u>Rotary</u>, <u>Rotary Foundation</u>, <u>Chamber of Commerce</u>, <u>Jay County Emergency Management</u>, <u>Local Emergency Planning Committee</u>, Honorary - Jay County Development Corporation, <u>Portland Country Club</u>

Volunteer over the last three to four years

Past President--Rotary, Chamber of Commerce, Past Chair--Library Fundraiser - private funds raised ($605,000), Housing Committee, United Way Fund Drive, United Way Patriot Brigade, Current Chair--Red Cross, Finance Committee, Arts Council Major Capital Fund Drive - all private ($1,750,000 goal), Red Cross secretary, Jay County Emergency Management Committee, United Way $1 a Week Campaign, Chamber Marketing Committee , Member Jay County Schools Focus Group

Awards

Jay County Citizen of the Year
Friends of the Library Citizen of the Year
Indiana Library Federations Citizen of the Year
Jay County Business of the Year (Twice)

Donations
1997

Jay County Arts Council
Jay County Community Center
Junior Class Parents Committee (Prom)
Jay County Swim Team
Jay County Friendship Company
Drag Racing Association of Women
Ft. Recovery Ambassador Park
Junior League Baseball

Crown City Cruising
IOF Foresters
Rod Masters
Fourth of July Celebration
Portland Rockets
Loblolly Days Truck Pull
Bryant Lions Truck Pull
WFBC TV 54
Jay City High School Alumni Association (one time)
Fireworks
Jay County Band
Portland Fire Department (National Fire Safety Council)
Red Cross (Chairs & Tables)
United Way of Jay County
Police League of Indiana
Jay County Hospital Foundation (Hole Sponsor)
Tri Kappa Mental Health (Hole Sponsor)
Youth for Christ (Hole Sponsor)
Redkey Fire Department
Rotary Foundation
Geneva Volunteer Fire Department
Chamber Golf (Hole Sponsor)
Jay County Emergency Management
Muscular Dystrophy
Youth Service Bureau
Indiana Firefighters Benevolent Association
General Shanks Elementary Reading Program
Tri Kappa Nursing Home Christmas Gifts
Youth for Christ Ministries
Red Cross
Special Olympics
Library
Arts Council
Fireworks

Chapter Fourteen

MORE ACCOLADES FROM COLLEAGUES

Financing Our Library by Ms. Rosalie Clamme
The Optimist by Ms. Donna Haggenjos
Going to the Races by Mr. Barry Hudson
On Leadership by Dean Jetter
Greg and Marianne Moser by Bob Quadrozzi
Greg Moser by Vicki Tague

Financing Our Library
by Ms. Rosalie Clamme, Director
Jay County Public Library
Portland, Indiana

Although I knew Greg before the Spring of 1994, I did not really KNOW him until he telephoned me one day out of the blue. The public library was in the financing stage of a project to construct a new library building. In order to issue a bond to be repaid by property taxes, a petition had been circulated to allow the Library Board to incur debt. Throughout the many months of planning, public meetings, and invitations to the public for input, no naysayers had appeared. However, a remonstrance petition was being circulated in opposition to the public debt when Greg called me that day. "How," he asked, "could anyone be opposed to such a worthy project? Let's talk."

A few days later we sat in his office, reviewed the statistics of growing library use, the nature of the project, and the apparent focal point for the remonstrators' objection--dependence on property tax. Greg voiced his desire--really, need--to take some action to advance the project. Unfortunately, the remonstrance juggernaut was too far down the track to deploy the 'chute.

The Library Board halted the financing process for one year, as required by law, but elected to proceed with fact-finding and consensus building. Within weeks of the defeat, a well-attended public meeting hosted by the Library Board heard strong opinions from both camps. In early fall, Board president, Bill Hinkle, recruited several members of the public to serve on an independent committee to review the needs, proposals, and solutions relating to the project. Greg, who was then president of the Chamber of Commerce, was one of his first recruits. The nine members represented a variety of occupations, ages, and interests, with the full scope of support--from the leader of the remonstrance to a long-time member of the Library Board.

Ah, the Review Committee process. What was sold to the participants as a "few meetings over a short period of time" grew to 16 sessions over five months. As committee members drove down several avenues of inquiry, Greg, true to his commitment, missed only one group meeting because of out-of-town business and devoted many non-group hours to the inquiry. The group could rely on him for both his analytical approach and paradigm-breaking nature.

One incident stands out in my mind. When the group discussed the costs of construction, with a $100 per square foot for a public building being the average suggested by the architects, Greg offered his opinion that there was surely a less expensive alternative. He suggested a conference with the company that had constructed his own manufacturing facility. Committee chairperson, Dean Jetter, whose company also had a relationship with the construction company, spent a day sleuthing with Greg and myself. We toured two new, conventionally-built public library buildings and then sat down with two executives of the construction company. While the company would like to have had such a large project to build, the officers discouraged our using their pre-engineered construction method. "It would not," they said, "be appropriate for a public building." They went on to say that the cost per square foot we had been given was accurate. Darn! The idea balloon deflated.

But here is the refreshing part. At the next Review Committee meeting Greg said, "I was wrong." No ifs, no buts, no uhhhs, just, "I was wrong." I think it was a watershed moment.

It was during the review process that an acquaintance asked what I thought of Greg. "How is he to work with?" he asked. Before I could answer, the person went on to say, "You know, he's the type of person you don't want to like. He's been so successful in his business that out of...jealously, I guess, you just don't want to like him. But, when you find out he works hard, he cares about people and he's generous with his time and money, it's hard to find something not to like. You can only admire him." True.

At the conclusion of the review process, the committee issued a unanimous opinion: build it as planned, but seek alternative funding to reduce the dependence on property tax funds.

With the "go raise money" mandate, Board president Hinkle again turned to Greg for assistance, asking that he chair the fund-raising committee. I recall Bill's excited call to me. "Greg said yes! I had prepared point-by-point remarks to coerce him into the job, and he said yes before I really got started."

Greg and Bill formulated a dynamic seven-member fund-raising steering committee. At the initial meeting, Greg announced that $200,000 to $250,000 would probably be needed to make the project go. "But if we can't raise a half million, we have no business being here." As soon as pledge forms were printed, Greg and Marianne's was the first to be signed.

The committee operated on a positive, no nonsense, no arm twisting basis. The response was overwhelming. Initially, ten areas of the building were earmarked for 'sponsorships' of $10,000 to $50,000. Before the campaign was complete, we had identified 24 sponsored areas: 22 of them were sponsored.

Two additional sources of money reflect Greg's attitude:

- He was adamant that everyone be afforded the opportunity to support the project and receive recognition, not just the big ticket donors. Inscribed bricks, to be laid in the entry sidewalk, were sold at $125 each. The result: 370 bricks were purchased by organizations, businesses and individuals. To encourage his own employees to buy 'a piece of history,' he allowed them to payroll deduct the cost over a matter of weeks.

- It was announced during the fund-raising campaign that the Corel Great Race, a cross-country race of vintage automobiles, would make a June 1996 pit stop in Portland. At the conclusion of the race, competitors would vote for the best pit stop city, with a $5,000 cash prize. "We can do it," he said, and the community did win the prize. What the community doesn't know is that Greg invested heavily in the event with is own company's materials and manpower. When someone asked him why he didn't just write a check directly to the library, he said, "That would defeat the point of it being a community effort to generate the money."

While I am ever so grateful that the library is now comfortably situated in a new structure with a sound financial picture, I do miss receiving Greg's phone calls. He took great delight in reporting new pledges. The call always started with a soft chuckle, and then an exuberant, "guess what" or "I've got more money" or "we are looking soooo good." And in the end, it did look good. A total of $605,000 was pledged.

At the conclusion of the campaign, Greg and Marianne hosted the steering committee members and their spouses for champagne at their new home. They had only recently moved. Stories had raced around town about its size and features, so I was anxious to see what my reaction to it would be. It is huge. It is stunning. But it's just home to a couple of people who have worked hard and are having the time of their lives. Two kids in a candy store.

Having been on the Indiana Library Federation Awards Committee in years past, I knew the high caliber of outstanding librarians, trustees, and citizens in the State of Indiana. In order for an award nomination to be successful, the track record of the nominee would need to be extraordinary. We had a winner with Greg. The state association honored him in the Spring of 1996 as its Outstanding Citizen, recognizing his volunteer efforts during the review and financing stages while continuing his numerous other civic commitments. And, as is typical of Greg, he credited everyone but himself for the success.

The library was dedicated in late October 1996. As news of our successful fund-raising campaign spread through the Indiana library world, I began to get calls. "What was your magic formula?" they asked. There isn't any magic formula, only magical people and Greg is the chief wizard.

During my son's senior year (1996-1997) in high school, he participated in the Interdisciplinary Cooperative Education (ICE) program. David, having done well in welding classes his junior year, wanted to develop those skills to see if it might be his career goal. He snagged a job at Moser Engineering and spent every school day afternoon learning and earning. David was elated the first day on the job when he learned there was no time clock. But the element of trust offered by the missing time clock created an employee who didn't watch the wall clock, who tackled whatever job needed to be done, and who couldn't wait to go back for another day of the same. Although a young man of few words, David frequently commented about how lucky he had been to become a part of the Moser team.

Months later the "T" word came up again. David laughingly told us about a practical joke coworkers left for him in his locker. "You don't lock your locker?" his father asked. "No. That place is run on trust." As generous as Greg is with his employees, his employees are with each other. All of them were quick to assist David on and off the job. They all work hard and play hard.

My only concern, as a parent of an 18-year-old who has spent a year at Moser Engineering, is that the level of camaraderie, trust, positive thinking, and employer-employee rapport will spoil him should he find himself working for another employer. That's an acceptable risk.

Through Greg's quiet encouragement and words of advice, a young man who had no post-secondary schooling aspirations is now on track to become a certified welder. Several months ago, David approached Greg about a full-time job following high school graduation. Greg told him he would not have a full-time position open then. "Go to school and then come back and see me. Go to school now, while it is easy to do. Marriage and fatherhood complicate matters later on." David was devastated, but his father and I seized the opportunity that evening to promote training at a nationally-known welding school. The next morning Greg called me. "I know the conversation with Dave would be coming, and I had intended to talk to you first. Did I say the right thing, Mom?" I don't think it would have mattered if the full-time job would have been available or not since Greg was concerned that David pursue more training. In fact, as I contribute this for Greg's book, we have learned that Greg heard of a scholarship to assist Dave in paying for his education, wrote a letter of recommendation, and Dave has won the scholarship!

As a woman, I would be remiss if I failed to mention Greg's respect for Marianne, his wife and business partner. "She's the brains of the outfit," he says, "I just know how to do mechanical things."

It is not a given that successful business people who are financially comfortable and in control of their own schedule will contribute money and time to the community. Nor is it required that they lend a hand or talent to help others attain a goal. There must be a willingness to share. With Greg it is not just a willingness but a need.

The Optimist
by Donna Haggenjos

Winning the race is a good phrase for Greg Moser's life. To me, Greg views life from the perspective of the half full glass as opposed to the half empty one. He is a very positive person.

It has been my privilege to work with Greg on several committees. One in particular, the Jay County Library Steering Committee, was quite an undertaking. In a county of 21,000 plus souls, we wished to raise $520,000. Greg's approach as chair was that the county has a good base of supporters and that the goal was achievable. The final tally was $605,000! Greg's commitment of time and leadership create a "can do" atmosphere and others follow.

He has used this formula to head a record year for the United Way of Jay County. He has challenged others to step up to the plate for the expansion of the Jay County Arts Council called Arts Place.

This short list of efforts (there are many more) exemplify his core commitment to his community. He believes strongly in giving to and helping build a better Jay County. It is this combination of the gift of time and money which can make all the difference.

Charitable work aside, Greg is a fun loving person. He is optimistic, loves a good story, and generally enjoys life. The library had a photo contest of ugly male knees. All the other contestants modestly displayed their knees in Bermuda shorts or with their pant legs rolled up. Greg's picture was of his knees, a hat to cover an area not in the contest, and him smiling like a Cheshire cat! It certainly put a more comedic slant on the personality.

Greg and Marianne invited me and my husband to join them with their racing team at Norwalk, Ohio. We both enjoyed watching Greg in his element. He is very focused and is intense about the sport he loves. Greg and Marianne have joined this love into a business which is an interesting story all by itself!

Greg loves his family, his community, and his work (which was, of course, a hobby first - so all the better!). Most of all he knows life is good.

Going to the Races
by Barry Hudson
President/Chairman of the Board
The First National Bank
Portland, Indiana

In early 1994, Greg Moser became the chairperson of a newly formed Jay County Housing Development Task Force. This group included several civic leaders, Mayor Maxine Lewis, Chamber of Commerce Executive Director, Vicki Tague, Jay County Development Executive Director, Bob Quadrozzi, a few others, and myself. We met monthly trying to figure out what to do about the housing shortage in Jay County. Greg's statement was, "We, the people of Jay County, are just selling to each other, bringing about no population growth." Greg did a great job in this position. People were willing to be moved along mentally as they felt Greg was sincere and had no ulterior motives for misdirecting or distorting any facts. I noted Greg was interested in these information gathering groups for city improvement reasons. On the other hand, if one listened, you could also hear Greg wanting to improve the potential for better housing for Moser employees. I have noted that many things the Moser's do come back in some way as possible improvements for their employees.

It was during these meetings that I became better acquainted with Greg. I asked him if he would keep me posted about drag racing so I could attend one. Greg replied, "You should attend the World's National Drag Race Finals to be held on August 27, 1994, at Norwalk, Ohio". He thought this was the race I should watch. So I took him at his word and looked it up on a map. It appeared too far for me to travel to see a drag race. The last race I went to was in 1958, the year I graduated from Portland High School. You can note by this attendance of every forty years how great a race fan I am. An idea came to me one evening to make this a "fun hog event," at which a bunch of people just go and have fun. I called Dr. Stephen Myron, one of our First National Bank (FNB) Directors, to see if he would attend. I also knew that Steve had a Cessna Twin Engine 421B airplane. Steve said he could not go, but suggested that we take his plane as he would be willing to furnish a pilot. What a guy that Steve is!

After getting the plane, I rounded up Jack Ronald, Editor of the local newspaper, two local businessmen, Bill Davis and Ed Williams, John Samples, REMC Executive, and Dr. Mark Haggenjos. I think he went along to make sure we brought his medical partners' plane back in good shape. We all donned our Moser racing T-Shirts and neon FNB hats and took off early one Saturday morning from the Portland Municipal Airport. The Moser's had it all set up. We were met at the Norwalk private airport which must have been part of the drag strip at one time. From the air, we could see the racers gearing up so as we landed we hoped no one came close by at 100+ mph.

The van driver taxied us to golf carts so we could drive in style to the Moser food tent and the Moser race truck. We could not believe our eyes. Back in 1958, it was just a bunch of kids dragging their dads' car or a friend who had a job and poured all of his hard earned cash into a car for one Sunday afternoon run. Norwalk was loaded with trailer after trailer of fine machines, mechanics, and equipment. The paint jobs on the cars cost more than our old 1958 hot rods.

As we were all standing there with our mouths open and our eyes shining like little kids, old Greg came by. He looked us over and then announced to me, "Well, this is why I wanted you to come to the World's National Drag Race . . . to see the wall to wall money involved and see I am not the only crazy car person in the United States".

We never thought he was not too crazy. The following month I proposed Greg's name for election to the Board of Directors of First

National Bank. I told the above story and Greg was unanimously elected.

On Leadership
by Dean Jetter
Fort Recovery Industries, Inc.
Fort Recovery, Ohio

Greg Moser gets to the point. When I asked him to tell me his thoughts on leadership, he had the following points to make.

- 1. Be Competent--When going into a new position, Greg looked for a way to change something for the better right away. This would establish credibility. It brought respect because the people around Greg would see that he was competent.

- 2. Give others responsibility--Once Greg established his credibility he would hand a responsibility off. He would not "bother" the person, to use his term. If the person needed or asked for help, that is when Greg was there.

- 3. Find ways to give credit and to take the blame--After someone has tried and failed you cannot believe how energized the person becomes when instead of being blamed he receives praise for effort and risk taking. Greg looks for ways to take the blame if something goes wrong. If he could have caught the error but did not, he is ready to take the blame.

- 4. Bring people along--Greg said he has seen people lose promotions because they were not big enough to bring others up. There was no one to step in if they were to be promoted.

- 5. Take responsibility for the welfare of the team--Greg feels responsible for those hired so he cannot simply walk away from the business or sell it like he thought he could. During the UPS strike, parts could not be shipped. Greg did not layoff. He figured the owners could afford to lose money more than the employees.

- 6. Focus on what is important--Examples:
- a. Remember how you wanted to be treated when you were at the bottom of the ladder;
- b. Only be paged for certain callers. If you are paged for

everyone, you cannot be out on the floor where the action is.

- 7. Do the right thing--That is:
-    a. Take actions which will allow you to feel good about the way you lived your life;
-    b. Know within yourself you did right;
-    c. Don't feel bad when in church because of actions the prior week;
-    d. Don't take advantage of anyone.

- These are the things Greg said so I asked him where the principles come from. His answer was his parents. Parents who spent a whole summer trying to convince Sears to take the money it had coming because Sears billed Greg's parents $5.60 when it was supposed to be $560.00.

- 8. Lead by example--That is:
-    a. Honesty--Do not take company pencils home;
-    b. Commitment--Normally first to arrive, usually last to leave;
-    c. Fairness--No favorites;
-    d. Straightforwardness — People want an answer, so give it to them now, good or bad. The idea is that you cannot procrastinate one minute. If you want Greg's opinion, you get it now.
-    e. Consistency--Be steady almost always...except when a machine is down. Then, get excited!

- 9. Be humble--Greg is embarrassed when complimented. It is not necessary.

- 10. Make lemonade--A quote from Greg, "If things do not go right it's just one big learning experience. Some of my best learning experiences came out of failure which means, I guess, they aren't failures." So when you're handed a lemon, make lemonade.

- 11. Win — Helping others makes you feel good. This is the payoff.

Greg and Marianne Moser
by Bob Quadrozzi
Executive Director
Jay County Development
Portland, Indiana

My relationship with Greg and Marianne Moser has been two-fold. First of all, I know them as the owners of one of Portland/Jay County's most successful and growing industries: the machining and manufacturing of auto parts for the car racing industry.

Moser Engineering provides some of the highest paying jobs in Jay County. Greg and Marianne are devoted to hiring local people who want to live and raise their children in this community. Their excellent wages allow these workers to do just that.

The attitude and work ethics of their employees are reflected year in and year out by continued growth in sales and production capacity at Moser Engineering. Their total devotion to the well-being of each and every employee is unparalleled in my 28 years as an economic developer.

Secondly, I am proud to know Greg and Marianne as a couple committed to the total growth and success of our community. Their volunteer work for the local Chamber of Commerce, United Way, Jay County Arts Council, Jay County Library Building Committee, Local Red Cross Chapter, etc., etc., has involved countless hours of dedication and has raised millions of dollars for our charities. Without this kind of support and volunteerism, many of our local projects and fund drives would have never left the starting line.

To know Greg and Marianne Moser has been my honor. They are two individuals who are always willing to help our community in many ways. Their personal and business contributions are usually in place before they approach others for the same.

One of my favorite quotes of Greg Moser came to me at a meeting where the latest "Welfare-To-Work" programs were being discussed as they related to comparable fringe benefits, i.e.; sick pay, vacation pay, personal time, holidays, etc. Greg's statement was, "Please, let's not forget that employers do hire and pay people to work!"

In my mind, Moser Engineering does just that and at the same time Greg and Marianne are very sensitive to the total needs and happiness of all their employees as well as our community.

For these reasons, and many more, I am proud to know both Greg and Marianne and I personally say, "Thank you for helping Portland/Jay County 'Win The Race.'"

Greg Moser
by Vicki Tague
Executive Director
The Portland Area Chamber of Commerce
Portland, Indiana

The president of the Portland Area Chamber of Commerce called the meeting to order. "On the agenda, ladies and gentlemen, you will note that our first order of business is to appoint a director to complete the final year of Doug's term following his resignation from our board." "The floor is open for nominations." After a moment of rare silence, one of the directors uttered, "How about Greg Moser?" Somewhere outside Mr. Robert's guidelines came the statement from the president, "Well, how about him? What I meant was, is that a formal nomination?"

Indeed it was, so the president asked for discussion. Being a community of 7000 people means that name recognition is generally a given and a nominee's committee history is usually known by someone in the room.

Another board member raised the obvious questions. How is he currently involved? Does he regularly attend meetings? Does he follow through on assignments? Is he a proponent of the community in which he lives and operates his business?

The second rare moment of silence for my sometimes overly zealous board. "Comments, please!!," the president urged. It was apparent that Greg Moser didn't have a track record.

"Well, he started his own business in his garage and look at his success story. Talk about motivation and commitment!" stated a director.

"Anyone worked with Greg on a committee?" asked another. A round of "not me's."

"I don't care if he doesn't have a committee history, I believe he would be a conscientious director of the Portland Area Chamber of Commerce," announced the original nominator. "We need new blood and someone with fresh ideas and an eagerness to be involved. I call for the question."

The vote was taken, and Greg Moser was unanimously and enthusiastically elected to directorship.

Thus began Greg Moser's service to the community of Portland/Jay County, Indiana.

Of course, Greg proved to be such a faithful member of the board that by the end of his one year appointment as a director, he was promptly nominated by the official nominating committee to a full three-year term on the board.

Over those four years, it was my pleasure to observe Greg as he became a community leader. I can remember the first few meetings with Greg. I wondered if he ever spoke. I attributed his quietness to a bit of shyness and reluctance to contribute in discussion in this new arena. But that fallacious assumption soon gave way to my understanding of Greg's thoughtfulness. He's one of those rare individuals who doesn't utter his opinion until it is well thought out. I soon learned that he is a man of few words but lots of action.

However, there were exceptions to Greg's quiet nature. I very much enjoyed the few minutes before our board meetings when he would relay, with much animation, stories (I don't believe they were tales) about the thrills and agonies of drag racing. My all-time favorite saga of his was about going somewhere in Texas to pick up his special Harley Davidson motorcycle. The details of his trip there and ride back home are a story of such speed that it rivals the Concorde.

Greg is an engineer by trade. He is one of those folks who sees everything as black or white, which made my relationship with him very interesting, given my bent toward too many words spoken in gray areas. Greg was forced many times beyond his comfort zone, when committee and planning processes took, what seemed to him, more time than necessary to work through goals, strategies, and outcomes.

During Greg's tenure on the Board of Directors of the Chamber of Commerce, I had the privilege of watching him develop into a true community leader. As you may well guess, Greg became president of the board. On that January in 1994, when he rapped the gavel and called his first meeting to order, he was once again in unfamiliar territory. But he was learning and he was growing, and the spirit of community was beginning to emerge and find its place in his life.

As Portland continued to prosper, housing became a serious concern. Greg agreed to chair a housing task force that was formed to address community housing issues. By now he felt comfortable chairing meetings, but he came face to face with a new entity: "the community system." Learning who the players were and how to manipulate his way through the sea of bureaucracy in order to reach a desired goal was not always easy for Greg. But he was growing in determination to do all he could for his community, even when it meant moving forward into some of the areas that were not just black and white.

Greg's desire to make his hometown a better place to live is an honest one. How many times I have heard him say, "Let's quit talking about it and do something." . . . the simple philosophy of a quiet man.

Do something he has! In the last few years, among other involvements, he has chaired and motivated volunteers in a successful United Way campaign, chaired the community housing task force, spearheaded the fund-raising effort for our new, elegant Jay County Public Library, and served as president of the Portland Rotary Club. He has also been instrumental in the effort to revitalize the American Red Cross in Portland's Jay County. Greg is now assuming additional responsibility as chairman of the fund-raising campaign for the expansion of the Jay County Center for the Arts. He continues his involvement with the Chamber through committee involvement.

In 1995 Greg was selected for the prestigious Chamber of Commerce Citizen of the Year Award for his tireless community efforts and philanthropic endeavors. That same year Moser Engineering was recognized as Business of the Year; deserving acknowledgment for an entrepreneur who built his business into a successful enterprise through hard work and tenacity.

When he rapped the imaginary gavel and called the January 1994 meeting of the Board of Directors to order, I knew the organization was in good hands. Greg was not only going to be a good leader for the organization, but he was developing into an outstanding leader for our community.

Greg Moser: Successful Businessman . . . Philanthropist, Community Leader . . . Role Model. The quiet, unassuming man who believes everyone has value and that no mind should be wasted; who wants desperately to get the message across to all young people that to believe in oneself, to set goals, and to establish a good work ethic provides each and every person with the tools for success.

Greg Moser: A man who loves his family, race cars, the challenge of the business world, and his community, each in their individual ways, but with the same fervor. Greg is a man who has grown into the role of community leader.

Did it all begin on that evening in the conference room of the Portland Area Chamber of Commerce when the vote was cast and his election was announced? Perhaps. But I would suggest that what actually happened over that four-year period was not a beginning, but an awakening of a humble leader, who was able to assist our community in moving in new successful directions.

Chapter Fifteen

LIFE AND TIMES WITH GREG MOSER

"Brace for Impact!" by Mr. Jeff Bicknel
Racing with Greg by Ron Miller
My Years with Dad by Cindy Moser
A Glimpse by Cindy Moser

"Brace for Impact!"
by Mr. Jeff Bickel
Plant Manager
Moser Engineering
Portland, Indiana

Hello, let me introduce myself. I am Jeff Bickel, the plant manager of Moser Engineering.

In the 1980's, Greg and I were both employed at Teledyne Portland Forge, a company that specialized in close tolerance closed die forging for the heavy trucking, agriculture, and automotive markets. I was in sales and Greg was our plant engineering manager. Greg was later to become the vice president of manufacturing and engineering.

Greg and I got to know one another at our monthly management meetings. We began to share stories and it didn't take long to discover that drag racing was his passion. As a youth I had also tried my hand at drag racing, although not to the extent or scale that Greg had. I was very interested in racing and soon found myself spending many hours at the races or at Greg's house working with him on the race car.

Greg competed in the top sportsman class of the International Hot Rod Association (IHRA) and attended only the national event level races, which meant that traveling great distances was usually involved. A normal race may be a nine hour drive away. The pit crew consisted of Greg, his wife Marianne, his son Rob, and me.

Through the racing season there are many demands on an individual's time. It was difficult to balance Greg and Marianne's newly formed and growing business (Moser Engineering), family, school, his position at Teledyne Portland Forge, and the racing operation. I felt very fortunate to be able to travel to a few of these races as a part of the pit crew.

I knew how important racing was for Greg as he used his allotted vacation a few days at a time so that he could attend the races.

It was in the summer of 1986 or 1987 that I was the only one able to go with Greg on a long drive to one of the races in the Carolinas. You will have to excuse my being vague on the exact date because, as you will read, I have reasons to try to forget this trip.

The start of our journey had an uneventful beginning. Greg drove us from Portland, Indiana, to Corbin, Kentucky, where we stopped for fuel, food, and a change of drivers as it was now my turn to take the wheel.

The tow rig consisted of a new custom Chevy van with a turbocharged diesel engine, and an enclosed trailer that housed the race car and all the associated tools and gear.

With me at the wheel, we proceeded south on Interstate 75. Less than an hour into my turn driving, I was passing a few slower moving semi tractor/trailers so that we could maintain momentum on the upgrade. The road curved to the right where there was an unseen dip in the road surface. There were many factors that could have been and did come into play at that time. There may have been wind gusts as I passed the other trucks. It may have been the speed at which I was traveling, the dip, the curve, the upgrade, or possibly the greatest factor . . . my lack of driving experience with a rig like this. Anyway, the trailer soon started pushing the van. In a heartbeat, the van was out of control. Instead of accelerating out of this push condition, I was trying to slow the rig. The van was like a dog being wagged by it's tail. We were being swung violently from side to side. I can still remember that at about the same time the left front tire caught some loose stone on the shoulder of the road, Greg put his hands on the roof above him and said, "Brace for impact!" As the tire caught, it slowed that side of the van enough that we spun completely around and eventually we rolled over.

In an instant, I had destroyed everything Greg and Marianne had worked so hard to achieve. We were alive and for the most part unharmed. The van was a total loss. The enclosed trailer was reduced to a twisted flat bed trailer. The race car itself was also damaged. Tools, parts, and debris were scattered everywhere. It was almost as if a bomb had gone off. Police and wreckers were soon on the scene.

The remnants were taken to a holding area. Fortunately, the van, even though heavily damaged, was still driveable.

We found a telephone and called home to tell everyone what had happened and that we were, for the most part, okay. In describing what had happened I eventually broke into tears. Greg took his turn and called home. I could only sit and watch and wonder what was going through his mind.

I wanted to find a rock to crawl under and die as I had destroyed so much of his life and his dreams.

We found a place to stay the night. Bright and early the next morning we went to assess the damage and see how we were going to make it home. The van was driveable although it had no windshield and a replacement could not be installed as the roof line and the windshield opening were no longer of the correct dimensions. We found some Plexiglas and duct tape at a local hardware store and fashioned a windshield from them. Then it was time for a trip to the impound area to see the trailer and race remnants. The trailer, although destroyed, would function as a flat bed trailer to bring home the damaged goods.

We secured everything, settled up, and thanked those involved in the recovery and storing of the equipment and started off for a very long and quiet trip home. What had started out as a fun and exciting weekend had ended tragically.

On the way home, Greg, the eternal optimist, was already thinking about a new tow vehicle and trailer so he could get back to the racing he loved so much. Fortunately, the race car itself received only minor damage. A new tow rig was purchased, a new bigger and better trailer was designed and built and things were mostly back to normal by the next race season.

When we arrived at Greg's home we were greeted with hugs. The statement that Marianne made summarized things very well: "I am glad that you made it home safe. You can't be replaced, the other things can. We could easily have lost as much with a blown engine in the race car. I am thankful that you are both alive and well."

The business (Moser Engineering) grew and grew and eventually became more than Marianne wanted to handle by herself. By this time, Greg was the vice president of manufacturing and engineering at Teledyne Portland Forge by day and helped with the business during his lunch hours and in the evenings. It was time for some tough decisions to be made. The business that had begun as an offshoot of drag racing had become a real enterprise. Greg made the decision to resign from Teledyne Portland Forge in the fall of 1989. Greg was looking to build the company and add product and services. To do this, he needed more people to help with the day to day operations, the sales, and customer service side of the business. I was asked to be a part of the future of the company and in June of 1990, I started work at Moser Engineering.

I have witnessed first hand Greg's caring for his employees, his selflessness, and his desire to win. The extent of his civic involvement is much too lengthy to list here. Greg is a man of great generosity, a sense of community, and a love of family. If there were more people like Greg, the world would be a better place for all of us.

Racing with Greg
by Ron Miller
Driver and Engine Builder
Lebanon, Ohio

    The first time I ever met Greg in was Bristol, Tennessee, at the 1986 Spring Nationals. We were both running in the same class. That was called "Top Sportsman." Greg had an altered car and I also had one. We competed right next to each other. I really didn't know Greg and he didn't know me but we kind of hit it off. I'd say we became friends fairly fast. We ran basically about five or six national events that year. I can remember some of the days we had to sit outside of the gates before they would actually let us in as sportsman cars. Greg had a station wagon and kind of an open trailer and I also had the same basic outfit. We were really low buck racers. I can remember staying outside the gates before they would let us in or to be checked in. We would sleep on the side of the road in sleeping bags. My wife and my young children both stayed with us and Greg had his son and a lot of times his wife would be with him. We can reminisce even today about some of those days. They were a lot of fun but they really were a low buck way of racing.
    Greg and I started to race together and against one another for about the next two years. In the next year, about 1987, I started doing some work for Greg in sports, building some of these engines and doing some sonar head work. I can remember at the time he was working at Portland Forge and he was also running a business resplining axles on the side. Basically, that is what supported his racing operation. Greg decided that year to have me do some work for him. I paid for my racing operation by doing outside work such as building engines, building race car engines, or whatever I could do like sonar head work. I taught school for a living at the Career Center in Lebanon, Ohio.
    Greg and I stayed in touch throughout the first two or three years that we knew one another. We raced against each other, and like I said, we raced in the same class. We had a lot of good times and it was a lot of fun. After we built Greg a new engine, he was running one of the fastest alters in the country. At the time, I was running a small block car, a small block dragster, and other cars.
    In remembering back to racing at various race tracks, I know Greg sometimes would run times that were faster than any of the big block alters.

It made him feel really good and it made me feel good, too, because I was doing some of the engine work for him. But Greg had a lot of innovations back then. He built a lot of things on his car himself and also on the chassis and the rear end components. Greg was very innovative even before he went into the business that he has now. We talk about it today and we can reminisce about the good old days that we had in the first two or three years together.

In 1988, Greg and I were both at the Sports Nationals and we were having a really good year in the class. I was going into that race actually number one in the point standings in Top Sportsman Eliminator. I had a small block engine dragster and Greg had an altered car with a 500 cubic inch big block.

Both cars were about equally matched in performance and we were at a track that was really poor. Greg's car was what they call a "solid mounted chassis." In other words, he didn't have any suspension on it. The track was in Marion, Ohio, at the Sports Nationals and we were making a qualifying run together with Greg in the right lane and I in the left lane. The right lane had a major dip in it just past the finish line. A lot of people don't understand this because they have never seen what some solid mounted cars do, but they have a tendency to bounce, especially on a bad race track. What happened was that we made the run, and when I pulled the parachute, I didn't realize that Greg had hit the dip that was in the right lane. It had caused many cars to crash. He lost control, and he tried everything in the world to straighten it out, but he hit me in the side. He practically T-boned my car. He put me in a 180 degree spin and we both proceeded to hit the guard rail on the other side of the track. The crash was serious, but luckily, we both got away with only minor injuries.

That was really the last time that Greg ever drove a race car. I don't think it had anything to do with that wreck, but I think he was really more worried about me and, at the time, I think he thought it was his fault. It wasn't really his fault. It was a bad race track and it could've happened to anyone with that type of race car. Greg really felt badly, not only about hitting my car but about putting us both in pretty bad jeopardy. But what was really good was that we worked all night together and were able to run again the next day after making repairs. Greg offered to pay for everything so it really wasn't a major deal. Greg didn't drive anymore after that.

One of the reasons was because his business just took off. The year was 1990 and Greg decided he wanted to get back into racing. I had stayed in touch with Greg through the years and he decided that he wanted to sponsor our car. We had a small block dragster and his willingness to support me really helped me out financially. Greg's business was really going well. By the end of 1990 we had set two national records and had run faster than any small block dragster that's ever been in the class!

In '91 and '92, Greg backed me again in the top dragster class and we decided to build a big block dragster. Both of our families went to almost every national event held in those two years. We were both working on the car, we stayed at the same motels, we ate at the same restaurants, and we were all family together. Greg paid most of the bills and we had a great year. In 1992, we were running top dragster and our big block dragster was the fastest that's ever run in the class with the records set in 1992 never having been surpassed to this day. That year, we won 12 quick-eights out of 14 national events and we won one national title in that class. The quick-eight is when the fastest eight cars run heads up on Saturday night with no break-out whatsoever. We won 12 of those races! We literally set records that year that even today are still standing. We really had a great time in 1992 and without the support of Greg and Marianne, we could never have had the year that we had as family together.

Also, in 1992, we were all at the Empire Nationals at Buffalo, New York. We entered that race in top dragster and we were about the fastest car in the class. On Sunday, they run the fastest 32 cars in a handicapped break-out type system. Cars like ours would never win those types of races normally. But at this particular event, we not only qualified number one with the 690 at 198 miles an hour, but we won the quick eight on Saturday night over Von Smith. On Sunday, we entered the car just basically to learn new things about the car. We wanted to try different things. We never intended to do well on Sunday because cars like this normally never did. Then we won the first round and we thought that was just a fluke. We ran a 690 and we were spotting cars over a second and a half. Then we won the second round so we decided to get serious about it. We didn't bother anything else on the car and just decided to go for it. We ended up winning the event and that was the first time that has ever happened! In fact, it is probably the only time that it will ever happen with a car like this being not only the number one qualifier but winning the quick eight and Sunday's event also. It was just a great weekend and both families were really delighted with what happened. Greg and I both couldn't believe it, and to this day we still talk about it, and so does most of the racing community. It was just a great day for all of us!

Highlighting that year in 1992, Greg and I went to the world finals in Darlington, South Carolina. We set the top dragster record at that event at a 683 at 199 miles an hour. To this day, the record still holds. The sportsman classes that Greg and I have won include four national titles. We have set 14 national records in various classes either singly or together.

After 1992, we had a great year in the sportsman class. In top dragster, Greg decided that he would like to try to run professional class and he talked about it quite a bit throughout '92 and we decided to go into pro-stock. Greg's lifelong dream for years was that he wanted to run a professional class and he has always really been fascinated with pro-stock eliminator.

A lot of people don't understand the different kinds of drag racing classes. I'll try to shine a little light on them. Pro-stock in drag racing is probably one of the most sophisticated classes there is. The class itself contains factory represented cars. In other words, Thunderbirds, Camaros, Monte Carlos, Cutlasses, and different classes of cars like that have to be American built. But after that, the silhouette of the car has to be just like a factory duplicate. But these are very high-tech, very expensive machines to run. The cars have to weigh a minimum of 2375 pounds with the driver. The chassis are very complicated as far as design and what's put into the chassis themselves. They have strict body templates that they put on so the car has to look just like that particular model year. The cars themselves are very sophisticated. Just the chassis alone is anywhere from $70,000 to $80,000 and that doesn't include the engine or the transmission or the drive line components or anything like that. The engine in our class is limited to 815 cubic inches. They cost, if you went out to buy one, anywhere from $75,000 to $100,000 each just for the engines. The engines make well over 1650 horse power.

We have a Jerry Haas race car now. We actually have two of them. We just purchased a '98 Monte Carlo. We have been running a '96 Cutlass this season. But to give you a little bit more about the class itself, in pro-stock racing they take 16 qualifiers. Generally in IHRA, the class that we are in, there are 30 to 33 cars that show up to try to qualify to become one of the 16 cars. For the class that we're in, especially in the last two years, the competition has become unbelievable as far as the qualifying fields go. Last year, for the three or four events that we were in, the separation of #1 to #16 qualifiers was under five hundredths of a second. Moving up from #8 to #6 spot in the qualifying field was sometimes separated by only one to two thousandths of a second. It is quite unbelievable when you have fields that tight with 16 or 20 different teams that are out there.

It has become a very exclusive class, both money-wise and technical-wise. The class has become some of the most competitive racing in the world. In terms of the money involved, you can't run these cars unless you have a budget of at least $500,000 a year to spend, and that is about as inexpensively as one can do it.

The big thing about pro-stock is the fans. They really love it throughout the country. We match race probably seven or eight times a year, and you can't imagine the number of people who come out just to buy a T-shirt or get autographed pictures of the car. It has become a very popular class with the fans.

Let me explain how Greg and I got into pro-stock. After 1992, we decided to go into this class. I had never driven a pro-stock car. Pro-stock was a new world for me because when I got into the class I was already 43 years old. I was a little reluctant because I didn't have any experience driving one of these cars. They are very difficult to drive. They run in 6 seconds to a little over 200 mph from a dead stop in a quarter of a mile. Some people ask what it is like driving one of these cars. It's like being shot out of a cannon! The g-forces are unbelievable. You pull about 5 g's when you leave the line, going from 0 to 60 mph in 8 to 9 tenths of a second, and from 0 to 160 mph in 4 seconds. That is the acceleration that these cars have got. They are very difficult to drive, shifting four or five times, wanting to get all over the race track with you. These cars are very tricky to get down the race track. I was really reluctant when Greg first talked to me about it. But, before the season was over, we decided to take a shot and try to run the class for 1993.

Greg and I didn't have any experience with it, but Greg was gung-ho just like he is in everything else that he does in the business world. He doesn't have a negative thought. Greg Moser is positive in every way. It doesn't matter if he wants to fly from here to the moon, he'll be positive about it and if it can be done, he'll try to do it. My job was to drive the car and to build the engines and make the horse power. We would learn as we go, so to speak. Basically, to put it mildly, 1993 was a flop. We had a very difficult time, having no experience in the class. We came out of a sportsman class and into a professional class. We thought we would do very well the first year, but we didn't. We qualified in only one event that year and that was in New Hampshire. We qualified #16, and we were thrilled to get into that race! But in none of the other races were we able to bump into the 16th spot, even running on Sunday. Anyway, I built the engine for the car. We didn't have any dyno facility and we didn't have any experience with those types of engines. But, overall, the first year we did fairly well for a non-experienced team. My son-in-law helped out on the car endurance parts and Greg's son, Rob, was doing most of the crew work that year. They did very well. We had another guy who works for Moser Engineering, Gary, who worked very hard on the car and did a great job. But Greg and Marianne, myself, my wife, Sharon, and son, Darren, Rob, and Gary basically learned as we went. And we learned very quickly that we would have to try some different moves if we were going to have any success in pro-stock racing.

That year we did our best, we learned quite a bit, but Greg decided we would have a brand new chassis built. The car that we bought that year was an older car. It was a good car, but it was a little outdated, so Greg had a brand new Rick Jones race car, a '94 Camaro, built for the next year. That same year, Greg made me an offer to quit teaching at the Career Center here at Warren County where I've been teaching for 17 years. I had tenure, I had a lot of security at this job, but Greg made me a better offer than I had at school to quit the job and to go into working on this car and working on engines full time. I thought about it seriously for several weeks before I finally made the decision. I decided to join Greg because I trusted him very much. I knew he wouldn't be asking me to quit a job that I already had with tenure, with good security, along with a little side business, if he hadn't been serious. Everything was going pretty well for me as far as money goes. But Greg made me a good offer to quit, and I respected that offer. I gave notice, retired from teaching, and went into racing full time.

In '94, we really didn't have a much better year. We did qualify twice, and we received the Best Appearing Crew Award because, although it is a family operation, we have very sharp uniforms and the whole operation is very nice. As part of our fine operation, our equipment, trailer, truck, race car, and rig take a second seat to no one out there, even to the most heavily financed teams in the business. Also, we received the Best Engineered Car award for our '94 Camaro, but we were trying to work out a brand new car which turned out to be a mistake in buying because we didn't have enough experience in the class. We were running against people who had 15, 20, or 25 years of experience, against heavily financed teams, against corporate sponsored teams, like General Motors and others. We weren't prepared and we didn't have a good year in '94.

So, in '95, we got another car, an Oldsmobile, and we started doing a lot better. We began running better and being a lot more competitive. The class also got a lot harder. The spreads became significantly tighter than they were in our first two years in the class. So in '95, the class kept getting harder to run every time we went out. It was mind boggling and a very stressful time! We were doing everything we could and we were getting faster and better prepared, but the class was getting tougher to run. A lot of the well financed and well prepared teams began dropping out along the wayside because the competition got way too hard.

Like I said before, Greg always stayed so positive. Even though at times I wanted to give up, Greg wouldn't and he stuck right in there, so we stayed right with it. Throughout '95 we struggled, but we kept getting a little faster and a little faster. In '96, we had the Oldsmobile running really well, and that year was one of our better years. Since '93, the power levels of the engines had come up quite a bit. In '95, Greg bought a new dyno facility for me in which to test the new engines.

With my knowledge of internal combustion engines, I feel that eventually we will be ahead of everybody as far as the engine goes. But for these first three years in pro stock, I have to admit, we just didn't have enough power in our engines. Basically, in pro-stock, there are two sources of engines. People go to either Sonny Leonard from Virginia for the GM products or to John Kaase from Atlanta, Georgia, for the Ford products. Those two guys are very smart. For years they have been the dominant force as far as building pro-stock engines, and each of them have about nine or ten customers who are buying or leasing those engines from them. These engines are between $75,000 and $100,000 dollars, and every time you take them back to have them freshened up, it costs about $15,000. So this is a very expensive project. Greg Moser could have bought Sonny Leonard engines when he went into this, but he refused to do it. He wanted to have our own engine program. He wanted me to figure out the horse power. He recognized my talents years ago as far as doing this. He had a lot of faith in me — a lot more faith than I had in myself. He refused to buy or lease other engines. We were going to do it ourselves and that was his whole game plan. So I stuck with it. I developed more things about the engine, but the research and development on the engines was coming a little slow.

We don't have a big elaborate shop, but we have a very nice dyno facility. We don't have a lot of man power to develop different things when it comes to the engine. When you get these engines and start working with them, they might look like a giant V-8 engine, but everything is hand-built. Everything is designed from the paper up. I've designed the sonar head, the manifolds, and everything that is on this engine. It has taken years to get to where we are right now. Greg financed all of this. He put in all the money, all the faith, and all the patience for me to get where we are at right now. For this, I am eternally indebted to Greg. He stuck with me when few people would have.

In '96, we had one of the fastest cars in existence, but we didn't win any races due to a lack of experience in getting the car down the race track, understanding the clutch combinations, and the chassis. There were things we still didn't know, but we did have a lot of horsepower, and we made some pretty impressive runs in '96.

In '97, we did a lot better. We had more power and we had the car in a lot better shape, but the class got much tighter. We were one of the few teams that was a family operation with unpaid outside sources coming in to race. Most of the other teams, including the Ford backed teams, the

Chrysler backed teams, and the GM backed teams, had their own engineers going to every race and their own clutch specialists. In '97, we were still running our family operation, still building our own engines, were competing against the best in the country, and were running them head to head. What was happening was that all these teams that we were racing against were getting faster and faster every year. The power was going way up and engines had a lot more horsepower. Greg explained it by saying that we were actually catching a running horse. In other words, they were making ground when we came in two or three years ago, and we were way behind them. But we were catching them even though they had a big head start and were running, at first, faster than we were. Now, we have caught them and are making the same amount of power as anyone in the country. We still need more experience, but we are getting that and are confident that in 1998 we will be one of the best teams out there.

This is what Greg's dream is. He loves racing, he wants to run in a professional class, and he wants to do it in different ways than some of your other millionaire entrepreneurs out there. He wants to do it as a team and family operation and he wants me to develop the power. He wants me to make the engine perform better than anything GM or Chrysler ever intended it to be. Basically, we have done this and in 1996, ESPN did a 30 minute special on us because of the fact that we build our own engines and are the only team out there that does this. In one of the most competitive classes in all forms of motor sports, we build our own engines and work on the car ourselves. This is a rarity today, but it was Greg's intention. He wanted it this way. He could have hired high dollar crew chiefs and he could've bought the best engines, but instead he wanted to do it this way. Greg has a way of finding the talent and getting the talent on the team. This is one of his expertises, too, in his business. That is basically a small highlight of what we have done up to this point in pro-stock.

Because Greg is an excellent machinist, he has made a lot and has designed a lot for the car which has made the maintenance on the car a lot easier. He also built the complete third member in the car. If anyone could ever see this who understands anything about mechanics and about the engineering of a car, they would really appreciate it. In building the third member, Greg started with a 12" by 12" chunk of aluminum and he machined the complete third member out of this aluminum, the carrier. He has also made components in the car, like a quick release coupler for the drive line. It is fascinating when you realize that this was all done on a vertical mill and it shows you the talents that Greg has in machining.

To me, Greg is a workaholic. If he isn't at his business in Portland, Indiana, then he's somewhere in the state working on his business. He's always making something, either for his equipment or for his shop. That's the way he is. That is what I really respect about Greg. He's not a three piece suit man who comes in everyday to work, sits behind a desk, makes a few calls to some people, and then goes home. Greg goes out hands-on, ready to work. Other people I've talked to say the same thing about him. They respect a man when they see him at his multi-million dollar business in jeans and a T-shirt. Not a day goes by when Greg isn't working out there in the shop. Even though he has several employees who can probably do the work, Greg has to see it himself because he's a hands-on person. There are too many phonies in the world, and Greg is definitely not a phony.

In pro-stock, I have no second thoughts and no regrets about quitting the job I had. I love the job I have now, even though Greg and I live about 150 miles apart. My job is to maintain and keep this operation going. We do everything on the car, but Greg is a hands-on person at the track. He is not just a car owner, and he is not just a sponsor. He helps, he watches the car, he drives me to the line every time I make a run. As a matter of fact, there have been very few races that Greg has ever missed. But when he has missed a race, I feel very reluctant about even being there because I trust his opinion so much at the races that I am kind of worried when he is not present. I really don't trust anyone else except for him to put me on the starting line because he watches everything, he turns the computer on, he watches the cars, he gives non-overbearing opinions about the car. We discuss everything after we make a run and look at the computer data that the car gives after the run. We talk about it, we make a logical decision, and then we'll make a change on the car. This has been the way that Greg and I have operated for years.

Like I said before, I consider Greg to be one of my best friends. It isn't just a work related acquaintance or a employer / employee relationship. Greg puts my logo with his on everything related to the car. "Ron Miller Racing" is on everything. It is on the car and on the uniforms. He has been that way since day one. Greg and I talk a lot on the phone, we discuss a lot of things about the car, and we make a lot of decisions together. It's not just a one person deal.

Greg, myself, and my wife, Sharon went to Washington D.C. to run in what is called the Pro-Stock Governor's Cup Classic. Every year they invite 16 cars to go to this race. It is usually in the middle of July or the first of August. We drove all night to get there. Greg drove about half the way and I drove about half the way. We got there really late at night and slept in the big truck we have, which is kind of like a mini motor home with a lounge. The next day we went out and qualified for the race. I remember the temperature got up to about 105 degrees. It was not only hot just standing, but it had to be 150 degrees inside the car. We didn't have any extra crew people that day, just the three of us, but we got runner-up, making it to the final round. Greg and I were working on the car, my wife was packing the parachutes, and the 33,000 people there were actually looking inside the car while Greg and I were working. We were just about worn out. But we didn't really mind the temperature because we ran well and got runner-up. That same night at about midnight we left the track and drove 9 hours to get home because Greg had to be at his business the next day. We got home at 9 a.m. on Thursday morning. Everybody was laughing because they said that we must not be "over the hill" yet to be able to do what we did. We drove 9 hours, got four hours of sleep, ran the race, got runner-up against some of the best cars in the country, and then drove all night to get back home. We all had a pretty good laugh over that. We showed some of the young guys that we could still do it by ourselves if we had to and they laughed. But we would have really appreciated some extra help, believe me!

As far as the future goes for us in pro-stock, I am a lot more positive now than I was two years ago. With Greg's support and his ambition, we will be the world champion in pro-stock. I hope that before I retire from driving we will be the world champion. I know that we will be one of the most competitive teams in the class, if not the most competitive, because we have shown other people, including our peers, national magazines, and other companies that we are the team to watch over the next two years. That makes us feel very good because when our competitors and other companies start realizing our potential and how good we can really be, it gives us a lot of confidence. I really believe that you'll see this team and Moser Engineering go all the way to the top in pro-stock before we're finished.

To sum-up everything, what I would like to give you are my feelings about Greg Moser. Greg may be a difficult person to know and to understand. Many of you do not even know Greg, but I will give you some insights about him as I have known him for over ten years.

Greg started a very small business, literally out of the garage attached to his home, and has built it into a business second to none. He built it from scratch into a multi-million dollar company! His new facility is a work of art. He has moved the company from no where to a place beyond the imagination. That is very admirable.

The people who work for Greg have only the best to say of the company and him. They are rarely absent, take no sick days, and do not quit. The Christmas bonuses and annual trips for all employees, spouses included, are not provided by most other companies. Of course, I am not totally knowledgeable about Greg's business, but I do race with him and consider him to be one of my best friends, if not my best friend.

Greg is one of the most generous men I have known. If you have any work ethic, he is there to try to help you. He has headed-up the United Way and has involved me in showing cars to raise money. He not only offers money, he donates his time as well. He has worked with the American Red Cross, has redone the community's library, and has received many citizenship awards locally and statewide.

No one else commands my trust more than Greg does. Anything he tells you can be taken to the bank. I feel that Greg is like a brother and I would not be as successful as I am today if it were not for him. He took me from where I was, sponsored me when no one else would, and opened up dreams for me that I would never have accomplished on my own. I have a lot of talent, but he is responsible for me achieving what I have thus far.

Greg likes seafood, unlike myself, and he takes me to fine restaurants, but he always orders me the steak of my choice. We have had many fine times together and we have gone to many fine places together, but it is only now that we have finally reached that point where we are one of the finest racing teams in the country and have some of the finest engines in the country and that is because of Greg Moser.

Greg is a self-made man, who may have some faults, but he sure doesn't have many. He is a man of his word, unselfish, and generous. I have been with him again and again where he has proven that anyone employed by him is a part of his family. He is not a greedy person, but very generous. My wife and family have found him to be everything I have said, too. Marianne Moser is a great women and assisted Greg in starting the business from nothing and building it into the success that it is today. I cannot express what these fine people mean to me other than to say thanks to them for all they have done. The world is a better place because of them!

My Years with Dad
by Cindy Moser

In the Beginning:

My earliest memories of my father come from a trip to Cedar Point in Sandusky, Ohio, when I was 7 years old. What I didn't know then was that the man who kept my head from hitting the sides of the roller coaster seats would make such a tremendous impact on my life. Not just as the father I had never had, but as a role model and mentor. I don't think I have ever met a person with so much desire to do what they love and so much love for what they are doing.

Dad had a regular 9 to 5 job, but that's not the person I saw. The man I saw everyday had passions and dreams that could never be realized while working for someone else. First, I think I need to give a little history. My dad, who is by far one of the smartest people I know, doesn't even have a college degree. But don't hold that against him! If anything it makes him that much more remarkable. He is, in the truest sense of the phrase, "A self-made man."

Anyway, Dad always had dreams and passions that went beyond his 9 to 5 job and were realized at home, with his family and hobbies. Dad has always been one who not only works hard, but also plays hard. Eventually, it became tough to find any differences between work and play, because he enjoys his life so much.

Over the years, I remember many late nights and long weekend days where Dad would be outside in his shop working on his race car. It seemed as if there was always something that needed to be done or some new idea that needed to be perfected. I'll admit, I still have only a small clue as to what Dad actually did out in the shop all those nights, but we were always welcome to help out and watch. As long as the race car made it down the track and went faster than a lot of the other cars, I was happy, but not Dad. He was always looking for that little something that would give him the edge. In reality, that's where the entire Moser Engineering axle business began — the business which has allowed him to give back to others so they can also realize their potential.

Sundays at the Races:

It was always such a great feeling to go to the races on Sundays. I really don't know why I enjoyed it so much. It's not like I understood much more than winning and losing, but racing on Sundays was always a family thing. We would pack up the back of the station wagon with food, drinks, and, of course, all the necessary race car equipment. Then we would load up the car on the trailer, and we would all get to help. At least I thought I was helping. Then we would set off for old Van Wert Raceway. It would be a typical Sunday at the races. We would get there, off-load the race car and unpack the necessary equipment from the back of the wagon--important things like the hood scoop cover and white shoe polish used to write the dial-in on the car. These were the important things to me because they were the ones that I could be in charge of if I wanted to be. Racing was always a family thing. I'll admit, I probably didn't want to go racing every Sunday, but those Sundays were always family time, even if it just meant being at the track! When I was younger, I had no idea what made one car faster than the other. I just know that I have always thought that Dad was the best racer out there.

When Dad decided to move up into the IHRA, racing involved a lot more travel and long weekends at the national events. I didn't get to go to too many races after that. I'll admit, my desire to go also began to diminish. But it has always been a great feeling to show up at the races and be able to say, "That's my dad!", whether he won or lost. Even now, it's great to go and watch the passion in my Dad's eyes for racing as Ron drives in the Pros. Every little detail matters to him, and every little thing needs to be perfected.

The Moser Engineering Days:

I watched Moser Engineering grow from Dad's hobby in the evenings — with Mom doing the entire shipping, receiving, technical services, and finance department — to the hiring of Greg Imel, our first employee, when the work load grew to where Dad could no longer finish it in the time after work. There were also the many years where Rob, my brother, was the shipping department. He would wrap the axles and get them ready to send out after school each day. Eventually, I decided I wanted to help out, too. I would get paid up to $1 per box to unwrap the boxes and then write down the description and address so Mom could type the invoices each day. I am guessing there weren't too many 13 year olds who could tell the difference between a Ford axle and a Mopar axle, know why a Chevy axle could not be resplined and also know the number of splines on the axle just by looking, but I sure could!!

It is amazing how quickly Moser Engineering outgrew our garage under my parents' guidance and moved into it's own building. Each year the company grew in double digits and more and more people became part of the Moser Engineering family. About this time, Dad also decided to retire from The Forge to work full-time in his business. I'll admit, those were occasionally tense times. Even though Moser Engineering was doing tremendous and both Mom and Dad were working full-time, it was strange knowing that everything depended on the success of the family's business.

Even after Moser Engineering moved out of the garage, Rob and I still worked there around our school and sports schedules. For this reason, I only worked in the summers. My parents may not agree with this statement, but I wouldn't trade the experience of working out in the shop for six summers for anything in the world. It is very important to me now that I had a hand in building the business from the ground up, even though it was only a small hand! In high school and college, while other kids were waiting tables and working as cashiers as their jobs, I was out there working in the grease and grime. But I wasn't just working to make money like they were, I was working for my family. There was always an added sense of pride and a desire to do the job well because it was also MY Name that was on every box that went out the door.

Eventually, Mom and Dad also started hiring other kids from our high school to work in the shop after school. I think that working for a company like Moser Engineering can also teach kids a lot about hard work and respect for what they are doing. I can guarantee that every kid who has worked at Moser Engineering, either wrapping or unwrapping boxes or cutting housings, realizes how important each person is to the overall success of a business such as Moser Engineering. Even if they have taken nothing else with them from this job, it's still a lesson well worth learning.

It is truly amazing what an impact a family business can have on you. You always hear stories of families where one child stays at home to run the business and the other can't get far enough away from it, although I'm not sure that has actually happened in my family. My brother and I both went far away from home to college, with Rob to Southern California and me to Massachusetts, but there are parts of the business that will always pull us home. Rob actually decided to return to Indiana to work for Moser Engineering after graduation. I, on the other hand, have not returned, but take the ideals instilled in me from my parents' business with me wherever I go. I have found that I look for the same qualities in my employer, managers, and co-workers that my father looks for in his employees and has instilled in his business. It's the little things that make the business run smooth:

> Listening to everyone's ideas, no matter who they are.
> Honesty!
> An environment where everyone's work is important. The job can't happen if everyone doesn't do their part.
> Respect
> Commitment
> and a Feeling of Ownership.

These are the values by which my dad runs his company. He is one of the few employers left who truly believes that if you treat your employees well they will also treat you well. Moser Engineering has always been a family business. Everyone who works there is part of our family.

As part of his operating culture, Dad also demands a certain amount of respect and hard work from his employees. In return, the company takes care of them. There are the little things like "Pizza Wednesdays" and "Donut Fridays", and the fact that there is always a stocked refrigerator with soda for the guys during the day. We have also always had company canoeing trips where everyone brings along a guest and has a great time on the river away from work. But the most unique gift that Moser Engineering gives back to its employees is the annual Christmas Party. Yes, all companies have Christmas parties. But not all companies pack up all the employees with their guests and takes them away to have a weekend of fun. Moser Engineering Christmas parties have occurred everywhere from Chicago and Detroit to Las Vegas and the Bahamas. These are the little things that give the employees not just a chance to be away from Portland, Indiana, for a weekend, but to see places they might not otherwise visit and have a chance to learn about a new place or explore a museum while also having fun bonding with each other.

Mom and Dad also give to their employees in ways most larger companies cannot. My parents have been able to help out by giving advice, loans, and an occasional reality check to the people who work for them. Most importantly, my parents have given the employees of Moser Engineering enough so they are not just "getting by," but enough that they can give something back to the community in which they all live. Moser Engineering gives them a feeling of worth that can be passed on to their children. It also gives people a reason to stay and raise families in Jay County, which in itself helps the community grow and prosper. I know that my parents realize what they are giving to the employees and community. I just hope that those who are on the receiving end also realize their good fortune.

The Sensitive Side:

To really see how sensitive my dad is, you have to see him with our cats. Here is this big, tough looking guy (yep, he scared away a few boyfriends while I was growing up!) who will just cuddle the cats like babies. I believe that it is the rarely seen sensitive side that has now compelled my dad to give back to the community. He wasn't always community minded, so I actually thought it was kind of odd when he started joining clubs and doing other things around Jay County. It wasn't until Moser Engineering had gotten off to a great start and our family became firmly planted in Portland that Dad started to give back. I think he realized that he had more to give than just jobs for a few people in the area. He has lots of ideas about how to make Jay County a better place to live and grow.

Through caring and hard work, he has earned the respect of all the citizens in Jay County.

A time that I'll never forget is when I first saw my dad cry. It was at my grandfather's funeral after he had died of cancer. It was at that point I realized just how special it is to have a father who is not only a father, but a friend. At that moment, Dad was saying "Goodbye," not just to his dad, but to a special friend. I hope this is the relationship that I will be able to maintain with my dad. Though I don't want to think of the day that I will have to say "Goodbye," I know on that day I will be saying it to My DAD, My Role Model, My Mentor, and My Friend. I am just glad that he has been able to share who he is with more of the world than just our family.

MOM:

An important feature of Moser Engineering may often get overlooked. That is my Mom. It is important to realize that Moser Engineering could never be what it is today without Mom. It's been said that you must surround yourself with trusted people who can bring to the company different strengths, but who still share the same values. Fortunately, my father found that person in my mother. She has spent many, many hours building the business behind the scenes. She started out as the core technical service department, shipping and receiving department, and financial department while also raising three children. When the business grew, Mom's responsibilities also grew as she became responsible for others working for her in the shipping and receiving department. She has always been there for Dad. He bounces ideas off of her and she gives him her input. My father never could have built Moser Engineering alone. But with Mom by his side the entire way, his dream, THEIR DREAM, has become a reality.

To Wrap it Up:

My dad is successful, not just because he has created a successful business, but because he has grown as a person along the journey. Dad's success cannot only be measured in the profits from Moser Engineering, but also by the size of his heart. He has grown from loving and caring about his family to including his employees and their families and now, the community in which they live and grow. This is the reason Dad is a truly successful man.

A Glimpse
by Cindy Moser

A man of greatness
A man of pride
You are fortunate to get to know him
And catch a glimpse of who he is inside

Caring and compassionate in his own ways
A hug from him can make your entire day
To cuddle next to him feels safe
To walk beside him feels strong

Very few can see the man beneath his exterior shield
But he gives to all in his own special ways
With words of wisdom
And examples to live by

Not many see the world the way he does
As a game to be played
For when you quit having fun
Obstacles are no longer opportunities
And barriers cannot be tools

To follow along behind him
Fills one with amazement and wonder
As a pile of metal becomes a machine
And that machine roars to life

He gives others opportunities
To live and realize their dreams
A chance to believe in themselves
A chance to do what he has done

For those who catch a glimpse
Or if they are lucky
A chance to fully see the man inside
A lasting impression will be made

For few can be a father

A role model and mentor
And forever remain
A friend

His impact is everlasting
For the fortunate few
Who catch a glimpse
Of the man inside.

Chapter Sixteen

WORKING WITH GREG MOSER

by Robert Read, Ph.D.
President
Second Opinion, Inc.
Portland, Indiana

When memory keeps me company it rarely has an accurate calendar. The further I penetrate the past the greater my confusion of exact dates. However, it is easy to recall the images and events that give Greg Moser a special place in my memory. I leave the hard work of exact chronology to the research of others. I will enjoy writing a few stories that define Greg for me.

Defining Greg was more than a fun challenge, it was my job. It began as an employment application and an interview. Portland Forge, a Teledyne company, needed an engineer, not just an engineer for the problems of the moment, but an engineer who could contribute to the replacement of an aging general management team. A good, practical engineer with leadership character who would come to Portland, Indiana, to stay. Greg Moser had the right stuff, and I remember the notes I made as we interviewed each other to see if we both had a good fit. I wrote, "Hard head, soft heart, will win or crash, would not flap in either case." (Had I known as much as I should have about Greg's drag racing passion, I would have realized how concretely true these thoughts were.) He had formal engineering education, but could care less whether he could calculate the moments of inertia of moving bodies. He knew he didn't need to make those calculations. He knew forging tools, a fuller from an edger, and an upsetter from a hammer. Above all, he could simplify rather that complicate engineering issues. His hard head was obvious. It was clear that Greg did not suffer fools or foolishness gladly. Foolishness prompted quick, good humored correction whether from a peer or from a potential boss who was interviewing. At the same time his soft heart touched him for his own errors as he relived his mistakes painfully. This was good stuff for sure, but to ice the cake he considered Jay County his family home. He might stay!

After Greg accepted our offer to join the Portland Forge management team, some early events were good omens for his future role. The Mosers soon purchased a modest, unfinished home just east of Portland.

Greg invited me to drop-by for a look, and when I arrived, I discovered an uncounted mob of Mosers cutting, staining, varnishing, and nailing woodwork for the entire house. Their good humor and enterprise were awesome. I remember leaving that home with some sense of pride. I had obeyed hiring rule number one, "get good people."

The "good person" attribute is often better measured by peers than by the boss. The favorable feedback came quickly, but not from everyone, with the occasional ruffled feathers which I often considered a good thing. He had that hard head and the straight forward making of an error, not with malice, but not necessarily honeyed either. As I listened to compliments and complaints and judged the source of each, it was clear we had hired a man of action.

I know that Greg made mistakes. I remember the details of very few of them. What I do remember well was that Greg was quick to admit his mistakes, and, in some cases took responsibility for errors of others. He would come into my office and slouch into a chair with a half-smile that tried to cover his feelings. I soon learned to know what was coming. After a long pause he would say, "Well, I screwed up." Patience was required to allow the details to come out, but come they would. Anyone who thought or thinks that Greg Moser is a happy-go-lucky type should sit with him when he relives an error. I think it is the reason he makes so few. Errors taught Greg, but never defeated him.

The entire atmosphere of Portland Forge factory management changed in the early 1980s. Managers became associates and team members among whom rank was unimportant. A stranger stepping into their shift review sessions could not have identified who was in charge of what, nor could he have been sure he was witnessing a serious management meeting rather than a party. The entire group assembled in Ernie Bright's office and tackled the day and each other with lie detectors completely displayed. Only close attention could determine whether the meeting was serious. Greg Moser not only fit into this management program, he more than fit into it. He made a major contribution.

One of Greg's early engineering assignments was an unpleasant challenge indeed. A substantial area of factory property had become a dump for unwanted factory equipment. It was overgrown with a thicket of trees and had attracted "dumpers." It was clear that junk is a magnet for more junk. It had been explained to me by several old timers that Portland Forge could not afford to clean this monster mess, and besides, it wasn't hurting anything. One morning the front page of the Commercial Review featured a photograph of a pair of wood ducks waddling down Meridian Street so covered with oil or tar that they could not fly. The Review knew,

I knew, everyone knew where the wood ducks had been.

Actually, I don't recall needing to give Greg a directive. He went at that problem with a vengeance. Trees and trash disappeared, a large transformer from another Portland factory was removed, PCBs and all, the oil was gone, and a new waste oil collection system was installed. In addition, drainage for the neighboring Coca Cola bottler was improved. Today, the grass grows and blows on the old trash site. Many helped to make it so, but Greg Moser lead the charge. It was done without nasty visits from the mayor or the EPA (Environmental Protection Agency). Had we waited for those events, we could have discovered the hard way what we could afford and what we could not.

As part of our clean-up we also bulldozed the old city dump east of the factory. We bought this unused liability from the city more to stop dumping in our backyard than for any hope of usefulness. We used our discarded bricks to fill holes, and Greg followed by making that property look much better. He made it look so good that in recent times it was slipped back to the city along with the liability.

For an engineer who likes to build, cleaning up a mess is no fun. There was one more major mess to tackle. I must admit that part of the long term success of Portland Forge was the built-in "string-saver" philosophy of many employees. Old dies were never completely scrapped. They were saved with the hope that a new die could be salvaged from the steel. We had tons and tons of old tools and machines of every sort, and even gear blanks for a Model A Ford transmission! When I would point to a specific pile and ask about its usefulness, there would follow much stroking of chins and, "You never know." In the early 1980s, we had a bit of a profit squeeze as business dropped like a rock. Major customers such as Mack Truck were shut down completely for the first time ever. To keep our owners happily at arm's length, we needed to dig in every gold mine we could find. The pile of metal blocking every path in the plant would be one.

This mining job had to be carefully done so that truly valuable parts or tools were not lost, and the "string-savers" were of little help because they could stand to see nothing go out the door. I was too ignorant to judge. On a Saturday I assembled those who should know what we could afford to scrap and let them go from south to north through the facility. "If you can't defend it, I'll spray it. If I spray it, we'll sell it next week." Without aggressive help from Greg, I doubt if we could have surrendered anything. With the sale of scrap metal and fuel oil reserves, pay cuts for executives, and voluntary time off without pay from all staff, we sent the owners a profit in a year when sales dropped over 50%.

Doing all the tough things may not have been fun, but they

established enough corporate confidence to allow us to invest in a future for the company. It also established that both Greg and I were part of a team dedicated to Portland and to the company's future.

It was easy to learn that the real strength of the company was a uniquely skilled and well motivated work force. But we could also see that the work force needed new and bigger tools to remain competitive, and that was contrary to the view of Teledyne who saw Portland Forge as a cash cow, year after year sucking out cash far in excess of depreciation, and depreciation having sunk to the pits because the equipment was old.

Slumping forging sales throughout the country followed by liquidation or bankruptcy of over 25% of our competitors in a short period did not make it easier to raise cash for any forging investment. Yet we were determined to bring in the tools and get them into operation. We were also determined to hang on to customers who were looking longingly at foreign supply hoping for lower prices and too often finding them. The programs we undertook to achieve this were successful as the result of contributions from many, but this is about Greg Moser and his contribution was valuable. He contributed very positively to the technical development of the plant, to holding customers, and to the general feeling that we had a future. Some of the bits and pieces illustrate.

One of the important pieces was the Portland College of Forging Knowledge. This piece begins with a sales problem. Any good industrial salesman knows that the prime sales task is to know exactly what customers want and need. This is no simple one-call job, for industrial needs are complex and fluid. To assure that wants and needs are accurately tracked, it is necessary to know, really know the customer and for the customer to know, trust, and respect the sales person and the supplier company. For years Portland Forge's premier sales vice president, Gordon Meeker, did a super job and built the customer base for a growing company. Gordon and his customers were never far from a golf course ör a dinner table, both of which were absolutely great ways to learn about each other. Gordon knew that sales depended on the flow of information, and detailing what customers needed and wanted was for many years gathered at the nineteenth hole.

Now comes the 1980s era of malpractice in many company offices combined with reductions in management due to poor business. Suddenly we were confronted with customer-buyers who knew nothing about the products they purchased except the price, and by customer company policies that would not allow managers and buyers from such old line customers as Caterpillar to take lunch with a salesman. Closer contact such as golf was unthinkable. Big companies put untrained people they did not like nor trust in charge of spending 30 to 40% of their revenues. If ever a need for an idea sat throbbing, this was it.

Then one evening John Young discussed his practice of bringing customers into his plant and teaching them how blue jeans were made. By the next morning his idea and my problem felt like a boil that needed lancing. Gordon Meeker, retired and bored to death, came into my office and it burst, the boil I mean. "How would you like to be Dean of a college?" Before I could finish he was out of his chair and the Portland College of Forging Knowledge was born. Buyers who were forbidden to have lunch with us came, were educated, examined, and had dinner with us three times. They came at their own expense. Their managers demanded that we accept them even when we were overbooked. They came to really know and be known by all our managers and many of our factory operators.

Greg Moser was one of the star faculty members. Not because he gave great lectures. I think he would rather be shot than to give a speech. He was best when meeting and talking one-on-one with customers who wanted simple and practical explanations. His confidence in what he was doing and where he was going was infectious. An engineer from Allison called me a few days after talking to Greg to ask how in the world we could be relaxed and confident when the whole manufacturing world was coming apart. All I could think was, "Thanks, Greg."

By the way, only a senior could guess that the school name was stolen from an old radio program, "Kaye Kayser's College of Musical Knowledge." Greg's real source of challenge and enjoyment was tooling up the plant for more products and greater efficiency. I can't begin to remember all the projects that combined in this effort, but some stick out. I suppose that the eight inch upsetter, the famous monster stranded in Lodi, Ohio, is the subject of a best remembered project. We wanted it, we needed it, we had no money approved to buy it, but we got it. Customers wanted bigger up forgings. (An upsetter is a horizontal forging press that forges a big knot on the end of a bar, in this case an eight inch steel bar.) I negotiated a delay payment purchase with the owner of an upsetter in Canton, Ohio, Teledyne reluctantly approved, and I asked Bob Snyder and Greg to get it rigged into our plant. Our contracted rigger attempted an illegal midnight run across Ohio with a load reckoned at 689,000 pounds as opposed to a legal limit of 40,000. He got caught and the rest is well known history. We performed uncounted favors for city, county, and state offices in Ohio and worked for six months to get our machine to Portland. We had only one problem with the Portland government. Mayor Luginbill came to see us with a plea not to bring it across the Meridian Street bridge. We didn't do that and we were grateful to Naas Foods who let us bring the machine to their rail head.

Our new machine became the Monster at Lodi because that is where the trucker got caught with the overload. Crowds traveled to see it on weekends all winter, the local restaurant owner sold shirts and hats commemorating the event, Readers Digest published a story, and Portland's own Tom Casey wrote and sang a country western song about it. But it wasn't funny when I had to go eye-to-eye with Teledyne about it in Los Angeles. Better than expected profits and cash flow sugared the vinegar.

Both Greg Moser and Bob Snyder wanted to take responsibility for the slight delivery problem. Greg still insists it was his fault. It was a team failure. Guess who was responsible for the team and who learned a valuable lesson?

Once the machine was delivered we suffered the usual shortage of funds needed for installation and start-up. Corporate accountants seemed to believe that the purchase of a production machine was much the same as the purchase of a new car, "buy it, start it, run it." I wish I could remember how many tons of concrete were charged to maintenance, or any account, and how much digging was needed to get that monster into place. It was a challenge Greg Moser loved. All that needed to be said to him was, "Do it."

One challenging aspect of the monster was that of engineering the operating system so that a reasonably strong and well coordinated person could operate it. It is hard to explain to those who may never have watched an operator wrestle a long, red hot, eight inch diameter bar of steel into the maw of a horizontal press and waltz it gracefully through the several passes to make a giant pinion gear blank. I don't remember who contributed the most to getting our new toy into operation. Maybe the reason I don't is because it was a team effort which included operators, managers, and engineers. I do know that Greg was important to the team process. I made two contributions. First, I left them alone, second, when one of the first operators complained to me that the system didn't suit him, I called to his supervisor and shouted over the racket, "This man says he can't handle the machine, get someone who can." The operator scowled at me as though he might wipe up the floor with me, stalked back to the machine, and refused all offers to be replaced. A work force of that caliber is irreplaceable.

Another equipment story concerns the purchase and installation of two 10,000 pound hammers. There's more to it than that. It began with the failure of one of the mechanical shears which cut bars of steel to forging length. We got approval to shop for a used replacement, since we could not operate without it. If memory serves, Bob Snider started collecting prices for a used shear. While he was doing that, and getting bids which I don't recall, I met a forging man in Philadelphia who was selling the equipment from a local, failed forging plant. He had a shear that met our needs, so I asked the price. He explained that he could not price the shear alone because the plant property had been sold and he had to sell all its contents as a package: a shear, a lot of furnaces and auxiliaries, and two 10,000 pound hammers.

His price for the whole mess was less than the best price we had for a shear alone. I explained that we could buy his plant if he would invoice us for one shear and auxiliaries (I had approval to buy a shear. Why confuse anyone? The purchase was duly reported later — after the first of the hammers was in operation. Arms length, remember.)

This all began before the upset story. However, the 10,000 pound hammer engineering problem persisted and may not have been over. I simply told Greg that we had no money for installation nor any room to install those hammers, but I sure would like to see them in operation. No question about it, Greg operates best if given an impossible problem to solve, and if he is left alone to solve it.

Mixed in with efforts to find bigger tools for our operators were efforts to find new customers and sometimes new kinds of products. We were hard pressed to make a profit on some products. For example, no one will forget learning to make slack adjusters for truck braking systems. I thought we had to take on some marginal products and learn to profit from them to hold our size and organization. We were one of the largest forgers in our market niche, largely thanks to the early efforts of Lee Hall, Gordon Meeker, and Charlie Barrenbrugge. Gordon continued to help with our college, but we needed to enhance our ability to provide more services to customers. That required maintaining a staff of good engineers and customer service people.

A crisis came when a group of senior managers cornered me one evening to make me understand that they were weary of the extra burden of new products and recommended that we stick to tradition. I recall replying that the "traditional" products were mostly new in the past 40 years. Nevertheless, we could remain profitable while retreating to the easier product line. To remain profitable while reducing sales, though, it would be necessary to downsize the company. "Downsizing will begin in this room."

Thinking back, I don't recall that Greg joined that party, but I do recall that Greg and Bob McCreery were the champions when it came to finding ways to make steady manufacturing cost reductions. We maintained Portland Forge as one of the best and one of the largest of the specialty forgers.

At some point I became aware of Greg's car racing passion. I am personally so uneducated about car racing that what he did tell me probably zipped over my head. Gradually, I learned that he made headlong weekend trips to exotic drag raceways in the south. If I had understood it better, I might have worried more. For the most part, I didn't annoy him about it and he didn't worry me. Then one day, almost in passing, Greg said, "You'll be glad to know that I've quit driving a drag racer. I wrecked my van, trailer, and car." I know Greg well enough to know that his half-smile and nonchalant appearance masked a real concern. Then I started worrying.

The racing business came up in another conversation when Greg explained his axle business which he operated in his garage. He believed his business was based on some proprietary ideas, and it was growing. I wanted some history because I feared that if he developed these ideas while employed by Teledyne, the company would claim ownership. Soon he was able to show me documentation that demonstrated his development of the axle making business before he came to Portland. I was relieved.

It wasn't much later that Greg again discussed his axle business with me. He explained that the business was growing so fast and was so profitable that he couldn't afford to work at Portland Forge. I sure didn't want him to get away, so I threw at him the only road block I knew. "Why don't you get someone else to make axles and stay here where you will find a real challenge." He did.

Now came a major change in Teledyne which was to have an unhappy effect on the Portland factory. Corporate management was aging and ailing and had never seriously sought replacements. However, they found a person to put forward. I think his name was Bill. As is so often the case during leadership transition, the old does not gracefully give way to the new on some appointed day. Reporting to two aggressive rivals is stressful, requiring more finesse than we at Portland had or wanted. Finally, both Bill and the current boss, Fred, came to Portland on the same glorious day. Fred sat in the office with me while Bill whirled through a plant tour. Fred's symptoms of Parkinson's were plain. It was a difficult meeting. I was torn between concern for an ailing boss who had promoted me and the obvious attacks of his apparent successor. When Bill returned to the office he sucked up all the air in the room, took charge, and challenged, "What did this place ever do for Teledyne? It's perfectly awful!"

"We sent cash, Bill. In two years alone we returned more cash than the total value of their investment. Since Teledyne purchased Portland Forge in 1968, we have never failed to send cash, and cash is what Teledyne wanted."

I was taking too much credit, but I now was part of the Portland heritage and was miffed. Bill's reply, "Sure, on depreciated assets," took a minute to hit me. But it did. Bill had given us an opening, probably without intending it. We could surely correct the problem of depreciated assets by spending some capital funds. I looked at Fred, he gave me the slightest nod and a wink. We had Bill.

"Well," I said, "I'm sure you will want to review the plans in preparation for a major new and modern capitol expansion. We will have them ready soon." A total novice had just stepped into the arena of corporate politics and started down the path with the wrong adversary. Bill blinked, but agreed to see our "plan."

Of course, we had no plan. Teledyne had barely approved funds to maintain the plant we had. But, by golly, we were going to get a plan, and soon.

Greg Moser and Ernie Bright were the pair chosen to lead the construction of a Portland Forge expansion plan. It was one of those times when Greg's eyes danced while Ernie just stared at the floor in disbelief. The charge to them was to go anywhere in the world, talk to anyone, study results, and determine the best equipment and manufacturing system for making forgings for the markets in which we found ourselves. Do not attempt to explore new markets, new products, and new production technology at once. Just figure out how to be the very best at what we do. Greg was the insightful manufacturing visionary. Ernie could quickly assess the operating skills implied. Since operating skill was the greatest strength of the company, it was well worthwhile to try to retain this advantage.

The days that followed were hectic and fun. Greg and Ernie here, Ernie and Greg there, followed by long sessions with Portland Forge management to critique conclusions. Equipment suppliers were brought to Portland for lengthy seminars for managers, engineers, and operators. We all enrolled in a cram course on new forging systems.

Trips to Europe by the Greg and Ernie team were a howl. I had traveled to Europe on business many times in earlier days. My boss had always explained that a trip of less than two weeks was a poor travel investment, and when in Europe there were no easy phone calls home. There was no way either of them could be persuaded to be gone for more than a week. By midweek there would be anxious calls from wives seeking reassurance of exact return plans. It was all fun and exciting, but most of all, it was educational for the pair and for all of us.

Toward the close of the project, we traveled together to Germany where we saw new equipment wasted on a poorly organized operation. We traveled to Massachusetts where we saw part of the future in a French owned plant forging shell casings for Egyptian cannons. Weird company, but they were induction heating bars for hot shearing slugs right into the window of a press and we liked that. (I throw that little bit of technology in to prove that I knew something about what had been happening at the time!)

The project team learned that European plants were generally no more modern than ours. The whole world of forgers was struggling to find an obvious path into the future. I suspected as much. I had attended a world congress of forgers in Germany as an invited speaker. It was obvious that in Japan or Germany or in any industrial country, forging was decried as an outdated art requiring an extraordinarily skilled and motivated work force to work in a noisy, dirty, muscle bending environment. That is what Portland had. But Portland had been the darling of the used tool trade for years. Our engineers and production managers had haunted used machinery shops until they became junk addicts. We had dreams of what this work force could accomplish with the latest tools for short-run forgings while other investors abandoned that market for automated equipment suited for lesser skills and tougher markets, like automotive.

In any organization, the selection of individuals to assume project leadership can create some envy and less than full cooperation from others. The enthusiasm and skill of the Greg-Ernie team combined with the generous application of experience by Bob Snyder, Lew Heffner, and many others resulted in the design of a new system for more precise and less costly forgings. The desired location was just north of the steel yard where we had ample space and proximity to auxiliary operations.

Now came a preliminary presentation of our scheme to Teledyne, which was not well received. I could grasp some of the reasons for rejection, so we set out to try again. One of the barriers to a new system in Portland was wrapped up in the complex "work rules" contracted between the company and the Blacksmith's Union, which knew how many workers would be engaged in each operation. For the most part, the company functioned well within these rules, and they did protect workers from arbitrary supervision. However, it was clear that the new system could only be effective if the work rules were modified. To explore the possibility that the union might agree to some modification, we began showing plans to union leaders to see how the wind might blow. It was a difficult time, because we were negotiating a new contract and we could not promise approval of new equipment. In the midst of labor negotiations, hat in hand, I presented a revised plan to Teledyne with assurance that union members would accept needed work rules modification. At the review session, a corporate attorney finally decided to shorten the proceedings by digging right to the root of the corporate objection. "We like your plant design, but we'll never build it in a location with unions."

"But it will cost much more to build without the support facilities already in Portland, and we need the skills to make it work!"

"Sure, but in the long run the lower operating costs will more than compensate, and you won't have to deal with the bad habits of an older management and work force. Why don't we look for another site?"

Somehow my hard head still failed to accept this decision, but within days the legs got cut out from under my argument. The Portland Forge unions went on strike. It was not the fault of particularly difficult unions but of some hearing problems among negotiators. It was quickly over as hearings improved, but it doomed plant expansion in Portland because it allowed corporate nits to take charge of something they little understood. One of them whose prissy obsequiousness with boss Bill was a corporate joke, hung over the Portland negotiations like a hungry buzzard adding confusion. If I had the courage and clout of Lee Hall, I would have run him out of the country as Lee had done with others in earlier years.

As expected, Greg Moser slumped in my office and took responsibility for the strike. He wasn't at fault. He was the least experienced of the negotiators and generally deferred to greater experience. I thought it was my fault. I had become a Group Executive with responsibility for several plants and believed it was time to delegate negotiations.

Final affirmation that a new plant was to be approved for a southern site was not long in coming. I never felt like I had failed so many who depended on me. That may be seen as an egotistical assumption, but it was the same ego that drove the plan.

Not everything that happened in the late 1980s was so tragic. It would be more fun to remember some lighter history. There was, for example, the great weight loss campaign. We purchased a good scale for weighing employees and placed it in the Human Resources office. ("Personnel office" for people my age. Have you ever noticed that folks who are not happy with what they are keep changing their name so as to disguise themselves? I could get into real trouble if I started naming examples.) Anyway, soon after the new scale was in place, the group of engineers and managers who gathered round Greg and Ernie started a contest to see who could lose the most weight in a short time. I figured myself a lost cause in any such game and stayed out. However, in a few weeks Greg and others, but Greg in particular, began to look emaciated. Still they continued dieting. Greg didn't even have the advantage of being a cigarette smoker while Ernie's smoke consumption soared, as often as not out of the pocket of an associate. In time, one of the contestants, I think it was Hal, surrendered to a week of pizza and the contest drifted away.

The lesson learned from the dieting war was that great care was needed in presenting challenges, particularly to Greg. I hoped this crew would never take up bungee jumping.

Greg also reveals part of his make-up on a golf course. Greg is not a golfer, nor does he probably care that he is not. But on the course he plays his own game, "Bet I can hit this ball further than any of you!" Often he can. If the rest of his shots are not the sharpest, it does not bother him. "How come all of you great golfers who practice everyday can't hit the ball as far as I can?"

As new boss Bill was struggling to succeed up the grand spiral of Teledyne command, he devised a great powwow of all Group Executives, Presidents, and noteworthy executives of all Teledyne manufacturing companies. Our smoke was to rise at a Florida resort, a Stanford shaman was engaged to guide us into the future, we were polled, checked, and laundered for the occasion. The avowed purpose was to convert our strategy from cash generation to internal growth. For four days we worshiped growth and burned the effigy of cash. Some played golf, some fished, but mostly we were inspired by the cheering squad who urged the birth of ideas for growth.

We at Portland Forge were already into the idea and did not need prodding, even though we were not happy with the location. At the end of the dance, we were glad that our momentum was established. The final speaker was George Roberts, co-founder and top gun. He made a very brief talk the essence of which was, "This growth stuff is great. Really great. Don't forget to send cash."

Funny? Yes. Tragic. That too. The long term life of Teledyne was thrown into doubt. Bill's effectiveness as a positive leader was compromised. But Greg and I had a good time in Florida.

When Greg built a new factory building for his axle business, he was still employed at Portland Forge. I remember asking him if he would take down the big sign with his name so prominently displayed. I did not want to lose Greg, but I wondered what would be thought by corporate folks who could not help seeing his sign if they flew into Portland. My worries were much relieved because Bill did make an attack on company executives who might have a conflict of interest. A successful Teledyne-owned iron foundry in LaPort, Indiana, had been assigned to my group. I had sufficient sense to stay out of their way so that their success continued. I knew, as the previous Group Executive had known, that the managers of the foundry owned and operated another, non-competing foundry nearby. My new boss, Bill, was livid. This had to be stopped. He dragged me with him to the real top gun, George, to see that this malpractice was revealed and stopped. From George we received a very lengthy and courteous lecture. As we left, Bill said to me, "I think we're supposed to stand down." I thought that if that meant get out of here and shut up, he was right. I worried less about Greg's conflict of interest. I was further relieved when another Group Executive took me to a restaurant which he owned and which was well known to Teledyne.

Finally, it occurred to me that all of our best employees had a conflict of interest. Whether it was farming forty acres of clay, volunteering at a church, or reengineering the country club, they all had conflicts. Why, some of them even placed family above work! My job was to keep them so challenged and interested that Portland Forge was effectively and efficiently managed. There never was a danger that any of them would enter into a business activity that damaged Portland Forge. The kind of loyalty found in Portland and LaPort is hard to conceive in a corporate office. It was great that George Roberts, from a small Pennsylvania factory town, did understand.

It's hard to close off my thoughts about Greg Moser and the work we did together. Summing up tries to end something that really isn't over. A helpful hint to those who work with him is that if you want to know how your boss or your buddy expects to be treated, watch him when he's with his boss. Greg treated his boss as an associate in every sense, and it was clear that he treated all employees as associates. Now, that does not mean that he was always super nice to all. He can be riled by incompetence or, and get this, by false obsequiousness, "sucking-up," if plainer language is needed. He doesn't do it, and he doesn't want it. So if your mama taught you to be very courteous, don't be surprised if Greg fails to respond as you expect. He will absolutely shield himself from gushing flattery.

One more thing is that Greg takes pride in self-sufficiency and expects that others feel the same. Those working with Greg often try a little too hard to lean on him for guidance and approval. He doesn't need a lot of it and doesn't give a lot of it. This makes him seem to be a loner to some. Don't worry, learn to watch more and expect to listen less. Greg is a good "fast start person," willing to make decisions when the time is ripe rather than to be forever waiting for more facts. But he is more implementor than theoretician. He would rather show how than tell how. Watch him.

As this is written, top gun Bill is gone, Teledyne is gone, the new plant has paid dearly for rejection of skills, but perhaps it has none of the bad habits of the Portland plant where a skilled but disappointing work force still generates cash for new owners. Greg is no longer emaciated because he now smells of his favorite perfume, exotic racing fuel. His enterprise has become a bright spot in an otherwise branch-plant town. I'm proud of whatever small contribution I made when I said, "Greg, come to work for us in Portland."

Chapter Seventeen

REFLECTIONS

**Always Innovate
Curtail Inflation
Learn to Challenge Tradition
Let's All Win
Recognize Family and Friends
When All is Said and Done
Final Thoughts
Psalm 23**

Something that I reflected upon recently, after talking to several people who have contributed to this book, was the fact that all my life, up until the early '90s, all I was trying to do was make a buck so I could go racing. I was really only concerned with myself and my family and trying to get ahead. After my sister was sick for two years starting in 1990 and then passed away from cancer, I suddenly realized that there is a lot more to life than making money. **In fact, helping people to make the world a better place is a lot more fun!** Since life should be fun, I sincerely hope that you can make your life fun by doing something that you are really good at doing and that you love to do.

Everybody's life should be fun. If it is not, you need to find something that you enjoy and do well so that you can have fun. The ironic thing is that ever since I started spending more time helping others and moved away from trying to make a dollar, and ever since I changed my philosophy of life, I am making a lot more money than I ever made working as a vice president or a plant engineer. **So I guess what goes around comes around.** Life is fun and you should ask yourself is that true for you. If not, maybe you should begin to apply the principles of winning the race as noted in this book.

Remember, too, that I haven't given up on my business because I am still totally focused on automation, increased productivity, cost reductions, and whatever it takes to remain competitive so that my employees have a lifetime job and a good retirement. **It is fun making equipment and it is fun running the plant. Life is just a lot of fun.**

WINNERS...

#147. make life fun by doing what they are really good at doing and love to do

And these things we write, so that our joy may be made complete. (1 John 1:4)

Always Innovate

Reflecting back to when I was a plant engineer at the Teledyne Portland Forge plant, I knew a fellow by the name of Mike Landers who was my electrical engineer and one sharp individual. He and I put together a lot of equipment, increased automation, reduced man-power, increased efficiencies, and, in general, made things work a lot better. We built equipment that made parts quicker, easier, and of better quality. One machine even descaled parts. We were always working on something.

One day we were walking through one of the departments that had just been redone to make it more efficient and there was a piece of cardboard stuck on the wall with the words "Tomorrow Land" written on it. I looked at that and thought, "That is strange. What is that?" I didn't give it any more thought at the time. A couple of months later we were in another department putting together another machine and there was another piece of cardboard glued on the wall and it said, "Fantasy Land!" This time I thought, "Now wait a minute. What is this?" I was speaking to some of the supervisors in the plant and said, "What about these Fantasy Land and Tomorrow Land signs? What is all this stuff?" They started laughing and they said, "Don't you know what the maintenance people call you?" I said, "No." They said, "They call you Walt Disney because of all the stuff you think up. They decided to name the departments after the different areas at Disneyland." I realized then the impact of innovation on everyone's life-- from those who work on the machines to those who clean them!

I have applied those same principles of innovation to my business. We have experienced fantastic growth through innovation just as computer companies are experiencing today. It is very rare, though, to find a metal working or a labor intensive type operation that has enjoyed the kind of success that we have had. But through innovation, all of the equipment, with the exception of the lathes that I purchased, was actually built in-house. Thus, we have had basically no money tied up in equipment. Everything has been constructed and built in-house to manufacture the product and to make the job easier for my employees.

All of my computer controlled mills are built out of old obsolete 1940 Kent Owens mills. I completely rebuilt them. New electronics interface a computer in them and we can actually machine parts quicker than anyone else can do in the same operation. A lot of my competitors think the way I manufacture my product is a negative. But in reality, through innovation, I am doing just what everyone else is doing in the auto making world. It is what they call "hard turning."

Years ago, companies would do all their work to a part, heat treating it, only to find the part would warp. They would then have to straighten it out, retreat it, retrue it, and grind the axle to make it serviceable because 10 or 15 years ago it was too hard to turn. Tooling wasn't available to turn parts. The key word in modern manufacturing is "hard turning." Nobody grinds anything anymore unless they are an out-of-date company. You don't use a grinder, you machine it. It is quicker, better, and cheaper. So we basically take our heat treated axle blanks and we turn them, we don't grind them. I have invented a way through innovation, the process to hold cold hob splines on axle shafts and up to 65 Rockwell material shafts.

It is amusing that my competitors think that my process doesn't work. "Well, this guy cuts these axles off and splines them." They are so far from actual truth and reality, since I have the best, state-of-the-art manufacturing process of a product that has ever been invented in the history of mankind. These guys are oblivious to that fact and that is how we can make axles so fast and how we can make them so cheap. I don't spend hundreds of thousands of dollars on my equipment. **I innovate, create Tomorrow Land, and believe in Fantasy Land!** Everything that we use other than the lathes has been manufactured in my facility.

WINNERS...

#148. constantly look to tomorrow, innovating through their imagination

"All our dreams can come true — if we have the courage to pursue them."
(Walt Disney)

We can cold hob 35 splines on a shaft in 65 Rockwell material in 2 minutes. That is 120 seconds! We can drill the bolt pattern in an axle, floor to floor time, picking the axle off the pallet, putting it in the machine, drilling it, taking it out of the machine, and putting it back on the pallet, 5 holes total, in 27 seconds. We can tap five holes in an axle shaft, taking it off the ground, putting it in the machine, tapping the five holes, and taking it back out of the machine, and putting it on the floor, that is floor to floor time, in 15 seconds. I just completed an access hole machine that will punch five 1 1/4 inch access or lighting holes in an axle flange in approximately 40 seconds floor to floor time. I have nothing in these machines, at least, I consider it nothing. The access, or lighting hole, machine that was completely built without any purchased products, other than two lathe chucks to grip the axle shaft, cost $1,000. The axle drilling machines, in which I have invested $14,000 each, do the work of a $100,000 C&C Mill, creating bolt pattern holes in 27 seconds. The splining mills will spline the 35 splines in two minutes and I have spent under $10,000 on each of them. So here we have a company built with worthless junkyard machines, purchased at auction for $500 each, renovated with a few thousand dollars, and I have got the latest, state-of-the-art manufacturing machinery anywhere.

This business actually started as a method to raise money to race cars. We operated out of our garage for several years and in 1987 we incorporated. That year we did around $75,000 worth of business. In 1997 we did around $7,500,000 worth of business. That is a growth of 100 times. When we built the 3,000 square foot facility in the industrial park we had one employee. We added on 6,000 square feet and then we added on 10,000 square feet, so we basically had 19,000 square feet. We presently have a complete dyno facility located in Lebanon, Ohio, and we have two employees there that do nothing but build horsepower and run the race team from that location. We have 21 employees who, together with Marianne and me, generate $7,500,000 in sales. That is a total of 23 of us doing that amount of business!

Our new state-of-the-art facility has 30,000 square feet. We have a business that generates $7,500,000 a year in sales with 21 actual workers, not counting the two that work on the pro-stock who have nothing to do with manufacturing, and we don't even have $200,000 on the books in equipment for the entire business. That is what you call "innovation." So many times I get these entrepreneurial books and business "how to" books written by people who have a business that has grown ten times to $10,000,000 in sales with 100 employees and the guy is named businessman of the year. I just can't believe it because that is not even remotely being successful. I don't believe I would be bragging about producing $100,000 in sales per employee.

Another thought on innovation is that I have over a half dozen products, and I am not even going to tell you what they are, that I have invented for my own race car to make it quicker. I don't let anyone see them and I do not apply for any patents for them. My race car is faster, and that's enough for me. I am way beyond the point of needing or wanting anymore money. By patenting something and selling it to my competitors, sure, you can make a lot of money. But the problem with that is that my competitors would know the competitive advantage that I now enjoy if I shared these inventions. So some of the trick things that I have engineered and designed, no one will ever see because I don't want anyone to see them. I really don't want the money either, so I will never make the parts available for the world. They are mine and mine alone and that is one way to maintain a competitive edge racing car.

There are so many race teams that develop all this trickery and all this horsepower. Then they get greedy, sell it to someone, and it is gone. It happened to Rher & Morrison. They had some great racing teams. They own probably the finest dyno facility in Texas. You get greedy. Someone offers you hundreds of thousands of dollars for one of your motors that you ran to win a national event, so you sell it. Well, guess what? You just sold your technology. I guess it gets back to my philosophy that if you don't have the money to be playing the drag racing game, and you actually have to sell some of your trickery to keep going, then you are in the wrong game from the start. You should not be doing something that is an afterthought. The money should be an afterthought. If you have to worry about your finances when you are playing the kind of games that we are playing, then you are playing the wrong game and that does not make life fun.

Curtail Inflation

Some people think it is pretty difficult to run a pro-type drag racing operation and to run a business at the same, but it really isn't because they both tie in so well with each other. Both racing and the business are after one goal, and that is to win. So we are constantly looking for ways to make the race car faster and we are constantly looking for ways to make the business more efficient. We are looking for methods to better serve our customers and to make parts cheaper. We have never raised a price in the last ten years, other than what we purchase from another individual and we have to go with how he prices parts to me. We have only lowered prices. We have lowered them because of better efficiencies in our machine operations and our manufacturing operations. We have always given our people extraordinary raises and now pay the highest wages in Jay County. We have a very good benefits package and, all this, without ever raising a price. We constantly equal or improve our bottom line profit margin each year, too.

In fact, I want to reiterate one of my philosophies of life. If everyone else in this world would do their best to improve their efficiencies before giving their employees raises, there would be no inflation whatsoever in the United States. There would be no inflation simply because there would be no people raising their prices to cover the cost of operations. This is just like UPS in the strike. Because of what they have given to UPS workers, UPS will have to increase their prices. This money has to come from somewhere. Just like General Motors, Ford, and Chrysler, they just keep raising the price of their cars. Why? They don't improve their efficiency one bit. The reason they have to raise the price on their cars is because they continually give more money to their work force for doing the same job and that is not right. All that does is fuel inflation. There would be no inflation if everybody demanded that if you are going to make more money, then you need to be more efficient.

That is the beauty of a small operation like we have. You can keep your eyes and your ears open to the customer's needs and what the manufacturing world is doing about it. It doesn't take a board of directors to talk about it for days, weeks, and months before you can act on it. You look at something and say, "Well, that is a good idea." Then you just do it because you know that you can do it more efficiently and that it will pay for itself.

It used to drive me crazy working for large corporations. You had to document on paper an idea on how to be more efficient and then spend months trying to sell it. Any fool could look at what you were doing and say that it would be more efficient to do it the new way and that the end result would pay for itself and make the company extra money. Now I realize big companies have to do things like that, but that is why our little company will always beat a large company.

Learn to Challenge Tradition

"We must dare to think unthinkable thoughts," said a speaker once to the U.S. Senate. "We must learn to explore all the options and possibilities that confront us in a complex and rapidly changing world. We must dare to think about unthinkable things . . ."

This speaker was not afraid to challenge tradition. Its key benefit is to avoid complacency and encourage creativity. This is an essential characteristic for those of us who wish to break new ground in our business, customer service, and everything else. **We must treat every occurrence in life as a learning experience, to think the unthinkable,**

whether you are racing cars or whether you are in business. Every time we go out with our pro-stocker or our top salesperson, even if the weekend race or sales call is successful or a total failure, we can always find something good in it to help us the next time we are trying to win. **In fact, there are so many things to learn and so many things to do, that life should be considered one giant learning experience.** It takes years to gain all the knowledge to be competitive in a class such as pro-stock. The same goes for business. Everything you do is a learning experience and an opportunity to think the unthinkable, and the beginner may have a thought or concept which could change the world, too, so do not discount any possible learning situation or source. The old rules maintained "you can't make a contribution until you know enough." Now you can make significant contributions anytime.

If you learn from your failures, then the next time they come your way they can be total successes, and that is what makes life worth living. Learning from everything that you do, both positive and negative, is the key. You have heard the expression, "If it ain't broke, don't fix it." That no longer applies, at least not in race cars and businesses that seek to go beyond the norm to win. Just because it "ain't broke," doesn't mean that it is as good as it could be. Innovate, invent, reengineer, and remanufacture!

WINNERS...

#149. view life as one giant learning experience to challenge tradition and think the unthinkable

"Nothing stops the man who desires to achieve. Every obstacle
is simply a course to develop his achievement muscle.
It's a strengthening of his powers of accomplishment."
(Eric Butterworth)

Let's All Win

What is the meaning of life? Life is a journey and about the only thing certain in life is death. You cannot get out of this world alive. Unfortunately, some people die young and fortunately some people die old. I believe the key here is quality of life. Live every minute of every day like it is your last minute. In the case where your life is short, you may or may not accomplish what you want to do. You should consider yourself very fortunate if you have a long life because then you can combine quantity with quality.

So what are we trying to accomplish in this journey of life? Is it preparation? Is it service? Is it success? Is it quantity of life? Is it quality of life? Is it winning the race; winning the race of life? Contrary to most of our beliefs, to win does not mean that somebody else has to lose. It means we are happy and finding life fun.

The chairman of Southwest Airlines was saying recently that a person should never consider himself successful. His favorite saying is, "About the time you think you are successful is about the time you become complacent, and that is about the time you get run over by somebody charging up from behind and you lose your business or you lose your competitive edge or you lose whatever." That is so true.

Another quote I like was said by Lee Iacocca, when he was on T.V. stumping for Chrysler products, "Either lead, follow, or get out of the way." Well, you get out of the way if you are not leading, because if you don't, you are going to get run over.

So what is the meaning of life and winning the race? Well, I guess you can scratch off success, at least in the context of trying to think you are successful. You should always try to work towards being successful, so if someone compliments you and tells you that you are, you thank them, but then let it go in one ear and out the other. My philosophy is that you really haven't seen anything yet because I am still working just as hard as I can to do all the things that I want to accomplish.

My four children are Rob, Cindy, Angie, and Danielle. Rob is the oldest at 26 and he graduated from the University of Southern California with a business degree. He is currently our sales manager. Cindy is 24 and she graduated from Worcester Poly Technical Institute in Worcester, Massachusetts, as a chemical engineer and is currently working as a scientist. Angie is 22 and graduated from Tulane University with a sociology degree and is currently tending bar. I am not sure she really knows what she is going to do in life. Our youngest, Danielle, is 14 and is an amazing combination of Marianne and myself in the sense that she is very intelligent. In fact, she took the SAT's as an eighth grader and scored higher than any of our other children scored as seniors. But the thing that just amazes me with her is that she has my mechanical ability. She has my wife's intelligence. It should be interesting to see where she goes in this world.

The reason I talk about my children is because to some people, that is what life is. Life is having children and raising those children to be responsible citizens, raising them to be successful, and raising them to live a quality life. For some people, that is their accomplishment in life and that is good. Other people wish to do that and more.

My premise is that right before you achieve your goal, you should move it out a little farther. Make the target a little harder to hit. That way you are always hungry and you are always moving forward. In a nutshell, set your goals, and as you approach them or accomplish them, realize that they may only bring you a short-lived happiness, and not a true lasting happiness.

What is forever? What are you looking for? Life is a journey. Try to accomplish and achieve your goals, but with some people, when it is all said and done, well, it is just a house. Or it is just a car. Or it is just a Harley Davidson motorcycle. They are nice, but you can't take them with you when you die. This takes us 180 degrees back to the quality of life. I do know one thing and that is that every time I drive by the Jay County Library, I smile. So maybe the true meaning of life and happiness is service to others. Maybe the true meaning of life is procreation — to have children that you can raise to have your thoughts, ideals, and integrity. They carry on their life like you have led your life. Maybe that is the true meaning of life and maybe those two things, serving others and raising your children to think like you think, allow you to win the race. By doing those two things, yes, you are still going to die but your philosophies of life will live on after you. Maybe, just maybe, that is winning the race.

The best advice I can give anyone is to have a good memory. Most people in this world didn't have things given to them and they had to work hard for them. **The best thing a person could have when he starts to manage people, when he is trying to raise funds, or when he is trying to get people to do what he wants them to do, is to have a good memory. Remember how it was when you were on the first rung of the ladder.** When you were on the bottom trying to work your way to the top. Remember how you wanted to be treated and never forget that!

WINNERS...

#150. value their memory
because it reminds them of where they started

It is better to be of a humble spirit with the lowly,
Than to divide the spoil with the proud.
(Proverbs 16:19)

Treat your employees and the people with whom you work the way you would want to be treated. (Remember the Golden Rule: "Therefore, whatever you want others to do for you, do so for them..." Matthew 7:12) You will be amazed how much you can get accomplished with that philosophy. As far as trying to be successful and a good business person, always keep things in perspective. I know that when I am trying to raise funds for projects, I have worked just as hard to get $100 out of a prospective donor as I have worked trying to get $100,000 out of another donor. They are all important, and they all add up. No matter how successful you have become, even though $5,000 or $10,000 means little to you, always remember that the same $5,000 or $10,000 might be another person's life savings. So keep the way you talk about your money in perspective, so that other people can maintain their dignity, their pride, and self respect. You will be amazed at how far you will get in life with this attitude.

When you're fund-raising, you may get $100 out of one person and then you may get $100,000 out of someone else. But when it is all said and done, both of them may have given you about the same percentage of their net wealth. Consequently, both of them should be treated with equal respect! This principle is effectively explained in James 2:24, "For if a man comes to your assembly with a gold ring and dressed in fine clothes, and there also comes in a poor man in dirty clothes, and you pay special attention to the one who is wearing the fine clothes, and say, 'You sit here in a good place,' and you say to the poor man, 'You stand over there, or sit down by my footstool,' have you not made distinctions among yourselves, and become judges with evil motives?"

Recognize Family and Friends

A few things need to be reiterated at this point. I was raised by two hard working parents, Joan and Paul Moser. I also spent some time with my grandparents. My mother's parents were Edith and John Montgomery, and my father's parents were Eva and Frank Moser. Both sets of my grandparents were farmers who knew how to work hard. At a very early age I learned how to operate tractors and drive pick-up trucks on their farms. I guess that is what got me started on motorized vehicles. I learned from my family that if you want something, you work for it. If you want something really big, you work a little harder for it. If you want something that nobody else has, get yourself another job or two. Up until 1992, I worked a minimum of two jobs and most of the time I have worked three. Just simply know what you want and go after it.

My parents and my grandparents would come first as I acknowledge those who have helped me in my life.. In school, I would have to recognize

Bob Follas, my industrial arts teacher, Forrest Albert, my advanced math teacher, and Colleen Snyder, my biology teacher, who involved me in science fairs. The Indiana Institute of Technology taught me college mathematics. I had all the math that an engineer is required to take. Honestly, mathematics has been the most important tool for me to master. There is not an hour of the day that goes by when I am not using mathematics. I calculate stresses on beams, and cycle times, tooling life, and surface speeds. Young people really need to understand the lifetime value of mathematics. I know all my children look at math and say, "Oh, this is terrible! I don't like math. I don't like this. I don't want to do that." They don't realize how important a total grasp of mathematics is and how easy it will make their life.

As I grew up, a few friends really helped me to be competitive. In high school, my close friends were Kirk Gary and Lonny Edwards. Jack Riley, Pat Bowers, Edgar Doster, Buzz Detmon, Steve Sprow, Tom Clemons, and Dewy Sanderson were all close friends, too. I have talked about Dewy before, but most of these fellows I ran around with raced dirt bikes and cars with me and made life a total competition at an early age.

Dewy Sanderson is the individual who taught me how to weld. He is an expert welder. At Maremont, I was a machinist and Dewy was a welder. The company shut down a giant oven and they wanted the whole thing completely rebuilt in a week. I think Dewy and I worked 16 hour days on it and welded in a whole new structure. I never welded before in my life, but when I got done, I was a pretty good welder. I always used to say, "I can weld overhead with a tee shirt on and not get burnt with a stick welder." I was proud of that!

Other people like Loran Zedyke, Rex Dangler, and Jeff Hunter, whom I have mentioned before, were really involved in racing with me. I really came to admire Henry Rose. I originally met him at the Maremont Corporation where he was a machinist. He was a rare individual. To look at him, you would not think that he had two nickels to rub together, but he was extremely wealthy, very talented as far as being a machinist, and was very intelligent. He had a fantastic sense of humor and still does today at age 80. But at age 60 when I knew him best, he was so strong that one of his favorite things to do when Maremont would hire a new machinist would be to walk up to the guy and say, "You got a pair of Channel Locks in your toolbox?" The guy would reply, "Yeah, yeah." "So let me see them." He would make sure they were genuine Channel Locks because they are the best. The guy would hand them to him, he would take them out and he would look at them and he would say, "I think these are defective." He did this every time. The guy would say, "Well, what do you mean these are defective?" He would take the lock, find something about an inch in diameter, clamp it on, and take one hand and break the jaws on it. He would just bust them right off! Well, I couldn't break the jaw with two hands. He did this all the time and he was 60 years old! He was one powerful individual and one nice guy respected by all.

Somebody whom I recently met in Portland, but who has now passed away, was Jeff Mumby. He was a businessman who poured concrete basements and driveways and did all kinds of concrete work. I learned a lot from Jeff. I learned a lot from my homebuilders, Neil and Karen Whitner, too. They taught me a lot about honesty and integrity.

Another wonderful individual whom I mentioned before was Virgil Dangler. He owned Dragway Automotive. Then there were Larry and Joanne Shaw who owned the Sohio station where I pumped gas all through high school and college. It was there that I really picked up my love for mechanical things and my ability to fix them and work on them. I worked there, fixed motorcycles in the evenings during the week, and pumped gas on weekends for Larry. While working there, I found out what it takes to run a successful business, what it takes to get customers, keep them happy, and how to keep them coming back.

Dave Ganger, who owned the Yamaha shop, allowed me to work for him for eight or nine years. I worked for him during my high school and my college years in the evenings whenever something needed to be fixed. I was his head mechanic. One thing I learned from Dave was the principle that he would always tell me, "You buy low and you sell high."

Bob Treinen and Bob Reed taught me a great deal, too. Bob Reed was the president of Portland Forge and Bob Treinen was a plant manager. I think the main thing that I learned from them was how to successfully run a plant and have fun doing it.

All of the people who have been influential in shaping my life are really too many to mention because I have met a lot of friends and interesting people while working on local projects. You never stop learning. You pick things up all the time. Life is just one big learning episode after another. In fact, it's a wonder that you don't overload your brain with too much information and have it explode.

When All is Said and Done

Throughout this book, "winning the race" has been discussed — success in business, climbing the corporate ladder, or becoming president of a corporation. Are these winning the race? Is being an entrepreneur, inventing a product, and marketing that product successfully, winning the race? Is making a lot of money winning the race?

When it is all said and done, I don't believe any of this is really winning the race. I do know, though, that you have to be able to generate money if you are going to give it away. You can't give something away that you don't have. So in that respect, you need to be successful. If you are going to keep people employed, your business needs to be successful. But in reflecting upon what has happened in my life, I think I can honestly say that when I reached the point in my life when I could do something for someone or I could donate money, time, or energy to help a total stranger and expect nothing in return, then I began to understand and believe that maybe now I was winning the race.

It is not a very well understood and accepted concept. A quick little story to illustrate this happened recently when a person I have mentioned in this book called me up out of the blue and said, "Hey, how are you doing?" We exchanged greetings, then he said, "I have a tremendous favor I would like to ask of you." "Sure. What do you want?" "Well, I know you have a Dodge Viper, an expensive sports car, and I have a daughter who is an attendant for the Homecoming in Paulding, Ohio." (Paulding High School was where I attended and graduated.) "I am trying to find an exotic car for her to ride in during the parade. Would you consider bringing your Viper up so she could ride in it?" Naturally, I said, "Sure!"

What he didn't know was the amount of work it would take. The car had less than 100 miles on it. I had to get my son's trailer because our race car trailer was way too big to haul it into a small town. I had to unload all of his race car stuff, load up the Viper, drive it up there, get it out of the trailer, drive it in the parade, and get it back home. I sincerely wanted to do this, but he spent the entire evening with me on the phone trying to compensate me when I really did it only to be nice. Most people need to understand the concept of giving and receiving. There is a time to give and a time to receive. If no one is there to receive, then there cannot be a giver. In this case, I was the provider (the giver) and he was the receiver, yet, he insisted on paying me back. I refused because that would have taken the joy out of giving! When all is said and done, winning the race is giving, but expecting and accepting NOTHING in return!

Final Thoughts

Alongside a road in Ohio there is a large oak tree that measures about three or four feet in diameter. This is the only tree on that entire road for about ten miles. Well, one night when I was 14, my best friend "borrowed" his sister's keys and car, went for a joy ride with four friends, ran off the road, and hit that tree head on. The driver, Buzz, was killed instantly. His shotgun passenger, who was Bobby Snodgrass, hit his head on the windshield and scrambled his brains. It took him years to recover from it and he still is not the same person that he was. The two guys in the backseat sustained some scratches and bruises but they were okay. Buzz was the first good friend in my life who died. The only reason that I was not in that car was because I had work to do and I had gone home to get some sleep. That was the only reason!

Buzz and I lived a wild life back then so I never gave the accident much thought. We did a lot of crazy things and I just kind of wrote off the incident by thinking that the only thing certain in life is death and that some people live longer than others and my friend, Buzz, just didn't make it. For some reason, I didn't change how I lived one bit. I didn't take any more caution in my driving and I continued feeding my need for speed. In fact, I was probably in my mid-30's before it really dawned on me that I could get killed doing some of the crazy things that I did. The teenage mentality is that you are going to live forever. You are invincible, you are immortal, and you will live forever. It took me a long time to realize that.

Actually, what I realized shortly after Buzz's death was the fact that the only reason I wasn't in the car was because I had to work. What I also realized was that I really needed to be in control of what was going on in my life. I don't know why he lost control of the car. I needed to have control of my actions or at least enough control of them so that I could get out of any situation without killing myself. I might wreck a car or I might roll a car, but at least I should have enough control over the situation so that I could live through it.

Looking back on that now, I think, boy, I was very fortunate to have had all those jobs because that is the only reason I am alive today, or else I might be alive but my brain would be scrambled. I remember saying to myself the day after the accident that it was a pure miracle that I wasn't in that car with Buzz. It is just another example that a sure fire way to get ahead in this world and to stay alive is through hard work. It keeps you out of trouble.

This also ties in with my theory of being at the right place at the right time. Only this is the reverse of that. I was at the right place at the right time by being at home in bed. If I had gone with Buzz I would have been at he wrong place at the wrong time. So, that is another one of my theories that holds true.

One other closing thought is that almost everything that I do in business always manages to work out. It's like, Wow! I can think up a machine and it will work! It works every time or is close enough to working that I can make it work when I'm finished building it. The decisions I make in business nearly always seem to work out for the best. It would seem that with a record like that, I could get complacent really quick. But drag racing, especially mountain motor pro-stock, is the one thing that I would call the "ultimate reality check." It is hard, it is time consuming, and it takes a lot of effort, but it is the ultimate reality check. A million little things can happen and not only do I not get to race, but I don't even get to qualify for the race. It brings me back down to earth and I realize, just like in my business, that I can never take anything for granted, I can never become complacent, and I can never think that anything is going to go successfully, even though it often does. I have my pro-stock racing as a very vivid reminder that nothing always goes right and then one day when everything does go right, it is such a fleeting moment that I want to hang on to it as long as I possibly can. Then, when I try to repeat what I did right, I find out that it is a very difficult thing to do. It's like the people who win the world championship in IHRA mountain motor pro-stock and then they don't even finish in the top ten the next year.

We have people in the pro-stock class who are so competitive that we have had four and five hundredths of a second spread from the number one to the number 16 qualifier. What that means is that first you have to make a really good run to even get the car qualified. You get four attempts at trying to qualify the car. But every season we have a person who wins a national event and he doesn't even qualify for the next one or two events. That is how competitive it is and that is why I call racing the "ultimate reality check." If you really think things are going well in your life and you really think you have it made, take up pro-stock racing. It will humble you really quickly and bring you right back down to earth, and then you will realize that you can take nothing for granted. You must keep plugging along because no matter how good it is going today, it doesn't mean that anything good is going to happen tomorrow. In fact, if anything, be prepared for something bad to happen so you can then turn the situation around and keep moving forward.

As a Christian, I believe in God as evidenced by the many verses in this book. Even though my attendance at church was very good as a child, it is not so good now. I am usually off racing on Sundays. I try to attend the Christian Racer's Association church services at national events when I can because I believe that God is my co-pilot. There is no doubt that is why I am still alive today after all of the crazy things that I did in my youth. I talk to Him frequently in prayer and He leads me and guides me in all my ways. No one can accomplish anything in this world without His help.

My favorite part of the Bible is the 23rd Psalm and I have

concluded with these verses. I do not wish to impose my views on anyone because everybody has a right to believe what they choose to believe and we are blessed to have that freedom in America today. Wisdom, knowledge, and understanding are worthwhile virtues to seek in life. As Proverbs 2:2-6 states:

> Make your ear attentive to wisdom,
> Incline your heart to understanding;
> For if you cry for discernment,
> Lift your voice for understanding;
> If you seek her as silver,
> And search for her as for hidden treasures;
> Then you will discern the fear of the Lord,
> And discover the knowledge of God.
> For the Lord gives wisdom;
> From His mouth come knowledge and understanding.

My wish is that everyone would praise God by following His Ten Commandments, and this is my word of wisdom for life: if we leave the world better than we found it, whether it be nature, people, or business dealings, then we will have sown the seeds of respect, responsibility, honesty, hard work, generosity, and integrity that will produce healthy fruit for future generations.

Psalm 23

> The Lord is my shepherd,
> I shall not want.
> He makes me lie down in green pastures;
> He leads me beside quiet waters.
> He restores my soul;
> He guides me in the paths of righteousness
> For His name's sake.
>
> Even though I walk through the valley of the shadow
>   of death,
> I fear no evil; for Thou art with me;
> Thy rod and Thy staff, they comfort me.

Thou dost prepare a table before me in the presence of
 my enemies;
Thou hast anointed my head with oil;
My cup overflows.
Surely goodness and loving kindness will follow me all
 the days of my life,
And I will dwell in the house of the Lord forever.

Glossary

Altered NHRA and IHRA: Type of drag car

Bracket Race: Everyone is equal, running off a dial-in. Faster cars have a built-in delay based on what ET is written on the window of the race car

Break out: Bracket racing term when you run under your dial-in and are disqualified

Bruce Litton: Top fuel driver

BTU: British thermal units

CEO: Chief Executive Officer

Christmas tree: Drag racing starting device

CNC Equipment: Computer Numerical Control Equipment

CNC mill: Computer Numerical Control mill

C.O.D.: Cash on Delivery

Dale Eicke: NHRA engine builder

Dial-in: Bracket racing ET that you are going to run off of that is written on your race car

Dyno: Dynamometer method of checking the HP of an engine

Dyno pulls: Making a test run on the Dynamometer

Eight inch Ajax upsetter: Horizontal forging machine with a forming capacity of 8"

11 Second Car: 11.00 to 11.99 ET in seconds

ET: Elapsed time it takes to race the 1/8 mile or 1/4 mile drag strip

Five 100: .05 of a second

Flange of the axle: Hub on the end of an axle where the wheel bolts on

Flat Track Racing: Racing in a circle, flat-out

480s: 4.80 ET in seconds

Funny Car Tires: Large slicks on a nitro funny car

Hard Tailed Altered: No rear suspension

Hare and Hound Racing: Cross country racing

High 10 second quarters: 10.90-10.99 ET in seconds in the quarter mile

Hill Climb Racing: Racing against yourself to reach the highest level on the hill

ICE Program: Interdisciplinary Cooperative Education Program

Ice Racing Motorcycles: Flat track racing on ice

IHRA: International Hot Rod Association

Jerry Haas: Chassis builder

Joe Clark: Head porter

John Kaase Motors: Mountain motor engine builder

LP: Liquid propane

Mid 10 Second Street Car: 10.40 to 10.60 ET in seconds

Mopar: Chrysler/Dodge parts/cars

Motor Cross Racing: Two, one-hour events--the person with the most laps wins

Mountain Motor Pro-Stock: IHRA rules maximum of 815 cubic inch motors

NHRA: National Hot Rod Association

OEM axle: Original Equipment Manufacturer

OEM axle shaft like 58-60 Rockwell on surface: Rockwell-hardness checking scale 58-60--very hard!

Open headers: Exhaust manifolds with no mufflers attached

Pro-Stock Racing: Heads up no break out racing following NHRA/IHRA rules

Pro tree: Unlike a regular (Christmas) tree, the three yellows flash together as one light. You do not have the transcending lights, and hence, no anticipation

Quad four: Hi-performance 4-cylinder General Motors engine

Quick eight: The quick eight is when they take the fastest eight cars and run them heads up on Saturday night with no break-out whatsoever or dial-in

Railroad spur: Railroad track that connects your plant or location to the main line

resplining: Remanufacture or recut splines in heat treated axles

Rick Jones: Chassis builder

Rickie Smith Car: World champion in 1989 IHRA pro-stock

Riding shotgun: Front passenger seat, derived from the stagecoach days

Roadrunner: Type of Mopar vehicle

Rocker Arm Ratios: Rocker arms activate valves, more ratio the farther the valve opens

ROI: Return on Investment

RPM: Revolution per minute

740s at like 180-190 in the Quarter: 7.40 ET, 180-190 MPH

Shot Gun Fords: Name given to the hemi head ford motors

Six Second Car: 6.00 to 6.99 ET in seconds

Sonny Leonard Motors: Mountain motor engine builder

splines: A series of parallel, 30 degree to 45 degree pressure angle grooves that mate with corresponding grooves in a spool or side gear

Street Racing: Unsanctioned, illegal racing on the street

Tag Trailer: Type of trailer where the tongue of the trailer is attached to the bumper or frame of the tow vehicle

10-60s to 10-70s: 10.60 to 10.70 ET in seconds

The Spread of the Bore on the Block: Distance between the bore centerlines of the block

Todd Payton's Alcohol Funny Car: NHRA/IHRA drag racing car

Top Fueler: NHRA/IHRA nitro burning unlimited drag racing vehicle

Top Sportsman Car: IHRA class of drag racing vehicle

Tricker Parts: Parts that make your car faster

Trick Heads: Heads that flow a lot of air

Twelfth in the Points: Position in which we finished the year racing

Wheelie bars: Rear mounted bars that keep a drag car from wheel standing when the car leaves the start line

Time Line
Greg Moser's Life and Career

1952-1961

Child growing up in Indiana and Ohio

1961-1970

News Carrier, Lawnmower, Snow Shoveler, Motorcycle Mechanic, Racer, and Service Station Attendant

1970-1973

Indiana Institute of Technology Student, Motorcycle Mechanic, Haviland Muffler Company Machinist, and Service Station Attendant

1973-1976

Maremont Tool Maker, Maintenance Superintendent, Motorcycle Mechanic, Racer and Service Station Attendant

1976-1978

Portec Plant Engineer and Plant Superintendent

1978-1981

International Harvester Manager, Motorcycle Mechanic, and Racer

1981-1992

Teledyne Plant Engineer and Vice President of Manufacturing and Engineering, Racer, President of Moser Engineering

1992 to Present

President of Moser Engineering

WINNERS . . .

Chapter One

#1. raise their children by example

#2. lead their employees, not by what they say, but by what they do

#3. work hard because they know what they want

#4. identify and meet others' needs and in return demand more from them

#5. train and motivate others to accomplish their goals

#6. know where they are going so others can help them get there

#7. build others by recognizing admirable traits and commenting on them

#8. accomplish what needs to be done doing their best at all times

#9. expect others to be winners and help them to be winners

#10. enjoy what they are doing and help others to enjoy what they are doing

#11. recognize how to be in the right place at the right time

#12. are willing to take a different path when a good opportunity arises

#13. will accept less pay to get the right job for the future

#14. create synergistic energy by finding others of similar mind

#15. are competitive and want to be the best

#16. take a potential negative and make it into a positive

Chapter Two

#17. find it easier to get a new job if they are doing well

#18. enjoy their job so much that working seems like play

#19. are entrepreneurs meeting needs by selling profitable products

#20. develop their leadership qualities to be the boss

#21. succeed by insuring product quality, price, and delivery (service)

#22. profit from their mistakes as well as from the mistakes of others

#23. surround themselves with responsible people who in turn do the same

#24. know and test their products and the products of their competitors

#25. increase productivity in order to give pay raises

#26   absolutely do not contribute to inflation by raising prices

Chapter Three

#27. do what they say they are going to do or communicate otherwise

#28. plan ahead to never waste time or procrastinate

#29. not only recognize opportunities but they take advantage of them

#30. get a lot of work done by doing the work that needs to be done

#31. do it right or don't do it at all

#32. do not vacillate in making decisions, getting things done, or being on time.

#33. recognize the importance of being able to get along with everyone

#34. gain strength from the One who is strong

#35. recognize God and are motivated by His power

#36. challenge themselves early on to make life easier for themselves later

#37. pay attention in school and get the best grades possible

#38. work smart to insure their success

#39. change jobs as frequently as necessary to remain effective

#40. thoroughly research a company prior to writing any resume

#41. Never lie on a resume and always dress to impress

#42. set their goals and know where they are going before getting married

#43. are in total synch with their spouse

#44. trust and respect their spouse

#45. unselfishly and constantly help their spouse to make life easier

#46. have their spouse as their partner

#47 accept spouse's decisions even when hindsight may prove them wrong

#48 do not marry for outward appearances, but for what is within a person

Chapter Four

#49. keep it simple by doing the job right with as few people as possible

#50. make more money by increasing the productivity of each employee

#51. create the ideal working atmosphere for their employees

#52. take care of their employees who in turn are diligent in their work

#53. give people what they need, when they want it, at the best price and quality possible

#54. are constantly looking to do it better, quicker, cheaper

#55. run hard to insure success but remain humble less they become overconfident and stumble

#56. watch the seconds to make every minute count

#57. believe in themselves, their employees, and their product

#58. get a good idea and move with it rather than sitting on it

Chapter Five

#59. are competitive to the point that they want to win every time

#60. experiencing loss are good losers learning from their mistakes

#61. are experienced to react fast in order to take the lead and win

#62. appreciate victory but are always anxious for the next challenge

#63. not only compete but actually search out better competition

#64. create to lead the pack rather than follow others

Chapter Six

#65. excel at what they are doing and enjoy it

#66. build their business on a foundation to last

#67. want to leave a legacy for future generations

#68. get things accomplished by making decisions as quickly as possible

#69. use positive attitude, confidence, and knowledge to take the lead

#70. accomplish much by focusing on what needs to be done and doing it

#71. do not fear failure because they are prepared when opportunity knocks

#72. are never satisfied due to their desire to always do better

#73. don't assume that something can't work, so in trying it, it does work

#74. are never satisfied at top speed because they know they can go faster

#75. approach goals only to reset them to accomplish much and stay ahead

Chapter Seven

#76. are eternally optimistic by viewing negatives as learning experiences

#77. consider luck to be where opportunity meets preparation

#78. always assess when projects are sinking and ensure that they don't

#79. complete projects within one year to ensure efficiency of operation

#80. sincerely trust others but utilize controls on a precautionary basis

#81. laugh in the face of failure the first time but cry if it happens again

#82. know what is right to do and do it without question

#83. earn integrity by always doing what is right

#84. have no need to worry because what they have done is right

#85. make the world a better place and find inner peace by helping others

Chapter Eight

#86. stay competitive through all possible means to win

#87. listen to their employees to change situations which need attention

#88. achieve victory by guiding their work force to innovate together

#89. increase productivity by creating a comfortable work environment

#90. know who they need, what they want done, and how to do it

#91. communicate precisely what it takes to make a winning team

#92. build a motivated team that regulates itself toward winning every time

#93. have high expectations of employees resulting in a winning team

#94. are honest and direct when needing to implement change

#95. hire intelligent, as well as dependable, individuals to build their team

#96. agree that good employees are worthy of their wage

#97. give and, in turn, receive much

Chapter Nine

#98. recognize the value of giving and in turn receive rich blessings

#99. rejoice when challenges arise because they know that patience and hard work will accelerate them beyond top speed

#100. are fearless leading others to accomplish the impossible

#101. are efficient in organizing work for today since tomorrow is unknown

#102. exhibit unusual confidence, do not doubt, and believe in what they say they will do

#103. do all they can, when they can, knowing rich results are the reward

#104. in accelerating to win, handle mishaps as best as they can to survive

#105. learn to stay calm even when the going gets rough

Chapter Ten

#106. realize that being first is all about the speed and quality of service

#107. know what their customers need and how to give it to them

#108. organize their finances making it easy to control money handling

#109. must have vision beyond present circumstances in order to be first

#110. find their responsibility increasing as others are willing to be led

#111. encourage civility and do not allow anger to rage among their ranks

#112. treat others like they would want to be treated

#113. do what is right with humility

#114. just do things rather than finding the reasons why not to do them

#115. believe that it is better to have failed than to not have tried at all

#116. enjoy life to the fullest by laughing in the face of failure

#117. succeed by meeting the needs, not the wants, of others

#118. know the value of marketing to the masses over a select few

#119. distribute products quickly that have perceived value and work

#120. keep their eyes on the customer identifying their needs continuously

Chapter Eleven

#121. realize that procrastination only leads to poor performance

#122. know to reconfirm all important communications with others to be certain that what has been stated is well understood

#123. please themselves and set the example by doing rather than dreaming

#124. trust others, congratulating them when they make the right decisions

#125. are asked to lead projects because success breeds success

#126. know who the leaders are and appreciate that they get the job done

#127. lead by example, sharing their expertise by assisting where necessary

#128. encourage fresh thinking by involving youth in problem solving

#129. look to others for better ideas and knowledge which they don't have

#130. are leaders planting good seed to harvest a plentiful crop

#131. desire to stay fit in order to have the stamina to lead and help others

Chapter Twelve

#132. move from project to project viewing them as games played with a purpose

#133. consider success to be the sharing of their rewards with others

#134. continually reach for new goals but have inner peace at all times

#135. know what happiness is and will focus on what it takes to achieve it

#136. are mentors to society and must live the part by setting the example

#137. return what they can to the world to make it a better place for all

#138. respond to God's calling not by questioning but by doing

#139. seek the truth

#140. lead in the spirit of giving to help others

#141. know that if all do their part in giving a lot more can be done

Chapter Thirteen

#142. release ill feelings immediately so appropriate action may be taken

#143. work behind the scene to ensure that all parties are participating

#144. speak to implement change or keep their thoughts to themselves

#145. find ultimate happiness in making others happy

#146. know that philanthropy is giving money expecting nothing in return

Chapter Seventeen

#147. make life fun by doing what they are really good at doing and love to do

#148. constantly look to tomorrow, innovating through their imagination

#149. view life as one giant learning experience to challenge tradition and think the unthinkable

#150. value their memory because it reminds them of where they started